THE CONQUEST OF POLITICS

BOOKS BY BENJAMIN R. BARBER

Strong Democracy, 1984

The Artist and Political Vision, edited with
M. McGrath, 1982

Marriage Voices (a novel), 1981

Liberating Feminism, 1975

The Death of Communal Liberty, 1974

Superman and Common Men, 1971

Totalitarianism in Perspective, with
C. J. Friedrich and M. Curtis,
1969

Benjamin Barber

The Conquest of Politics

Liberal Philosophy in Democratic Times

PRINCETON UNIVERSITY PRESS

PRINCETON, NEW JERSEY

All Rights Reserved
Library of Congress Cataloging in Publication Data will be
found on the last printed page of this book

ISBN 0-691-07764-9

Publication of this book has been aided by the
Whitney Darrow Fund of Princeton University Press

This book has been composed in Linotron Times Roman

Clothbound editions of Princeton University Press books
are printed on acid-free paper, and binding materials are
chosen for strength and durability. Paperbacks, although
satisfactory for personal collections, are not usually
suitable for library rebinding

Printed in the United States of America by
Princeton University Press
Princeton, New Jersey

To the memory of
LOUIS HARTZ

As soon as philosophy begins to believe in itself it always creates the world in its own image; it cannot do otherwise. Philosophy is this tyrannical drive itself.

Friedrich Nietzsche

Contents

Acknowledgments

EARLIER versions of chapters in this book appeared as articles in journals as indicated below. New material has been added to most, and all have been revised to some extent.

Chapter Two: "Solipsistic Politics: Russell's Empiricist Liberalism," *Political Studies* 223 (March 1973).

Chapter Three: "Justifying Justice: Problems of Psychology, Politics and Measurement in Rawls," *American Political Science Review* 69 (June 1976).

Chapter Four: "Deconstituting Politics: Robert Nozick and Philosophical Reductionism," *Journal of Politics* 39 (February 1977).

Chapter Five: "Unconstrained Conversations: A Play on Words, Neutral and Otherwise," *Ethics* 93 (January 1983).

Chapter Six: "Conserving Politics: The Political Theory of Michael Oakeshott," *Government and Opposition* 2 (Autumn 1976).

Chapter Seven: "The World We Have Lost," *The New Republic*, September 13, 1982.

Chapter Eight: "The Politics of Judgment," *Raritan Review* 5 (Fall 1985).

I would like to thank Sanford Thatcher and Gretchen Oberfranc of Princeton University Press for their careful editorial assistance. I am also grateful to the American Council of Learned Societies, the Rutgers University Research Council, and the Guggenheim Foundation for timely awards that permitted work to be done on earlier versions of the manuscript.

THE CONQUEST OF POLITICS

ONE

The Conquest of Politics:
Philosophy Against
Practice

When man first begins to think, he thinks of himself first.
Henri Bergson

THINKING about politics creates a unique dilemma, for it seems
inevitably to lead to thinking about thinking; and the more we
think about thinking, the less we think about politics. Human
thought has a natural tendency to narcissism, and narcissism dis-
poses it to reflexivity. Like the uncomprehending pet spaniel who
stares curiously at his master's pointing finger rather than the direction in which the gesture is intended to move him, we humans
are often led to dwell introspectively on the processes of our own
consciousness rather than to gaze outward at the myriad objects
that are its presumed targets. This tendency, although it nurtures
metaphysics, theology, and art, can play havoc with the human
sciences.

In much of what we have chosen to call political philosophy in
the liberal postwar era, philosophy has flourished while politics
has wilted. Because the constraints on how we define and understand philosophy are not necessarily commensurable with the constraints on how we define and understand politics, politics frequently ends up as a creature of absolutist philosophy—and one
that bears only slight resemblance to the public activities and
goods associated with common power and common citizenship.
Reflection is not action, but a political philosophy severed from
its connections to action and reflexively preoccupied with its own
philosophical character may conflate the two, as when the philos-

opher construes every form of human "activity," including thought itself, as a species of "action," thereby obfuscating common-sense differences between thinking and doing. Wishing to conform to the highest cognitive standards, such a philosopher may find himself reducing questions of political practice (What shall we *do*? What is just?) to questions of adequate epistemology (What do *I know*? What is truth?) and then insisting, as Marx observes on his way to pillorying Proudhon, that by manipulating his categories he can change the world.

The historical aim of political theory has been dialectical or dialogical: the creation of a genuine praxis in which theory and practice are sublated and reconciled, and the criteria yielded by common action are permitted to inform and circumscribe philosophy no less than philosophical criteria are permitted to constrain the understanding of politics and inform political action. Yet in much of what passes for political philosophy in the age of liberalism, reductionism and what William James called "vicious abstractionism" have too often displaced dialectics and dialogue. The outcome has been neither political philosophy nor political understanding but the conquest of politics by philosophy. If, as Hannah Arendt suggests in "Truth and Politics," there is a nonpolitical or even antipolitical character to truth, then the philosophical pursuit of truth, or of clear epistemological criteria by which truth might be measured, will necessarily distort politics.

This is obviously not true of philosophy in all of its modern guises. And when we recall how many modern guises there are, we will be careful lest we impeach the genus for the defects of one or another of its species. Pragmatism, phenomenology, and hermeneutics, to name but a few, have all assiduously nourished an understanding of the political that does not reflexively assume that the political is to be subsumed under or reconstructed as the philosophical, or that philosophy can thrive by conquering politics and reducing it to a problem in epistemology. Nevertheless, a number of Anglo-American moral and legal philosophers appear to prefer metatheory to theory. Inverting Aristotle's prudent dictum calling for a method appropriate to the subject under study, they have sought a subject appropriate to the philosophical method at hand.

4

When that subject—in this case, politics—has resisted the method, it is the subject and not the method that has been adjusted. The result is a distortion of our sense of the political that has undermined our politics at least a little and our philosophical understanding of politics a good deal more.

In the 1950s, a certain anxiety about the future of political philosophy appeared among its practitioners, manifested in essays announcing the "decline" or the "death" of political theory. Sir Isaiah Berlin's 1958 jeremiad "Does Political Theory Still Exist?" represented one famous attempt among others to put a lid on this spreading anxiety. Similarly, those English philosophers who initiated the well-known series at Blackwell's on "Politics, Philosophy and Society" regarded themselves as engaged in a salvage operation on behalf of a form of political understanding under assault both from positivism (the old philosophical positivism on the model of T. D. Weldon's *The Vocabulary of Politics*, and the new social science positivism of the American behaviorists) and from the historicist reductionism of the Marxist left. Neither positivists nor historicists seemed to take politics very seriously, causing the great historian Alfred Cobban to quip that political science was mostly a device for avoiding politics without achieving science.

Today political philosophy is in no such dire straits. It has easily outlasted its detractors, thanks in part to the ministrations of liberal political philosophers of the kind examined in this book: thoughtful and committed theorists working in the fields of moral, legal, and political philosophy. If the character of political theory is still in question, its survival is not.

Yet the revival of political theory in its liberal form raises new questions. If positivist political science was the conquest of politics by scientistic hubris, resuscitated liberal theory has often appeared to be the conquest of politics by hubristic philosophy. Where political science avoided politics without achieving science, political philosophy voids politics by achieving philosophy. But philosophy, while it may offer up maxims that are philosophically true, too often confirms Burke's rule: as maxims are philosophically (metaphysically) true, they are morally and politically false. One need not agree with Burke that "nothing universal can

5

be rationally affirmed on any moral and political subject'' in order to recognize that general maxims must be adjusted to circumstance, time, place, and people and that, in doing this, political theory will often have to abandon its own rigorous standards for the rough–and–ready realities of the world. Even such universalizing philosophers as Rousseau acknowledged the need to adapt ideal political solutions to concrete political realities—to take men as they are and only laws as they might be.

Among the philosophers under examination here (with the exception of Oakeshott), Burke and Rousseau are not favorite sources. As philosophers, these modern liberals suffer from what John Dewey disparaged as the quest for certainty—what we might call, in keeping with more recent philosophical usage, the seductions of foundationalism. The foundationalist wishes to establish unimpeachable epistemological foundations for political and moral knowledge in a bedrock composed of either irreducible empirical data (empiricism, positivism, behavioral science) or indefeasible a prioris (rationalism, idealism, analytic philosophy). His goal is to render political knowledge certain by associating it with the putative certainties of prepolitical knowledge. It is of little moment whether this certainty is found in a hypothetical natural condition or in the ''facts'' of ''human nature,'' in innate ideas or in immutable mental categories, in intersubjective sense impressions or in specified constraints on ideal human choice. Indeed, there may be little for the foundationalist to choose between the metaphysics of rationalism and the metaphysics of empiricism: the object in both cases is to ground politics in something less contingent and less corrigible than politics itself tends to be.

Liberal political philosophy does have much to recommend it. To abjure liberal foundationalism promises an anarchy of unwieldy, free-standing alternative structures easily blown away by the winds and whims of mundane politics. Relativism, contingency, particularism, and radical subjectivism typify the architecture of such structures. Indeed, critics of foundationalism such as Richard Rorty, Michael Walzer, and this writer are most often assailed for their vulnerability to relativism and subjectivism, tendencies that are thought to uproot liberal values from the philosophical bedrock that gives them their political staying power. Politics bereft of philosophical foundations can quickly deteriorate into the rule of unreason or majoritarian tyranny. Foundationalist philosophy, on the other hand, offers a grounding for notions like liberty and right in the inviolable domain of natural and higher law or in the sanctuary of formal reason. In the absence of such firm prepolitical grounding, these and other cherished liberal values may be placed at permanent risk—not least of all from the arbitrariness of politics itself.

John Rawls and Robert Nozick entertain widely divergent ideas of the meaning of justice, but they are as one in believing that it must arise out of a notion of right that is prior to politics and that the task of philosophy is to establish such a notion free from the contamination of particularism and subjectivism—free, in other words, from politics. For both men, philosophically constructed notions of liberty and justice are made to produce a politics; neither understands those notions to be produced by a politics. Today, both progressive and conservative liberals are united in decrying the dangers posed to the rights and liberties of the private sector by democratic majorities that legislate free from the constraints of a higher law embodied in a constitution and administered by a judiciary. Progressives may emphasize the civil rights of minorities while neoconservatives stress the economic rights of individuals or corporations, but they will concur in opposing the right of the public to try to discover and legislate a common weal.

The primary political target of foundationalism is in fact democracy itself, the conceit that a public has the responsibility to legislate not only its own common destiny but also the standards by which what is common and what is individual (what is public and what is private) are determined. Here, philosophy, law, and morality—and those who read, write and teach them—are deemed better guardians of the public weal than the public whose weal is at stake. Academic philosophers are content to speak only to one another on this subject (even that great advocate of democratic discourse, Jürgen Habermas, writes books that are unintelligible to all but the most dedicated professional philosophers). In debating and resolving theoretical questions, they seem to assume that

7

they have resolved practical matters for confused citizens. On the whole, however, they are discomfited by the practicalities of party politics and political movements (few would emulate Edmund Burke or follow Charles Taylor into the morass of his nation's party politics). Robert Nozick goes so far as to announce (in the Preface to *Anarchy, State and Utopia*) his embarrassment at the stripe of conservative ideologue his ideas have attracted—as if ideas were games not to be taken seriously and ideologues had made a category mistake in taking him at his word.

Terms like "liberty," "politics," "power," "government," and "justice" are something more than pieces in an intellectual puzzle, however. They are the handles by which politicians and citizens (and philosophers who are citizens) try to capture and treat with the conflicts and commonalities of their intersecting lives. Since all citizens are trying to adjudicate conflicts or make decisions or get along with neighbors or pay for common services, and since it is finally common action that concerns them, they show little interest in truth or certainty or the epistemological status of moral propositions. Nozick is bemused at the incompatibility of his principles as philosophy (neoconservative) with his inclinations as a citizen (more progressive). A citizen would scarcely hesitate before dismissing abstract principles that were at odds with her civic convictions. "If my principles make my civic soul sick," she would reason, "there must be something wrong with my principles." The philosopher, on the other hand, is quick to surrender the civic convictions born of his citizenship if they violate the philosophical mindset required by his principles. This places him in a bind: he wishes to legislate for the body politic and to have thought count as action, but he expects to be exempted from accountability for his legislation because he is only thinking in the abstract. He thus pleads to be taken seriously even as he begs to be ignored.

The theorists who are the subject of the essays that follow are almost all philosophers first; philosophers of moral, legal, and political philosophy second; and students of or participants in politics per se only in some remote, tertiary sense. That is to say, their first loyalty is to philosophical clarity, their second is to the structure of moral and political argument, and their third and last is to the meaning (or lack of meaning) of *res publica* (the public good, the Republic) in and for itself. Michael Oakeshott alone qualifies as a teacher of politics, and that is the peculiar consequence of a long intellectual journey he has made from pure philosophy to political history, using politics as a kind of swaying bridge across the chasm dividing them. And of course Oakeshott rests his political theory on the presumed distinctiveness of the domain of politics from the domain of philosophy, insisting that the two can be merged only at the cost of endless confusion as well as a politics of peril. He is certainly no foundationalist. Perhaps he is best understood as a conventionalist, a distinction explored in Chapter Six. When he plays the political teacher, he sheds his philosophical garb—or, at least, pretends to.

Readers will search in vain among the others for signs of salient historical interests, sociological artifacts, or political practices. Even Alasdair MacIntyre, who makes the very historicized and socially embedded idea of a practice his central political norm, ascends in his quest for relief from modern relativism to an ethical stratosphere that leaves the real world of politics behind. He dictates mores and morals to the masses, but from the heights. His practical political advice can be taken seriously only by recluses.

As in so many marriages then, the marriage of philosophy to politics has been tantamount to the subjugation of one partner by the other. Politics reconstructed as theory has been trained to obey the rules of philosophy: to yield coherence by mimicking philosophical intelligibility. As women who seek credibility in a patriarchal world may sometimes behave not quite exactly as men behave but as they think men behave, so students of politics, in trying to establish their philosophical credentials, carry on in a fashion they imagine is appropriate to their aggressive philosophical suitors. If philosophy's categories are reflective, then action must be made to resemble reflection; if philosophy aspires to certainty, then justice must cease to be a flexible rule of thumb for practical human conduct and live up to certainty's demanding metaphysical standards; if philosophy is the sovereign discipline, then politics must permit itself to be subdued and conquered by it.

9

Thus does the quest for a useful *political* theory give way to the conquest of politics *by* theory.

The messily practical features of the world of common action that journalists, politicians, novelists, and mere citizens often associate with things political and that ought, one might think, to be the subject of an appropriate philosophical understanding are in fact as overshadowed in the marriage of politics to philosophy as a young woman's gifts and talents once were overshadowed in the traditional marriage of maiden and patriarch. Burke noted that the lines of politics and morality cannot be assimilated to the ideal lines of mathematics: they are, he observed, broad and deep as well as long, and they admit of exceptions and demand modifications. Philosophy is too often an absolutist science of straight lines, uncomfortable with exceptions and wary of modifications of its own standards. This is evident in the philosophical analysis of critical political terms such as "action," "autonomy," and "sovereignty." In conceptualizing them, philosophers often end up adapting, altering, or transmogrifying them, rather than penetrating or embracing them. Where he ought to be trying to tease out the intrinsic political character of such crucial notions, the analyst ends up imposing a stipulated philosophical character on them or putting them aside in favor of constructs more nearly suited to the constraints of his philosophical apparatus. As Nietzsche writes in *Beyond Good and Evil*, as soon as philosophy begins to believe in itself, it always creates the world in its own image. The questions we must now deal with are: What precisely is the image of philosophy? And what effect does this image have on philosophy's recreation of the political world?

Philosophy is, first of all, a reflective activity and is thus inclined to treat politics as a reflective activity. It is also reductive and is thus stymied by the irreducibility of politics, an irreducibility closely associated with political autonomy and political sovereignty. Finally, philosophy is reflexive and thus preoccupied with epistemology and inclined to cognitive imperialism. It is correspondingly resistant to the sovereignty of the political sphere. The "tyranny" (again Nietzsche) of these philosophical traits (and it is not the philosophers but philosophy per se that appears, as

Dewey suggests, "absolutist") is apparent when we review the political notions of action, autonomy, and sovereignty.

Take the notion of action. The embeddedness of politics in action suggests a temporality and contingency, as well as an engagement in the world of ongoing events that rebuffs facile philosophical reconstruction. Action means doing, and philosophical abstractions have a difficult time with doing, often undervaluing the extent to which it entails activity, energy, work, and participation—values little emphasized in liberal foundationalist theory. Such a theory, which construes politics in terms of accountability, representation, individual rights, and formal autonomy, consequently tends to suffuse the *vita activa* of politics with an untoward and enervating torpor. In *The Poverty of Philosophy*, Karl Marx observes how the solution of present problems does not lie for the philosopher in public action but in the "dialectical rotations of his own mind." In changing his categories, the philosopher thinks he alters the political world. Too many of our subjects in the chapters that follow celebrate the purity of categories, neglecting what Marx calls the profane origin and the profane history of the ideas they manipulate. Alasdair MacIntyre urges us to choose the ethics of Aristotle over the nihilism of Nietzsche. John Rawls recommends the discipline of the original position. Bertrand Russell wishes us to think our politics as we think our skepticism. Bruce Ackerman believes if we only talk aright, we may act aright. And Robert Nozick would have us reify our rights and recondition the rest of the political world accordingly. Nonetheless, politics remains something human beings *do*, not something they possess or use or watch or talk or think about. Those who would do something about it must do more than philosophize, and philosophy that is politically intelligible must take the full political measure of politics as conduct.

In the same spirit, politics as a domain of action needs to be characterized by the constraints of necessity and the accompanying logic of necessity. Specific actions are enmeshed in a chain of cause and effect already at work in the world and must be judged accordingly. To fail to act in these circumstances is also a form of action for which responsibility must be taken. Political actors are part of a continuing history, the inertial momentum of which, for better or worse, helps to define what it is they are "doing," as "nondecision" theory has made clear. In foundationalist philosophies, which are wedded to the quest for certainty and its attendant abstractionism and are seeking fixed and unambivalent meanings for things political, these kinds of complexities get pushed aside in favor of a comforting but spurious clarity—a clarity that illuminates not politics but some more easily lit two-dimensional political facsimile. Some students of the theory of social action are of course sensitive to the special properties of the political (Charles Taylor, Richard Bernstein, and R. A. Louch leap to mind, and one could do worse than to consult Machiavelli or Montesquieu or Rousseau), yet much of their effort is spent correcting the misdirected reductionism of foundationalist philosophy. Nor have such neopragmatist critics of foundationalism as Richard Rorty developed explicitly political theories of action, perhaps because the pragmatists they admire were themselves so remarkably unpolitical. Dewey was the exception among the classical pragmatists; but, other than Michael Walzer and perhaps Jürgen Habermas (if he is counted as an admirer of Peirce), there are few notably *political* modern critics of foundationalism in the pragmatist mold. Certainly the French poststructuralists from Foucault to Lacan and Derrida who are currently so fashionable lack an explicit political teaching (which is perhaps why they are currently so fashionable).

Autonomy would seem to be a more tractable political construct for philosophers. Its champion was the most eminent of German classical metaphysicians, and its theoretical defense has most often been built from philosophical materials. Yet, in its political incarnation, it is the child not of Kant but of Rousseau, a parentage that suggests an understanding of autonomy as social self-determination and common self-government. Rousseau's particular inspiration was to envision a form of political interaction—conditioned by consensual mores and a simple and austere socioeconomic environment—in which the psychology of particular interests guided by appropriate participatory institutions could produce public goods (the general will) even where individuals

12

qua individuals failed to distinguish these public goods from their private interests. Where, for Kant, the right issued out of the good will, which depended in turn on a commitment to rationality, for Rousseau the right issued out of the common will, which was produced by politics. Common willing, not private reasoning, was to be the key. Autonomy for Rousseau was a concomitant of political interaction, produced in part by it, rather than its necessary prelude, just as self-legislation was a feature of common action rather than of individual self-scrutiny. In short, for Rousseau the problem was not one of private knowing but of public doing, which is presumably why Rousseau preferred a Sparta that knew how to act aright to an Athens that knew how to think aright.

For philosophers of Rousseau's political-mindedness, if autonomy is to have social significance in the real political world, even questions of meaning that normally fall under the scrutiny of philosophy must be subordinated to processes of political deliberation and decision. Political autonomy in fact entails the autonomy of the political domain: the autonomy of the politicians or (in democratic regimes) the citizens in establishing common meanings and common ends, common agendas and a common language. The neo-Kantian philosopher wishes to make autonomy a feature of the nonpolitical person—the abstract agent—whereas the citizen sees in autonomy a product of membership in the polity. For him, autonomy is less the premise than the consequence of his citizenship. For the philosopher, the language of autonomy issues in the language of prepolitically grounded rights (universality, inviolability, individuality, abstract rationality, formal and negative freedom from external constraints). For the citizen, the language of autonomy issues in the language of commonality and community (deliberation, communicative discourse, political reason, freedom of association and membership, liberty to act on behalf of perceived goods and goals). This is the critical difference between Kant and Rousseau alluded to above. Ironically, although Kant celebrated him as the Newton of the moral world, he did not quite get Rousseau right. In translating Rousseau's language of the self-transforming, communal world of politics, where men are taken "as they are, and laws as they ought to be," into his own philosophical language partial to universals and immutables, where men are taken as they ought to be (rational and thus capable of individual good will) rather than as they are (self-interested, though capable of common will under the right political arrangements), Kant could only distort and ultimately abandon the genuine political meanings of Rousseau's crucial terms, "autonomy" chief among them.

As defined by action and autonomy, politics denotes a realm in which we continually re-create the abstractions of our thought in the new and often necessarily ambiguous terms of our evolving consciousness as members of a community held together by the necessity of common judgment and common action. By this understanding, the vaunted inscriptions found on the philosopher's stone must themselves become susceptible to politics, that is to say, to political deliberation and transformation. To try to re-create in the image of philosophy a domain that takes our philosophical understandings as it own mutable subject matter, at least where these understandings impinge on common action and are marked by dissensus, is to get things the wrong way around—although philosophical denizens of remote towers (ivory and otherwise) will perhaps be forgiven for thinking that their ruminations in private are somehow lexically prior to the people's in public.

To speak of the autonomy of the political is in fact to speak of the sovereignty of the political. For by sovereignty is meant not merely the dominion of the state over other forms of association, but the dominion of politically adjudicated knowledge, under conditions of epistemological uncertainty, over other forms of knowledge. To be sure, this sovereignty over knowledge is wholly residual: it comes into play only with the breakdown of ordinary cognitive consensus, and only where some public judgment is required by the need for common action. Where knowledge can prove itself certain, or at least where consensus is for the time being undisputed (as in the case of mainstream science, for example), or where the absence of consensus has no impact on public action (as in matters of private taste, for example), the political domain claims no sovereignty. But where scientists disagree on the public outcomes of experimental technologies (genetic engineering, for example), or where matters of taste are seen to have public consequences (the design of a national flag, for example), or where theoretical inquiry raises issues of common import (the dividing line between a fetus and a legal person, for example), the political realm necessarily becomes sovereign over the contested realms of science and taste and inquiry in which such disputes are ordinarily conducted. For at this point science, taste, and theoretical inquiry are reduced to *opinion* (*doxa*), and it is over opinion that sovereignty, defined by public judgment, necessarily holds sway, albeit only by default. Neither scientists nor artists nor theorists, consulting what in the face of their own inability to agree can only be regarded as contentious private opinion, will be left to their own uncertain devices to render private decisions about safety standards for molecular biology laboratories or color schemes for flags or rules for conducting abortions. The sovereignty of the political becomes the sovereignty of political knowledge (however partial or provisional or similar to opinion it appears) over philosophical knowledge (however orthodox or lexically prior or far from opinion it claims to be) wherever the philosophers fail to agree among themselves (most of the time?), or fail to offer arguments persuasive to the affected public, on issues that have import for public action. This lesson about the nature of political sovereignty can be reduced to a simple priority rule: whenever private theorists disagree on matters of public import, then the normal epistemological priority of truth over opinion is overridden and reversed in favor of the political priority of public over private. In other words, where knowing becomes doing, public opinion agreed upon overrules private "truth" disputed. The philosopher may trump the drop-out in private; but the citizen, even when he is a drop-out, trumps the philosopher in public.

Now it is clear that philosophers may feel uncomfortable, even outraged, in addressing the standards and procedures of a political domain to which their own epistemological criteria may be subordinated, particularly since they will regard their criteria, however contested, as both lexically prior and cognitively superior to

15

those deployed by the political public. They will no doubt wish to clarify the disreputable and inchoate standards of the political by subjecting politics itself to the test of their own more rigorous standards. But what they will discover is that their rigorous standards, if they are contested and are of political consequence, will always be subjected to the politics they aspire to suborn. It is not just that they *ought* to be trumped under such circumstances: it is that they *are* trumped and always will be, because that is the meaning of political sovereignty.

I hope it does not appear that I am merely rehearsing the voguish strategy associated with radical versions of the sociology of knowledge, where all scientific and philosophical agreements are deemed illegitimate spoils of conspiratorial political interaction among scientific and philosophical elites. Nor am I saying that truth is always a function of power. I am concerned with legitimate power (hence, politics), not brute force. And I am happy to cede the larger part of the realm of scientific and philosophical discourse to putative "truth" or whatever pale sociological reflections of truth are methodologically admissible under current philosophical standards (consensus, intersubjectivity, dominant paradigm, not yet falsified hypothesis, and so on). It is only in that small residual sector where philosophers and scientists fail to achieve consensus, and where the matters on which they disagree affect public action, that their conflicting views are necessarily subject to self-conscious political arbitration. This subordination is integral to the meaning of political sovereignty. For science, this issue occurs only on the frontiers, where paradigms are under active challenge. But for philosophy, conflict would seem to represent a perennial condition, reflecting philosophy's metascientific mode of argumentation and its lack of success in achieving either unimpeachable foundations or indefeasible paradigms for morals or politics (or much of anything else, for that matter). Hence, philosophers must expect absolute right or justice as fairness or neutral dialogue or the character of a practice to be fair topics of deliberation and decision for publics whose will ultimately imposes cloture on debate in a way the philosopher never can. That is why the priority rule makes politics the sovereign epistemological do-

16

main—not in order to arbitrate questions of truth or establish criteria of certain knowledge, but in order to permit public judgment and action in the absence of truth or cognitive certainty.

This rule helps to explain why experts can inform political decision making but cannot displace the decision makers. Expertise is a matter of access to specialized data and of positing causal linkages (science narrowly defined), whereas fundamental political decisions are a matter of evaluation and judgment of common values and community ends. In the realm of judgment, although data and linkages must be surveyed and factored in, there are no standards independent of those of the decision makers, otherwise known as the sovereign citizenry. (For a full discussion, see Chapter Eight.) Politics, then, does not displace philosophy, but it challenges philosophy's cognitive imperium where disagreement among philosophers prevents philosophy from resolving human dilemmas of action and where expertise falls short of the required evaluation and judgment. Because disagreements of this kind bedevil a great deal of philosophical discourse, the cognitive imperium of philosophy is challenged much more often than philosophers might wish, and the residual imperium of politics often extends further than citizens would ideally want.

Foundationalist and reductive philosophy of the kind we have been looking at here finds itself in a bind. It wishes to speak intelligibly about a domain whose categories are self-generating, subject to a process of transformation and legitimation that is ultimately more political than philosophical. As we have already noted, there are competing philosophical methods that recognize the limitations of formal thought and that attempt to fit philosophy to the cut of politics rather than the other way around. Hermeneutics is presumably a philosophical attempt to recognize the self-referential nature of the political and to render it intelligible by teasing out of it the self-referential language it has created from within. Pragmatism is an attempt to be true to the political by developing a language of consequences and ends appropriate to the domain of human action. Dialectics is an attempt to discover an all-embracing language of praxis in the collision and interaction

17

of philosophy and politics, thought and action, universality and particularity, and the ideal and the historical.

Nevertheless, liberal political philosophy in England and America continues to shape politics to the mold of its own cognitive requirements. We have already noted the costs to understanding and thus to thought and philosophy. There have also been some costs to the politics of liberalism, costs that I have remarked on at length elsewhere (in the first section of *Strong Democracy*). These costs include a demeaning portrait of the human being as an abstract monad and as *homo economicus*: man as beast, as interest-monger, as disinterested agent or grasping consumer, as hostile competitor and predatory aggressor. They also include an antipathy to democracy and its sustaining institutional structures (participation, civic education, political activism) and a preference for "thin" rather than strong versions of political life in which citizens are spectators and clients while politicians are professionals who do the actual governing—in other words, an understanding of democracy not as collective self-government but as the rule of elites who are periodically legitimized by elections. Additional costs are an unrealistic belief in politics as a processor of predetermined values and ends rather than as a producer of such values, an absolutist approach to rights that ignores their socially embedded character, and an understanding of the individual as a solitary rather than a social being, someone with a fixed nature (hedonism) beyond the reach of history or circumstance.

For all of these political weaknesses, liberal philosophy possesses important political strengths—above all, the capacity to endow its institutions with stability and to provide rights and liberties (including property) with a powerful bulwark against statist tyranny. Nowhere were its strengths more visible than in the struggles for emancipation from feudalism, hierarchy, and absolute monarchy that were the political signature of the seventeenth and eighteenth centuries. Liberal theory as dissent theory created an ideology of emancipation crucial to the emergence of the modern democratic state. Yet in democratic times, when the initial emancipatory struggles are concluded, philosophies of resistance lose much of their political force. To posit and then theorize the indi-

18

vidual as an abstract solitary may be helpful on the way to loosening feudal bonds and demarcating a clear space for rebels attempting to individuate themselves from a hierarchical and oppressive order. But it may appear as an obstructive exercise in nostalgia in an era when the extent and quality of citizenship are in question and when the bonds that hold together free communities are growing slack. For centuries, there was a need to stake out a circumscribed private ground in an otherwise statist, mercantilist, all-too-public world. In our own day, the need would seem to be to identify and fence in some small public space in an individualistic, anomic, all-too-privatized world. The philosophical conceits and emancipatory metaphors of liberal theory have little to offer to the anomic survivors of a post-emancipated society. Liberal philosophy helped to propel the West into democratic times, but democratic times call for something more sustaining than liberal philosophy.

There is a paradoxical, even contradictory, aspect to my criticism here, for I seem to argue both that liberal theory is too remote from its subject matter to capture it with understanding—that it is in a certain sense irrelevant to politics—*and* that it has quite literally captured politics by remaking it in its own image—that it is determinative of (and thus destructive to) politics. Yet it is precisely both of these things: in its abstractness and philosophical rigidity, it has failed to get hold of and render intelligible crucial features of a free polity (for example, autonomy, action, sovereignty); but at the same time it has reshaped our politics in the mold of its abstractions, at the cost of a lively and sustainable democratic political life. In their quest for a foundation for politics, most philosophers seek what John Rawls called reflective equilibrium. Alexis de Tocqueville, as astute a political philosopher as any of our contemporaries, argued the contrary. In contrast to the moral and philosophical worlds, where everything is classified, systematized, foreseen, and decided beforehand, he observed that in the political world everything is agitated, disputed, and uncertain. In such a world, we require not a sturdy foundation to prevent politics from moving, but a seaworthy vessel to ensure that philosophy moves. Reflective equilibrium may suit philosophy, but for the tumultuous realm of politics, where life means constant motion and change is the only certainty, what is required is reflective disequilibrium.

AN ARGUMENT as broad and general as this one will obviously appear forceful only to varying degrees as it is applied to one or another of the particular philosophers who are the subject of the chapters that follow. Yet it is an argument as much to be drawn from as to be applied to liberal theorists; at least, that is what I hope to demonstrate. Bertrand Russell is, for example, the first twentieth-century philosopher to endorse explicitly a theory of liberalism rooted in the epistemology of empiricism, and the portrait of him in the next chapter sets the framework for the chapters that follow.

John Rawls and Robert Nozick, among the best-known philosophers of justice in our own time, come at the political question of justice from opposite ends of the political and philosophical spectrum. Yet, as my examinations in Chapters Three and Four argue, they are united by a reductionist approach that refuses to take politics on its own terms. Different as the two philosophers are ideologically, their common methodological commitments converge to expose all of the difficulties of foundationalist liberalism.

Bruce Ackerman, aware of the perils of abstractionism and writing in part to overcome them, nonetheless falls short of establishing a completely adequate language of politics because he remains a reluctant captive of the philosophical ideal of neutrality. I have treated him in a peculiar but fitting manner by taking his love of dialogic talk to heart and constructing Chapter Five as a mini-drama.

Alasdair MacIntyre rejects modern liberalism in the name of Aristotelian practice but develops an antidote to modernity that is without political relevance. I am in sympathy with his despair at the privatized, vapidly ambitious commercial culture that has grown up alongside of democratic political institutions, and I share his fear that liberalism bears some of the responsibility for that culture's vices. But in his despair, he is reduced to nostalgia

20

and cynicism. What his work achieves as cultural criticism it forfeits as political criticism, ironically at least in part because it shares in the indifference to the politics of democracy that is the mark of modern philosophical liberalism.

Michael Oakeshott is a special case, a genuine political philosopher, but one who establishes his politics by declaring its radical separation from philosophy. Oakeshott is hardly a democrat; but in his responsiveness to the inadequacies of liberal modes of discourse he does offer a model of a more appropriate kind of political understanding.

What political understanding actually is, I confront directly in Chapter Eight, the concluding essay on political judgment. Political judgment is, I shall argue, a political rather than a cognitive faculty; this makes it the centerpiece in a philosophy of politics that is at the same time necessarily a philosophy of democracy. Indeed, the essential argument of *The Conquest of Politics* is that political theory and the politics of democracy share a profound and provoking kinship. Both are rooted in the quest for a language that must be common and conversational, a language by which the imperatives of common conduct can be both informed and rendered intelligible.

TWO

Solipsistic Politics:
Bertrand Russell and
Empiricist Liberalism

> In our day, as in the time of Locke, empiricist Liber-
> alism is the only philosophy that can be adopted by a
> man who . . . demands some scientific evidence for
> his beliefs, and . . . desires human happiness more
> than the prevalence of this or that party or creed.
>
> Bertrand Russell,
> "Philosophy and Politics" (*Unpopular Essays*)

THE CONQUEST of politics by philosophy began well before the age of liberalism. It began at least as early as the seventeenth century with the English Dissenters' search for a secure moral foundation for resistance to absolutist tyranny. This search became a quest after a natural and thus a divine sanction for the rights and liberties of a people who wished to delegitimize monarchical absolutism and legitimize constitutional rule. If the legitimacy of a government was to be measured by its service to the maintenance of prepolitical liberty that defined men by nature, then politics could be understood only by examining man's prepolitical or natural condition. Politics issued out of the metaphysics of naturalism. Whether natural law was rooted in a naturalistic psychology of motion (Hobbes's hedonism) or in God's providence reflected in the state of nature (Locke's naturalism), its rightfulness as a political standard reflected its antecedents. Right was a natural rather than a human contrivance, and neither kings nor (later) democracies had the authority to challenge or infringe it. Power and sovereignty might depend on will, but legitimacy and right were functions of a higher order of being.

With the success of ideologies of dissent rooted in naturalism, the need for metaphysical grounds for rebellion against traditional forms of nonrational authority was attenuated. Nevertheless, in our age of liberalism, an age made possible by dissent but one that no longer requires ideologies of resistance, philosophers still look to independent grounds for the rooting of their political norms. They no longer can appeal to metaphysical naturalism—Hume and Kant saw to that. Nor can they adhere to simplistic forms of empiricism (in which the incorrigibility of facts and the irreducibility of data are thought to be grounds for cognitive certainty about things political)—Hume and Kant also disposed of that temptation, although positivist social science has continued to chase the chimera of an empirically grounded "science" of politics. Yet a powerful connection persists between what philosophers think is required by the criteria of cognition (philosophy as epistemology) and what they think ought legitimately to "count" as politics.

From John Stuart Mill to Sir Karl Popper, liberals emancipated from the requirements of dissent and rebellion have continued to focus on the implications for liberal politics of cognitive skepticism of a particular postnaturalist kind. One might have thought that the modern crisis in philosophical certitude would free politics from its dependency on liberal metaphysics; and indeed, for certain pragmatists, relativists, and deconstructionists this has been the case (see Chapter One). But for many liberal philosophers, the opposite has been true. The skeptical critique of liberal metaphysics has itself become a new basis for linking liberal politics to philosophy. Nowhere is this more presciently seen than in the writings of Bertrand Russell, an extraordinary philosopher who not only wrote at great length about politics but who believed that political understanding must necessarily mirror philosophical understanding.

Among the multiple products of Bertrand Russell's panoptic intelligence, his writings on politics have been slighted. Admirers of his analytic lucidity are content to celebrate his mathematical philosophy and some of his later work in the philosophy of science and the philosophy of mind, while those stunned by his persona and touched by his moral courage dwell on his life—his practical engagement in the great issues of suffrage, pacifism, nuclear disarmament, and world peace. Consequently, his political thought, falling somewhere between pure theory and vigorous praxis, is often treated as a function of his journalism. The political books, on this view, are a kind of tribute exacted by his political principles, popular "potboilers" (Russell's own term) to pay the bills academic emoluments might have met had he kept his politics to himself and lived passively as a distinguished academic logician. A. J. Ayer thus pays Russell's political thought little heed, passing over it entirely in his *Russell and Moore* and just grazing it in his *Modern Masters* account. The assumption would seem to be that Russell's politics was neither informed by nor reflected in his philosophy and so could be safely ignored by students of his philosophy. Similarly, devotees of his politics freely ignored his philosophy, which they presumed existed in pristine splendor, unadulterated by his worldly political opinions.

It does not help that Russell's political writings fail to evince much systematic continuity or that relative immunity to time and topicality that, because it suggests philosophical wisdom, attracts permanent attention. The early works assail Bolshevism with a spirit of ardent individualism, principled pacifism, and a hint of anarchism. Later, power and authority emerge as dominant concepts, while the quest for liberty seems overshadowed by the quest for peace—almost at any cost. Each book thus seems to speak its own language, develop its own inflections, and create its own context depending on the relevant issues of the day and the pertinent subject at hand. Each is to some degree a *livre d'occasion*, although Russell's lively independence assures that the *livre* is always a good deal less fashionable than the *occasion*. Finally, Russell's political theory may seem even to the sympathetic observer to be superficial, journalistic, inconsistent, eclectic, and unoriginal—too often the hostage of Russell's practical engagements, too seldom addressed to the great discourse that defines the history of mankind's political thought.

Yet such a judgment would undervalue Russell's political writing egregiously. To begin with, charges of inconsistency and lack of continuity seem quite beside the point. The leaps that carried

Russell from pacifism to humanistic patriotism, from visions of mutualist utopia to reluctant advocacy of American or Russian world hegemony in the name of survival were no more staggering and certainly no less explicable than the leaps that carried him from early Platonism to scientific empiricism and, after a glancing encounter with mysticism, to radical empiricism, to skepticism, and beyond. A man who lives nearly one hundred years, if his mind does not predecease his body, had better change his views several times—in politics and in metaphysics. There is nothing like a timely death to lend rigor and consistency to a life's work. Russell had to contend with staying alive; and by the time he was ninety, consistency must have seemed to him less like the hobgoblin of little minds than the hallmark of a short life. Indeed, as I argue throughout this book, the power of political analysis depends in no little part on its hostility to the universalizing tendencies of philosophy and on it willingness to forgo consistency when consistency obstructs our capacity to comprehend the particularistic and circumstantial character of the political world. Russell's inconsistency was, by the standards of particularism, no different than Montesquieu's or Rousseau's or Burke's, a virtue rather than a defect.

There is a further compelling reason not to dismiss Russell's political thought on grounds of inconsistency or particularism: Russell himself regarded that part of his work with utmost seriousness. Although he was amply self-critical about certain of his political works, he regarded the thesis of *Power* as being of great importance and was disappointed that, despite the book's popularity, it was not always treated with the seriousness he thought it deserved.[1] He testified repeatedly to the continuity of theory and praxis in his own life, observing in his contrived "obituary" that "Russell's principles were curious, but, such as they were, they governed his actions."[2]

For all of Russell's political particularism—the mercurial nature

[1] *The Autobiography of Bertrand Russell*, 3 vols. (London: Allen and Unwin, 1969), 2: 193.
[2] *Unpopular Essays* (London: Unwin Books, 1968), p. 158.

of his political opinions—the continuity between his political theory and his philosophy remained quite striking. Perhaps the most unfortunate consequence of the neglect shown Russell's political thought has been the failure to perceive and understand the vital connection between his radical empiricism and his persistent liberalism, a feature of his thought central to our theme of the conquest of politics by philosophy. Russell was one of the last of that long line of British philosophers whose work epitomized an extraordinary alliance, both dynamic and fruitful and at the same time misleading and corrosive to politics: the liaison between empiricism and liberalism. Perhaps he was even the last of the line, "the last survivor of a dead epoch" as he mischievously suggested.[3] If we count Hobbes as a dubious forefather and trace the lineage from Locke and Berkeley down through Hume and Mill, then Russell is indeed the last empiricist liberal, the last to try to wring from the justificatory enterprise arguments that both describe the world and prescribe human conduct in the social setting, the last to try to render the metaphysics of sense experience consistent with the politics of liberty secured by power, the last to try to answer the question "What can Man do?" by asking 'What can Man know?'' Yet, if Russell was the last of the old liberals to link liberalism with the particular metaphysics of empiricism, he was the first of the modern liberals to insist on a connection, *some* connection, between modes of knowing and the politics of conduct, between philosophical cognition and political understanding. Empiricism is no longer regarded as the appropriate linkage by his successors, but the necessity for rooting political prescription (theories of justice, for example) in philosophical foundations of one kind or another (rationality, for example) has become a leading dogma of liberal political philosophy.

When we take Russell's self-appellation "empiricist liberal" seriously, then, we provide a context for apprehending his political thought that clarifies its essential liberalism, that throws into sharp relief its relationship to the polarized premises of the empiricist metaphysic, and that forges a template for the relationship of

---

[3] Ibid.

politics to philosophy that has survived Russell and continues to operate in the present day in a great deal of what we still regard as liberal philosophy. In fact, many of the strengths and not a few of the deficiencies of liberal thought derive from the close kinship that ties the empirical and liberal traditions together in British and American philosophy and politics. Russell's political ideas are made comprehensible in their almost schizophrenic treatment of liberty and power when they are examined in the context of the interface between these traditions.

II

That Russell is a liberal requires elaboration rather than demonstration. He often depicted himself as a "British Whig, with a British love of compromise and moderation,"[4] though moderation was not, as I will argue, well served by his liberalism. In describing early liberalism in the *History of Western Philosophy*, he might almost be describing himself: "[E]arly liberalism," he contends, "was optimistic, energetic and philosophic . . . it appeared likely . . . to bring great benefits to mankind . . . it was opposed to everything medieval, both in philosophy and politics . . . the distinctive character of the whole movement [was] . . . individualism."[5] The liberal political program was, in its major thrust, Russell's political program; its dilemmas were his dilemmas. Jean-Jacques Rousseau posed the dilemma in paradigmatic liberal terms (although his solutions transcended liberalism): "[T]he problem is to find a form of association which will defend and protect with the whole common force the person and goods of each associate, and in which each, while uniting himself with all, may still obey himself alone, and remain as free as before."[6] This is the liberal challenge: to accommodate conflict and ameliorate competition without surrendering individuality, to employ power in the service of liberty, to contain the aggressiveness that issues

---

[4] *Sceptical Essays* (London: Unwin Books, 1960), p. 9.
[5] *The History of Western Philosophy* (London: Allen and Unwin, 1961), p. 578.
[6] J.-J. Rousseau, *The Social Contract* (London: J. M. Dent, 1913), bk. I, ch. 6, p. 12.

out of man's individuality without destroying the liberty that is individuality's chief virtue, to accommodate the requirements of order and legality and yet remain as "free as before." Rousseau attacked the problem by violating the framework, that is, by transforming liberty and recognizing the human condition as one of inescapable dependency (chains). But Russell, true liberal that he was, felt pressed to preserve the dilemma in its pure and thus most intractable form. In an early letter, written during his visit to the nascent Soviet state, he grasps the dilemma's poignance in movingly personal terms:

> I know that for collective action the individual must be turned into a machine . . . yet it is the individual soul that I love . . . its loneliness, its hopes and fears, its quick impulses and sudden advances. It is such a long journey from this to armies and officials; and yet it is only by making this journey that one can avoid a useless sentimentalism.[7]

In *The Practice and Theory of Bolshevism*, he puts it with less agony but greater simplicity: "Government and the law, in their very essence, consist of restrictions on freedom, and freedom is the greatest of political goals."[8] Yet he is also clear (later, in *Power*) that "there must be power, either that of governments or that of anarchical adventurers. There must even be naked power, so long as there are rebels against government, or even ordinary criminals."[9] There must, in brief, be liberty—that is the end, the aim, the object of politics. Yet there must be power—for that is the essence, the substance, the sine qua non of politics. The natural issue of liberty uncontained is anarchism; the natural issue of power uncontained is dominion. The liberal dilemma is simply how to preserve liberty without falling into anarchy, how to use power without falling into dominion. "Every community is faced with two dangers," according to Russell, "anarchy and despotism . . . [both] are alike disastrous."[10] Liberty denies power, but what

---

[7] *Autobiography*, 2: 105.
[8] *The Practice and Theory of Bolshevism* (London: Unwin Books, 1962), p. 82.
[9] *Power: A New Social Analysis* (London: Allen and Unwin, 1938), p. 106.
[10] Ibid., p. 211.

then will deny anarchy? Power thwarts anarchy, but what then will thwart dominion?

Anarchy or despotism—this polarity seems built into liberal theory, giving it its characteristic instability, its restlessness, its ambivalence toward both liberty (a virtue frought with vice) and power (a vice that may serve virtue). It might appear that power can, in liberal thought, never have any other end than the security of the individual and the guarantee of his liberty. "It is the individual," Russell is certain, "in whom all that is good must be realized, and the free growth of the individual must be the supreme end of a political system which is to refashion the world."[11] Yet the individuals in whose name power is always exercised often seek power as an end in itself. They are closer to beasts than to gods—"pole-cats and foxes" even in Locke's somewhat civilized gloss on Hobbesian man. Russell's conception, infused with Freudian irrationalism, is little different. Politics issues out of the needs of passion-impelled individuals who are distinguishable from the beasts not by the transcending but only by the boundlessness of their desires. Whereas animal desires are specific and satiable, human desires are "essentially boundless and incapable of complete satisfaction,"[12] giving rise to adverse conditions that make politics both necessary and possible. From mankind's "infinite desires," from its endless lust for power, which, in a "Titanic combination of nobility and impiety," drives it to attempt to "be God," comes "competition, the need of compromise and government, the impulse to rebellion . . . [and] the need of morality to restrain anarchic self-assertion."[13]

The individual creature who lurks behind liberal political formulas is an awesome animal, evoking our approbation as he excites our fears. He is a "wild beast" whose "primitive lusts and egoisms" must be curbed,[14] but whose saving individuality must be cherished and protected. Contemplating the beast can lead a

[11] *Roads to Freedom: Socialism, Anarchism and Syndicalism* (London: Unwin Books, 1966), p. 97.
[12] *Power*, p. 7.
[13] Ibid., p. 9.
[14] *Roads to Freedom*, p. 73.

liberal to "abandon political thinking as a bad job, and to conclude that the strong and ruthless must always exploit the weaker and kindlier."[15] It can lead him, in other words, to acknowledge dominion as man's natural fate.

A part of Russell remained in permanent revolt against the ugliness of the portrait of man drawn by his Freudian realism. During the First World War and again in the 1930s he had to grapple with a paralyzing despair that suffused him with melancholia and nearly immobilized him. In a bitter letter, written during the height of Britain's war hysteria in 1917, he wrote: "I hate the world and almost all the people in it . . . I hate the planet and the human race—I am ashamed to belong to such a species—And what is the good of me in that mood?"[16] Yet for a "vigorous and temperamentally hopeful" liberal, man the beast cannot entirely eclipse man the individual.[17]

Like all aristocratic liberals, like that runaway liberal aristocrat Nietzsche, Russell despaired for man the species even as he harbored hope for man the individual. Indeed, it is precisely the hope of liberal politics that man the individual can be rescued from man the animal species. Government for Russell, as for his liberal predecessors, is calculated to secure natural individuality by restraining individualism (anarchy). It is thus always prudential, a manipulative instrument in the service of minimalist objectives like security, justice (narrowly construed), and conservation, rather than a creative vehicle for achieving progress or promoting welfare or uncovering a public weal.[18]

Consequently, Russell's liberalism tends to be only incidentally egalitarian—interested in justice but indifferent to democracy per se. Nineteenth-century aristocrat that he was, he had little patience with the masses. He shared completely John Stuart Mill's distrust of the "few wise and many foolish individuals called the pub-

---

[15] Ibid., p. 79.
[16] Letter to Colette, *Autobiography*, 2: 77.
[17] *The Practice and Theory of Bolshevism*, p. 79.
[18] See *Authority and the Individual: The Reith Lectures for 1948–49* (London: Unwin Books, 1964), p. 67.

lic,"[19] warning in "The Need for Political Scepticism" that "an honest politician will not be tolerated by a democracy unless he is very stupid . . . because only a very stupid man can honestly share the prejudices of more than half the nation."[20] His cynicism is even more extravagant in *Power*, where he notes that "the most successful democratic politicians are those who succeed in abolishing democracy and becoming dictators."[21] If power is always perilous, popular power unchecked by wisdom, prudence, or limits on its exercise is positively devastating. Remonstrating with critics of leisure, Russell reminded his readers in *In Praise of Idleness* that the leisure class, whatever economic oppressions and political tyrannies it may have fostered, "contributed nearly the whole of what we call civilization. It cultivated the arts and discovered the sciences; it wrote the books, invented the philosophies and refined social relations . . . without the leisure class, man never would have emerged from barbarism."[22] The few save the many from themselves and thus preserve the best in mankind from the worst. Individuality is threatened by the plurality of individuals, necessitating the forms of power and control. But power exercised plurally (that is, democratically) continues to threaten individuality and the excellence upon which civilization depends. Thus, individualism is, in the typical liberal fashion, pitted against itself, adumbrating the tension between quality and equality that has characterized all liberal democratic regimes.

Self-contradiction is also built into the liberal idea of power: the beast who is father to the individual needs to be both tamed (controlled by power) and preserved (insulated from power). Politics is human zoo-keeping of a particularly delicate kind: too many cages, though they keep the animals from one another, destroy their natural character; too few, though uninhibiting to be sure, unleash the beasts upon one another. Power, in its liberal manifestation, is thus the means by which it curbs itself as an end, the

[19] J. S. Mill, *On Liberty* (Everyman Edition, London: J. M. Dent, 1910), p. 83.
[20] In *Sceptical Essays*, p. 99.
[21] *Power*, p. 47.
[22] *In Praise of Idleness* (London: Unwin Books, 1960), p. 19.

device arising out of desire that permits desire to be limited. Because it coerces in order to free, power serves man's individuality by subduing man's will.

These contradictions and ambiguities can be found everywhere in Russell's liberalism. To some degree, his entire political career—the whole of his political thought—is devoted to a largely unsuccessful search for answers to the Confucian riddle from Lao-tzu that serves as the epigraph to his early *Roads to Freedom*: "Production without possession, action without self-assertion, development without domination. . . ." And, one might add, excellence without inequality, individuality without anarchy, and power without dominion. How to use power to emancipate man from the yoke of nature's scarcity and from his own insatiable desires (of which scarcity is but nature's reflection) and yet prevent his enslavement to the instruments of his liberation? How to preserve freedom by curtailing it? Where to find a lion bold enough to contain the strife of pole-cats yet mild enough to be trusted by them? These are dilemmas that arise at every step in the development of Russell's liberal thought and that remain endemic to the liberal way of thinking about politics. Russell is a liberal, then, not simply because he is an individualist and an instrumentalist who sees in politics a necessary but dangerous instrument of prudential power, but because for him the road to freedom is always paved with a form of power that is insidious to freedom. He is a liberal because, for all his temperamental moderation, he can find no middle ground between anarchy and despotism. He is a liberal because democracy strikes him as being more necessary than it is desirable. And he is a liberal because power draws him with an awesomeness that horrifies him, defines man's nature with a decisiveness that appalls him, captures the purposes of human life with a finality that fills him with despair. His life is a struggle with, for, about power: the need to express, to do, to change, to manipulate, to cause, to overcome and to liberate. "Power over people's minds," he writes, "is the main personal desire of my life."[23]

---

[23] Letter to Lucy Donnelly, *Autobiography*, 2: 59.

The goal may be liberty, but power, finally, is what politics is all about. Indeed, it is a virtue of Russell's liberalism that he still sees in power a crucible of politics. For the liberals who come after him, the preoccupation with the philosophical conditions of legitimate political understanding often seems to extirpate both politics and its critical constituents, such as power. But if power was too much on the mind of Bertrand Russell, it has been, as we shall see, too little on the minds of such philosophers as Rawls, Nozick, Ackerman, and MacIntyre.

III

The argument that the form taken by liberalism may reflect the shape of empiricism suggests that there ought to be a significant relationship between the liberal dichotomization of liberty and power on the one hand and elements in the empiricist metaphysic on the other. Empiricism was in part a response to and a concomitant of the disappointment with revelation, naturalism, and rationalism that attended the emergence of modern science. Revelation was mired in superstition and authoritarianism; naturalism had been too generous with its favors, giving sustenance to far too many divergent normative systems; reason, as an active faculty seeking out the forms of external reality, was declared unfit either to inspire discovery or to certify knowledge. Sense experience, on the other hand, although it narrowed the notions of what was to qualify as knowledge, extended epistemological confidence in the status of what could be known. The observational method engineered by the early empiricists penetrated the world by withdrawing from it, enlarged the realm of intersubjective communication by restricting the realm of communicative discourse. Reason was appropriately devalued, reduced to an instrument of ratiocination without the power to apprehend, to posit, or to evaluate. The Kantian attempt at reconstructing reason was dismissed as an unfortunate detour on the journey to epistemological clarity—a journey resumed by post-Kantian empiricists such as Russell himself, who in *The History of Western Philosophy* portrayed Kant as a foolish dissenter from Hume's empiricist wisdom.

Russell was, on these terms, a complete empiricist. In *Human Knowledge*, he writes, "individual percepts are the basis of all our knowledge, and no method exists by which we can begin with data which are public to many observers."[24] Although he was increasingly skeptical over his lifetime about the ontological status of the external world, he was certain even in his more confident moments that its existence depended on "unobservable entities" that could (at best) only be inferred from percepts.

The pertinent question is then: What sorts of common patterns, if any, are to be found in Russell's empiricism and in his dilemma-strewn liberalism? I am not solely concerned here with the well-discussed parallels of such Hobbesian pairs as logical atomism and individualism, mechanistic reductionism and state of nature reasoning, or physical mechanics and psychological hedonism. I want rather to get at those features of empiricism that may help to illuminate and perhaps even account for the central polarity between liberty and power (anarchy and dominion) that I have depicted as the chief dilemma of Russell's liberalism. I want to show that empiricism is itself characterized by a deep psychological (and perhaps logical) ambivalence toward certainty and mankind's capacity to know the world that mirrors to some degree the dichotomic elements in the liberal dilemma. And finally, I want to demonstrate that Russell's empiricism was particularly inclined toward this ambivalence in ways that help to illuminate the ambiguity of his attitudes toward liberty and power. I will be satisfied if I can suggest certain striking parallels in the conceptual structures of empiricism and liberalism. Whether these parallels reflect a causal interplay between the two, either historically or psychologically, is beyond the resources of my argument.

The ambivalence toward uncertainty that I have claimed is endemic to empiricism issues directly out of its methodological solipsism—its preoccupation with subjective sense data as the necessarily privatistic starting point for all knowledge. For solipsism is psychologically disposed toward both passivity and aggression.

[24] *Human Knowledge: Its Scope and Limits* (London: Allen and Unwin, 1948), p. 22.

It proclaims its humility ("all knowledge is subjective") in the language of hubris ("subjective knowledge is *all* the knowledge there is"). In the interplay of humility and hubris in the empiricist metaphysic lie vital clues to the interplay of liberty and power in liberal political thought.

Solipsism's inclination toward humility appears to be a psychological reflection of certain logical features in its philosophical structure. Sensory experience is very much a trap: it not only closes persons off from the "real world" that percepts can project only inferentially but also denies them direct access to the experimental content of other persons' percepts. In Russell's descripton of Locke's empiricism, "we cannot know of the existence of other people, or of the physical world, for these, if they exist, are not merely ideas in my mind. Each one of us, accordingly must, so far as knowledge is concerned, be shut up in himself, and cut off from all contact with the outer world."[25] We can know what others experience only as mediated by our own experience, which is to say that we can never really *know* what others experience. This paradox belongs to Russell as well as to Locke. Ultimately, it compels him to conclude that "all human knowledge is uncertain, inexact, and partial. To this doctrine we have not found any limitation whatsoever."[26] This bleak conclusion, rendered inevitable by methodological solipsism's lack of ontological confidence in the self, is radically discomforting in its implications. It leads Russell eventually to adopt a position "not unlike that of Berkeley," but far more depressing because it is "without his God and his Anglican complacency."[27] Humility is eventually converted into desperation: "Solipsism," he recalls in the *Autobiography*, in a passage redolent of Carl Becker, "oppressed me [during the early 1930s] . . . it seemed that what we had thought of as laws of nature were only linguistic conventions, and that physics was not

---

[25] *History of Western Philosophy*, p. 591.

[26] *Human Knowledge*, p. 527.

[27] *Autobiography*, 2: 160. In reaching this sober diagnosis, he notes, "the best years of my life were given to the Principles of Mathematics, in the hope of finding somewhere some certain knowledge. The whole of this effort, in spite of three big volumes, ended inwardly in doubt and bewilderment."

really concerned with an external world. I do not mean that I quite believed this, but that it became a haunting nightmare. . . .[28] Russell summed up the nightmare in a "pessimistic meditation" written at Telegraph House during this period:

> The revolutions of nebulae, the birth and death of stars, are no more than convenient fictions in the trivial work of linking together my own sensations, and perhaps those of other men not much better than myself. No dungeon was ever constructed so dark and narrow as that in which the shadow physics of our time imprisons us, for every prisoner has believed that outside his walls a free world existed; but now the prison has become the whole universe. There is darkness without, and when I die there will be darkness within. There is no splendour, no vastness, anywhere; only triviality for a moment, and then nothing.
> Why live in such a world? Why even die?[29]

Yet if solipsism issued in skepticism and promoted a dark, despairing passivity, if it was finally a "dead end" (as Russell suggested in the *History of Western Philosophy*)[30] terminating in nihilism, it was also capable of nourishing assertiveness. In denying our capacity ever to know directly the external world other than through the subjective senses, it brought the self, the subjective perceptor, into new prominence—not, as happened with idealism, as a metaphysical surrogate for the world, but as a methodological avenue leading back into the world. The reflexivity that was to become so characteristic of modern liberal philosophy surfaced here in Russell with the attempt to find in the self an epistemological standard the world could no longer offer. In this, reflexivity promised that modesty might have its rewards, that epistemological humility might actually facilitate scientific conquest—the conquest of politics itself. The renunciation of the epistemologies of revelation and rational naturalism had, after all, had as its aim not

---

[28] Ibid., p. 158.
[29] Ibid., pp. 158–159.
[30] *History of Western Philosophy*, p. 634.

the cultivation of skepticism but the enhancement of certainty. Traditional epistemology, for all of its bold claims, had finally stood in the way of mastery over nature. As Russell noted late in his philosophical career, "it is not by prayer and humility that you cause things to go as you wish, but by acquiring a knowledge of natural laws . . . the power to be acquired in this way is very much greater than the power that men formerly sought to achieve by theological means."[31]

If methodological solipsism provoked a certain skepticism, more often it seemed to generate hubris. At the time he wrote *The Problems of Philosophy* (1912), Russell was still confident enough in the existence of the external world to warn against the dangers of assertive solipsism in the most dramatic terms: "Greatness of the soul is not fostered by those philosophies which assimilate the universe to Man . . . the view which tells us that Man is the measure of all things, that truth is man-made, that space and time and the world of universals are properties of the mind, and that, if there be anything not created by the mind, it is unknowable and of no account to us . . . is . . . untrue [and] has the effect of robbing philosophic contemplation of all that gives it value, since it fetters contemplation to Self."[32] Although Russell was clearly concerned with forms of subjectivist idealism, his strictures apply with equal force to subjectivist empiricism, for empiricism affects to know the world by reducing it to a measure of the self even narrower than a priori ideas, namely, sensations or percepts. And it was modern science's preoccupation with sense observations, with percepts as basic data, with a reading of the world taken in the first instance through the senses or instrumental (technological) extensions of the senses that made it successful. Not induction but observation, not verification (or falsification) but sense perception, not the positing of objectivity but a surrender to subjectivity—these were its secrets. If methodological solipsism as an attitude is as disposed to certainty as to skepticism—as disposed,

[31] *Autobiography*, 3: 29.
[32] *The Problems of Philosophy* (Oxford: Oxford University Press, 1959), pp. 92–93.

practically, to mastery as to abdication—then, although "the external world may be an illusion . . . [and] order, unity and continuity . . . human inventions just as truly as are catalogues and encyclopedias" [solipsism as skepticism], nevertheless, "human inventions can, within limits, be made to prevail in our human world . . ." (solipsism as mastery).[33]

Empiricism's ambivalence—the paradox of solipsism—thus comes full circle. Man exerts ever greater control, thanks to empiricism, over a world that, thanks to empiricism, disappears before his inquiring eyes. The cosmos is mastered by techniques arising out of the premise that it cannot be shown to exist; and the more effectively it is mastered, the less warrant there is for believing it does exist. So we finally arrive at the ultimate irony of Hiroshima, where forces known to us only as abstractions, resting on a physics that wrests from philosophers the last vestiges of a belief in the existence of an orderly external world, nonetheless manage to lay waste to a city, decide a world war, and revolutionize the course of human history—threatening, as it were, to reunite us in mundane practice with the nothingness to which our skepticism commits us in metaphysical theory. Russell, his life fairly swimming in such ironies, thus feels compelled by modern physics both to abandon all philosophical certitude about the world *and* to plunge nobly into the world to save it from the practical consequences of the self-same physics that has inspired his doubts.

In one of those frequent jeremiads with which he tempered his natural optimism, he went so far as to suggest that solipsism was a form of insanity.[34] Russell's primary target was idealism, but there is also a sense in which solipsistic empiricism seems to move toward insanity at both ends of its ambivalence: toward the insanity of nihilism as it moves toward skepticism (where "the lunatic who believes he is a poached egg is to be condemned solely on the

---

[33] *The Scientific Outlook*, pp. 101–102.

[34] "The success of insanity, in literature, in philosophy, and in politics, is one of the peculiarities of our age, and the successful form of insanity proceeds almost entirely from impulses towards power." *Power*, p. 270.

ground that he is in a minority"),[35] and toward the insanity of annihilation as it moves toward mastery (where "unless power can be tamed . . . all must die").[36] The two extremes converge somewhere in the realm of nothingness: nihilism insists there is, there exists, nothing for certain, as annihilation guarantees that there will in time certainly be nothing.

The empirical approach has of course resisted these extremes; it aspires to a common-sensical moderation that can secure it against the excesses to which it is logically disposed. Yet the empiricist metaphysic that has nourished both skepticism and science appears inherently unstable, forever on the verge of lunacy, seemingly unable to accommodate notions that are life-affirming but nonimperial, that are modest yet immune to nihilism. Indeed, methodological solipsism has been as incapable of moderation in resisting the twin lunacies of nihilism and annihilation as liberal political theory has been in resisting anarchy and despotism. And that is precisely the point of this comparative exercise: for it is here that the metaphysic of empiricism and the political theory of liberalism exhibit certain decisive parallels. To put it provocatively, what they seem to share is a common insanity, an insanity that is all the more ironic in light of the liberal's claim to reasonable moderation. This insanity is defined by an incapacity to occupy the middle ground, to elude the seductiveness of logical extremes, to adduce epistemological or political constructs appropriate to the middling realities of the common human condition and the politics by which we essay to mediate that condition.

In both philosophical empiricism and liberalism, methodological solipsism gives to the subjective self a paramountcy that leads either to the total denial of an external, law-governed world, or to its assimilation and conquest—nihilism or annihilation in the metaphysics, anarchy or despotism in the politics. It might even be said that the quest for certainty, the attempt to buy verifiability by surrendering intelligibility, the substitution of epistemology for ontology, the entire enterprise of trying to overcome the world by

[35] *History of Western Philosophy*, p. 646.
[36] *Power*, p. 39.

knowing it in some limited but certain way *is* in its political expression the quest for power, for order, for security, and for dominion, and that, by the same token, the flight into skepticism, into particularism, into subjectivity *is* in its political expression the flight into anarchism, radical individualism, and a nearly misanthropic self-sufficiency. Confronted with the world as Whirl, the sensory self in whom the empiricist reposes total epistemological confidence can only deny it, by relegating it to the unknowable and thus depriving it of ontological status, or overcome it, by conjuring science from patterns putatively arising out of percepts. What it apparently cannot do is to live in and with the world in noetic equilibrium, able to apprehend without dominating, able to doubt without negating. Confronted with other humans, the atomistic, self-sufficient self in whom the liberal reposes an equivalent political confidence can only deny them, by asserting its own solitary freedom, or overcome them, by obtaining total dominion over them. What it cannot do is to live in and with fellow humans in social equilibrium, able to maintain autonomy without surrendering mutuality, able to secure order without risking despotism, able to reconcile self and community by constructing a communal or social self. Indeed, it would sometimes seem that what distinguishes liberalism is that, where other approaches to the political have been concerned to show how men do or ought to live together with one another in just polities, the liberal has tried to show that they can live only alone (the state of nature) or under sovereign domination—in splendid libertarian isolation (suggested by such liberal constructs as "privacy," "natural rights," and "freedom"), or in chains (suggested by terms such as "sovereignty," "power," "sanction," and "the greatest good for the greatest number").

Just as skepticism and mastery are natural tendencies in an epistemology rooted in individual sense perception, so anarchy and despotism are natural tendencies in a political philosophy rooted in individual hedonism and private interest. Solipsistic imperialism reflects the same consciousness, the same climate of opinion, the same unstable attitude toward certainty, whether it expresses itself in the sovereign artifices of empirical science or in the sovereign artifices of the liberal state. And solipsistic skepticism reflects the same doubts, the same particularistic subjectivity, whether it is recommending epistemological humility or dictating liberty, privacy, and tolerance. In this sense, to describe Russell as an empiricist liberal verges on redundancy; in this sense, his liberalism and his empiricism become inseparable facets of a single approach to the human condition; in this sense, the dilemmas of knowledge expressed by Russell the philosopher converge with the dilemmas of politics expressed by Russell the political theorist.

IV

Having said this much, I must add that I can hardly conceive of a more provocative or controversial way to treat Russell's political thought: it is at once too neat and too perverse, too all-encompassing and too idiosyncratic. Yet what may seem incautious as interpretation turns out to be Russell's own mode of expression. For in describing the politics of liberty and the politics of power, Russell himself dismantles the barriers that keep politics and epistemology apart.

The relationship between power and manipulative science is a theme throughout Russell's work, but it is perhaps most clearly stated in *The Scientific Outlook*, where Russell advances the blunt claim that "scientific thought . . . is essentially power thought."[37] This is so because "the fundamental impulse to which [scientific thought] appeals is the love of power . . . the desire to be the cause of as many and as large effects as possible."[38] The equation is simple enough: power is the production of intended effects (as defined in *Power*), and science is the art of understanding how to produce effects. Science is thus a critical mode in the exercise of power. It lends to the "natural" human quest for power, a "new ruthlessness" born of "intoxication" with its modern technological possibilities.[39]

[37] *The Scientific Outlook*, p. 167.
[38] Ibid., p. 179.
[39] Ibid., p. 167.

Science, regarded as knowledge in the service of mastery over nature, thus becomes a direct extension of man's aggressive nature, defined (in Russell's Freudian-Hobbesian imagery) by insatiable and boundless desires and an interminable quest for "power after power that ceaseth only in death." Despite the changing contexts and evolving concerns of many different books, Russell managed to make power the central element in every definition of human nature he proffered over half a century. In *Roads to Freedom* he cites "competitiveness, love of power and envy" as the defining traits of humanity.[40] In *The Practice and Theory of Bolshevism* "acquisitiveness, vanity, rivalry, and love of power" are the "basic instincts."[41] In *Marriage and Morals*, "power, sex, and parenthood" are decisive; of these, "power begins first and ends last."[42] And in *Power*, not surprisingly, it is the impulse to power and to glory that rank first. Power and envy, power and vanity, power and sex, power and glory—but always power, always the unquenchable thirst to drink from the fountains of the gods. Power not only provides the key to human nature, it defines the character of social relations. "The laws of social dynamics are only capable of being stated in terms of power in its various forms," Russell writes in an early section of *Power*, hoping to combat the authority of economists, lawyers, and idealists who were foolish enough to think that utilities, legal institutions, or ideas could somehow sufficiently convey the essence of politics.[43] Indeed, to Russell, *Power* constituted a significant attempt to convince social scientists that "power, rather than wealth, should be the basic concept in social theory," a claim he had first advanced decades earlier in *The Practice and Theory of Bolshevism*.[44]

We might say Russell succeeded too well in that subsequent social scientists from the 1930s through the 1960s became so preoccupied with power that few other constructs found a place in their new science of politics. But he failed finally to make his case

[40] *Roads to Freedom*, p. 109.
[41] *The Practice and Theory of Bolshevism*, p. 64.
[42] *Marriage and Morals* (London: Unwin Books, 1961), p. 149.
[43] *Power*, p. 13.
[44] *The Practice and Theory of Bolshevism*, p. 63.

to philosophers, who, since the 1960s, have pursued their attempts at reducing, deconstructing, and conquering politics in a manner that denies or ignores the essential power character of the political domain.

There was in Russell's discussion of power a typical liberal ambiguity. Power might, in one sense, be an undesirable perversion of man's nature, and science, in consequence, a catalyst of unsavory transmutations. Yet power is also a necessary feature of man's condition and a defining aspect of the political process and thus can hardly be regarded as entirely perverse or wholly undesirable. It was, after all, an object in Russell's own life, though presumably only as a means.

The attempt to distinguish between power as a means and power as an end is at the core of the liberal ambivalence about power. Hobbes had commenced, innocently enough, with an apparently instrumental definition, stipulating that power is merely "a present means to obtain some future good." This was to make it little more than a synonym for generic instrumentality—little different from John Rawls's idea of "social primary goods" or Bruce Ackerman's "mana" (see Chapters Three and Five). But Hobbes's usage quickly moves beyond mere instrumentality to comprehend darker forces. Men are destined, by the portents of this more grim psychology, to lead lives that are little more than "a perpetual and restless desire of power after power, that ceaseth only in death."[45]

In Russell, power as a prudential facilitator seems to confront power as a kind of deontological lust with no other end than its own sprawling perpetuation. Neither Hobbes nor his liberal successors had quite been able to reconcile the two, and although Russell is at pains to distinguish "power desired as a means and power desired as an end in itself," he never seems altogether certain which of the two is endemic to human nature. He would prefer it to be the former, but his own portrait of human psychology, human history, and human politics can only persuade us that it is the latter. In *The Practice and Theory of Bolshevism* he acknowl-

[45] The first definition is found in *Leviathan*, pt. I, ch. 10; the second, in pt. I, ch. 11.

edges that power was being used as a means to desirable ends by the young Soviet state, he but feared the means might too easily become the ends. Power as a means is energized by the lust for power as an end and thus can never be conjured into use in the service of civilization without fear of awakening the beast civilization aspired to tame. In *The Semblance of Peace*, Yeats wrote: "Civilization is hooped together, brought / Under a rule, under the semblance of peace, / By manifold illusion." What was illusory, if Russell's account of human nature is to be our guide, was the hope that the beastly in man (power) might somehow subdue the beast—that, in the Madisonian formula, power could be its own remedy. Not that Russell ever had a great deal of confidence in the forces dwelling in the human heart. Drawn to darkly impassioned writers like D. H. Lawrence and Joseph Conrad, he had continually to resist the seductions of an anguished morbidity. Too often, his anatomy of the human soul portrays eyes glinting with avarice and envy, a will yearning for power, and a heart shrouded in darkness. Russell the perennial optimist was forever averting his eyes, but despair remained at the periphery of his vision. In his blacker moods, science seemed to him not only to enhance power but also to threaten a world of perverse insanities. In *The Scientific Outlook*, he left readers with a dismal prophecy:

> Gradually the world will grow more dark and more terrible. Strange perversions of instinct will first lurk in dark corners and then gradually overwhelm men in high places. Sadistic pleasures will not suffer the moral condemnation that will be meted out to the softer joys . . . in the end such a system will break down either in an orgy of bloodshed or in the rediscovery of love.[46]

For all of its dangers, however, we cannot finally elude power. To act in the world, to treat effectively with the human condition, is to use power, to rely on science as a means to other human ends. The love of power is, after all, a part of normal human nature and neither can nor ought to be wholly shunned. Prudently used,

[46] *The Scientific Outlook*, p. 267.

power can remake not only the world but mankind as well. The beastly in human nature is ultimately capable of doing more than taming the beast in mankind: it may extirpate it.

Here, Russell the neo-Freudian pessimist is challenged by Russell the liberal optimist, the advocate of man's perfectibility. Beastly though it may be, human nature is not for Russell "a fixed datum, but a product of circumstances, education and opportunity operating upon a highly malleable native disposition."[47] Without a notion of malleability, human nature would represent an incurable disease rather than a compound of malignant and benign potentialities. Without it, Russell's own political involvements would have been absurd, and the idea purveyed implicitly in late writings, such as *Unarmed Victory* and *Common Sense and Nuclear Warfare*—that individuals can make a difference in the international process—would have been risible. However rooted in desire, lust, and compulsion human affairs might be, Russell had to concur with such liberal predecessors as John Stuart Mill: moral suasion, rational argument, and liberal education could, under the appropriate civic circumstances, affect those affairs. Science, used for ends other than itself, was once again the model. If the world was governed by necessity and a set of fixed laws extending even to man's own nature, man nonetheless was capable of rising above necessity and directing his own evolution by acquiring knowledge. Recall, "it is not by prayer and humility that you cause things to go as you wish, but by acquiring a knowledge of natural laws."[48]

The essence of this form of power remains manipulation, but manipulation for ends other than power itself. It is power used to secure liberty, power used to overcome necessity, power used to civilize man, power used to move man away from power and toward perfection. It is not man insisting he *is* God, as pure solipsism suggests, but man aspiring to *become* that which is godly in him.

This less nefarious form of prudentialism cannot, however, en-

---

[47] *Roads to Freedom*, p. 109.
[48] *Autobiography*, 3: 29.

tirely escape solipsism. When it is contrasted with classicism's contemplative tenor and the ancient Greek wariness of the sense world rooted in unfounded opinion (*doxa*) or with Christianity's otherworldliness and distrust of human pride and pride's propelling hubris, even a restrained instrumentalism devoted to humanistic ends appears arrogant. Liberal politics may employ power only to curb power, may manipulate human nature only to rescue the best in it from the worst, may command men only to liberate them, but it still refuses to leave the world alone. It still confronts human imagination and human understanding as tools designed to conquer the world. Whether expressed in prudential or deontological language, the modes of thought that have pervaded scientific understanding and political action in the post-Renaissance world have been action, assertion, aggression, manipulation, conquest, and mastery—the active self seeking to gratify itself while satisfying the claims of other self-gratifiers, the active mind overcoming the senselessness of a sense-mediated world by erecting a manipulative science on precisely those percepts that have rendered the world senseless. These are the parallel products of solipsistic empiricism's assertive side.

Solipsism, as I have argued, has another side as well. Radical empiricism promotes the self as sense perceptor, but it also denies the external world, the objective world of Other. Hubris issues naturally out of the promotion of self, but skepticism tends to follow from the denial of our capacity to know the world in itself. Skepticism and doubt, introduced into the political realm, offer alternatives to power and manipulation and give to liberalism its defining laissez-faire color. John Stuart Mill states the political consequences of skeptical fallibilism this way:

> that mankind are not infallible; that their truths, for the most part, are only half-truths; that unity of opinion, unless resulting from the fullest and freest comparison of opposite opinions, is not desirable, and diversity not an evil, but a good, until mankind are much more capable than at present of recognizing all sides of the truth, are principles applicable to men's mode of action, not less than to their opinions.[49]

[49] Mill, *On Liberty*, p. 114.

If we can never know with certainty, we have no right to compel with authority; if reason is incapable of apprehending truth, then politics cannot legislate truth by fiat; if there is no philosophical warrant for maintaining that there *is* a world, there can surely be none for dogmatic assertions about what the world is or ought to be like. The fatal admission "I could be wrong" entails the principle "The enforcement of right is unjustified." If, as Hume says, "moral distinctions are not the offspring of reason," then reasonable men will be tolerant, pluralistic, and open-minded, distrustful of governments that speak in the name of right and sympathetic to minimalist constructions of political authority. In Russell's own words, the quasi-skeptical confession that "almost all knowledge . . . is in some degree doubtful . . . [has] in the sphere of practical politics . . . important consequences" that include tolerance, an unwillingness to inflict present pain in the name of future good, a bias against violent coercion in the settlement of disputes, and other similar liberal values.[50]

The contention that empiricism in its fallibilist manifestations is linked with liberalism in its minimalist inclinations is not an unfamiliar one. Sir Karl Popper, whose understanding of empiricism is radically fallibilist, transforms skepticism into a foundation for the politics of the open society. One bite from the apple of knowledge may nourish pride and corrupt the species, but to eat the fruit whole, Popper seems to say, has the opposite effect. Knowledge pursued to the limit reveals its limits; and reason rationally explored exposes its impotence, leaving us finally certain only that we must forever live with uncertainty.[51] The sole habitat fit for a race confronting in perpetuity the reality of its meager noetic ca-

---

[50] "Philosophy and Politics," in *Unpopular Essays*, p. 23. The same kind of argument is advanced in *Power*, where Russell writes that "a diffused liberal sentiment, tinged with scepticism, makes social cooperation much less difficult, and liberty correspondingly more possible" (p. 308).

[51] Popper writes: "There is no return to a harmonious state of nature. If we turn back, then we must go the whole way—we must return to the beasts . . . but if we wish to remain human, then there is only one way, the way into the open society. We must go on into the unknown, the uncertain and insecure. . . ." K. R. Popper, *The Open Society and Its Enemies* (London: Routledge and Kegan Paul, 1957), 1: 200–201.

pacities is an open society where neither dogma nor authority are permitted to legislate what reason shows can never be known.

Russell notes pointedly that Locke, "who first developed in detail the empiricist theory of knowledge, preached also religious toleration, representative institutions, and the limitation of governmental power by the system of checks and balances."[52] Order without authority, he concludes, can be taken as the motto of both science and liberalism. Minimalist politics that are justified only to the extent they serve liberty and private interest, representative institutions that permit numbers to adjudicate what reason cannot determine, and sufficient tolerance, diversity, and constitutionalism to hem in public authority and safeguard the individual upon whom the system is erected—these are the only political measures warranted by a temperate skepticism whose goal is order without authority.

It must be said that Russell never wavers in thinking that skepticism is politically viable only when informed by temperateness. He thus writes: "the temper that is required to make a success of democracy is, in the practical life, exactly what the scientific temper is in the intellectual life; it is a half-way house between skepticism and dogmatism. Truth, it holds, is neither completely obtainable, nor completely unattainable; it is attainable only to a certain degree, and that only with difficulty."[53] Yet, I have argued, liberal politics no more lends itself to this kind of epistemological temperateness than methodological solipsism lends itself to noetic equilibrium. However attractive a median point may be, there is no logical stopping place between dogma and skepticism once knowledge has been reduced to private sensory experience and politics has been reduced to the science of power in paradoxical pursuit of liberty and the ethics of liberty paradoxically exploiting power. Russell himself had no easy time holding the middle ground. In his youth he was drawn to anarchism; in his senatorial years he acquiesced increasingly to the necessity of power—even naked power—in the quest for an orderly interna-

[52] *Unpopular Essays*, p. 22.
[53] *Power*, pp. 312–313.

tional system that could guarantee human survival.[54] When Robert Paul Wolff concludes in his essay on violence that "philosophical anarchism is true" because "there is not, and there could not be, a state that has a right to command and whose subjects have a binding obligation to obey," he is doing no more than carrying skepticism to its logical political end (although he is not, as I have argued elsewhere, carrying it to its politically logical end).[55] Skepticism is infectious, as Hume well understood: those who deploy it to undermine an adversary authority soon find that it destroys their own advocacy as well. The aim is to curb authority, but the result is the annihilation of all legitimacy and thus of even minimal order. Every minimalist notion of politics that views mutuality as a form of necessary but pernicious subjugation is inclined to anarchy; every instrumentalist notion of politics that conceives of power as a means to security and of government as the only barrier between man and his defining bestiality is inclined to despotism. A theory that insists on both notions is hopelessly schizophrenic, torn between incompatible strategies aimed simultaneously at libertarian independence and a power-forged orderliness.

It is the liberal heritage out of which Marx and Lenin come that accounts for their conflicted approach to power and liberty, and what is true for Marx is more decisively true for liberals like Mill and Russell. Russell's liberal schizophrenia leaves out the very moderation to which he aspires; it precludes that halfway house which he rightly sees as indispensable to liberal democratic politics. Finally, Russell's liberalism omits politics itself, understood as a collaborative activity manifesting man's social inclinations

---

[54] Underlying an apparent vacillation in his later years in his attitudes toward the Soviet Union (which seemed to be the object of his fears in the late 1940s) and the United States (which received his opprobrium in the later 1950s and 1960s) was a constancy of principle: the need for world hegemony by *some* power to secure world peace, whether under the auspices of the Soviet Union, the United States, or an international body. See *Common Sense and Nuclear Warfare* (London: Allen and Unwin, 1959) and *Has Man a Future?* (London: Allen and Unwin, 1961).

[55] R. P. Wolff, "On Violence," *Journal of Philosophy* 66, no. 19 (1969), 607. My objections to Wolff, which are reflected in the final part of this essay, can be found in my *Superman and Common Men: Freedom, Anarchy and the Revolution* (New York: Penguin, 1972), pp. 34–35 and passim.

and serving the common ends of justice and the public weal. For all its humanistic rhetoric, and despite the considerable success of the institutions whose experience it reflects, liberalism has left modern man with a legacy of discontent. Its predisposition toward anarchy has manifested itself in practice as anomie. Its preoccupation with asocial liberty has precipitated an estrangement that has alienated men and women both from their fellows and from their public identity as citizens. Its refusal to develop public norms in the face of metaphysical uncertainty has left man as a social being without standards, vulnerable alike to meaninglessness and authoritarianism, defenseless in the face of heteronomy, contingency, and mere accident. Its fascination with power both as a means and as an expression of the species' defining self-assertiveness has run the twin risks of megalomania and subservience. Without norms, without a legitimate notion of public justice, how can power have any other issue than domination? Without a concept of mutuality, without common goals, how can liberty produce anything but misanthropy, envy, greed, and war? Skepticism and mastery, liberty and power, can create passive, solitary loners or secure slaves (though some think themselves masters), innocent misanthropes or craven followers in pursuit of craven masters.[56] But they cannot create citizens, and without citizens there can be no politics.

If men are to be regarded as something more than beasts and something less than gods, an alternative to empiricist liberalism's ambivalent polarities must be found. That alternative is politics itself, but a politics that demands a different mode of thought. Philosophies that reduce or deconstruct or conquer the political will not help us to construct a political domain capable of mediating thought and action or of bridging the cognitively impossible objectivity our minds seek and the behaviorally necessary standards of reasonableness our conduct requires.

Russell is more sensitive to this line of argument than his lib-

---

[56] Russell suggests that political men tend to fall into two discrete classes—leaders and followers—neither of which, I would argue, encompasses citizens. See *Power*, ch. 2.

eralism might suggest. Like Hume, who recognized that skepticism can be thought but not lived, Russell regarded it as "logically impeccable" but "psychologically impossible." "Knowing and feeling," he writes in *The Scientific Outlook*, "are equally essential ingredients both in the life of the individual and that of the community."[57] As John Stuart Mill had once been drawn to Coleridge, so Russell was drawn to Conrad and to Lawrence. Part of him remained in permanent rebellion against the austere logic of skepticism, compliantly yielding to the seduction of passions he could nonetheless not quite trust. Love of power and the irrational quest for dominion were, after all, expressions of the passionate soul no less than compassion or friendship. "If social life," he warns in *Power*, "is to satisfy social desires, it must be based upon some philosophy not derived from love of power"[58]— no easily filled prescription for Russell, since materialism, idealism, and pragmatism all appeared to him to be power philosophies. The problem is how to generate a politics of love, of community, and of justice that is immune both to anarchy and to dominion—a politics that will neither permit power to overwhelm liberty nor permit liberty to undermine mutuality.

Russell aspires to a solution, but the dichotomies springing from his empiricist perspective make it difficult for him to conceptualize the issue in any but polar terms. His dilemma is evident in *The Scientific Outlook*, where he writes that "it is only in so far as we renounce the world as its lovers that we can conquer it as technicians. But this division of the soul is fatal to what is best in man. As soon as the failure of science as metaphysic is realized, the power conferred by science as technique is only obtainable by something analogous to the worship of Satan, that is to say, the renunciation of love."[59] To live in the world, Russell seems to say, is to master it; but we pay for our mastery with our souls. To love in the world is to leave the world alone; but we pay for our abstinence with frustration and impotence. He can offer only the

---

[57] *The Scientific Outlook*, p. 278.
[58] *Power*, p. 273.
[59] *The Scientific Outlook*, p. 273.

choice between an impotent if reverent passivity—an unproductive anarchy that will not sustain life—and an aggressive manipulativeness that in the pursuit of efficient productivity and secure order abjures love.

I believe, to the degree these dilemmas are not endemic to the human condition, that their resistance to resolution arises in part out of the liberal but much mistaken belief in the unity of epistemology and politics. The very continuity that implicates his political theory and his philosophical empiricism in common dilemmas dooms Russell to an unsatisfactory politics. To insist, as liberals have always done, that the criteria by which we elucidate standards of knowledge must somehow correspond to the criteria by which we fashion a common life is a particularly pernicious kind of folly. It makes impossible demands on philosophy and creates impossible expectations for politics. In seeking to create a politics as well grounded as foundational philosophy, it fails to grasp the actual virtues of the political. To think that the attitudes with which we approach nature must somehow reflect the attitudes with which we approach the civic polity promotes an extremism of the mind incompatible with the social requirements of common living. Thinking about what we know and how we know it and thinking about politics are both *thinking*, to be sure; but political thinking makes special demands that suggest it may be a unique activity. The trouble, then, with empiricist liberalism is precisely its redundancy, its incapacity to distinguish between epistemology as a descriptive activity that makes a science of self-consciousness, and politics as a prescriptive activity of citizens in search of common purposes—a science of ''other-consciousness'' as it were.

Russell's genius lent to everything he wrote about politics a wisdom that argument cannot deny, and his moral courage invested his activity with a nobility that is irreproachable. Yet the conundrums in which his liberalism involved him and the polarities forced on him by his empiricism closed him off from the political alternatives toward which his soul instinctively leaned.[60] He

_____

[60] It is a sad irony that Russell was least able to understand those political phi-

aspired to a transcending humanity, but his liberal psychology insisted that men are beasts or gods, not mere humans. He hoped for a politics of love, but could anticipate only a politics of anarchy or a politics of dominion or some weak, unstable compound of the two. He wanted to forge new solutions, but could raise only traditional problems in the inflexible language of traditional rational-skeptical philosophy. Finally, his philosophy confounded his genius.

In the preface to the final volume of his *Autobiography* Russell wondered morosely whether his last words would be "The bright day is done / And we are for the dark," or, as he sometimes "allowed himself to hope," "The world's great age begins anew, / The golden years return. . . ." He longed for golden years and prophesied darkness, unable from the uncompromising perspective of empiricist liberalism to comprehend that men live in a twilight where the human soul burns too ardently ever quite to be extinguished by shadows but too languidly to overcome the restless night that awaits us all.

---

losophers who sought a way out of the liberal dilemma. He was vicious as well as wrong about Rousseau and wholly unsympathetic with Kant, Hegel, and the Continental tradition—a tradition that has been an important source of recent critical reactions to liberal politics in Hannah Arendt, Jürgen Habermas, Leo Strauss, and others (see Chapter 8).

THREE

Justifying Justice: John Rawls
and Thin Theory

> Those metaphysicians who, in making these abstrac-
> tions, think they are making analyses, [are men] who,
> the more they detach themselves from things, imag-
> ine themselves to be getting all the nearer to the point
> of penetrating to their core.
>
> Karl Marx

FROM THE bleak years following World War One, when Bertrand
Russell was drawn by his philosophical skepticism into political
cynicism, to the epoch of renewal after World War Two, when
John Rawls began his optimistic quest for a secure philosophical
foundation for certain intuitively attractive liberal principles of
justice, one feature of philosophy remained constant: its ambition
to render the political world intelligible through the reduction and
assimilation of politics to philosophical categories. Wittgenstein
in his later years had grown doubtful of the capacity of linguistic
analysis to reduce the mundane world to palatable bite-size mor-
sels the abstract mind might devour and digest. But philosophy
incarnated as linguistic analysis, logical positivism, and eventually social science positivism claimed that politics could be formulated in terms (purely analytic or wholly value-free, for example) that would suborn it to the dominion of unambiguous
understanding.

When in 1958 Rawls published a terse and compelling essay
entitled "Justice as Fairness," an important new chapter in the
history of philosophy's conquest of politics opened.[1] Rawls

---

[1] "Justice as Fairness," *Philosophical Review* (1958). The definitive revision
appears in Peter Laslett and W. G. Runciman, *Philosophy, Politics and Society*,
2d ser. (Oxford: Basil Blackwell, 1962). An even earlier, partial statement of

54

evinced little concern either for Wittgenstein's complex doubts or for the stipulativist tendencies of the positivists, who domesticated and thereby neutered morals and politics by removing their normative vital organs). Nor did he display much sympathy with the French effort, which would issue in deconstructionism, to sever the tie between text and interpretation and thereby abolish traditional understandings of political and moral knowledge. Rather, he set out to rehabilitate philosophy by demonstrating its potency as a tool for securing foundations for political justice. That straightforward and modest little essay, which seem composed with an almost Benthamite simplicity (though its intentions were averse to Benthamism), aspired to root intuitively attractive notions of justice in a framework of rational consent no reasonable person would reject. Traditional antitheses between right and utility, individual and community, and private interest and the commonweal were to be overcome by an approach that would demonstrate to nonaltruistic, self-interested, but nonetheless rational individuals the intrinsic worth of principles of justice that otherwise could be dismissed as supererogatory.

If Bertrand Russell had insisted that the politics of liberalism necessarily reflected the prepolitical epistemology associated with philosophical skepticism, Rawls apparently set out to show that the politics of liberal justice could be grounded in the prepolitical rationality of abstractly conceived individuals existing in a hypothetical "original position" whose primary feature was that it was purged of everything remotely suggestive of politics, social psychology, morals, and history. Principles of justice with an attractive but debatable social utility would turn out to be what self-interested individuals would select under specified and very special conditions—thereby satisfying the demands of both utility and right, of both individual and society, and yet maintaining the priority of liberty (the individual) that was liberalism's chief distinguishing mark.

The Rawlsian project was perhaps never as clearly visible as in

Rawls's position came in his "Two Concepts of Rules," *Philosophical Review* 64 (1955), 3–32.

that early, uncomplicated, and unqualified essay. Later elaboration in magisterial, book-length form, although it clarified and extended the principles introduced earlier, also signaled Rawls's gradual withdrawal from the pure philosophical conception of justice.[2] In *A Theory of Justice*, Rawls already seemed to be moving very slowly toward a more political conception, which was to find full expression in the later essays "Kantian Constructivism in Moral Theory" and "Justice as Fairness: Political Not Metaphysical."[3] Accompanying this withdrawal from pure philosophy has been an increasing preoccupation with neo-Kantian versions of moral constructivism, which we shall review toward the end of this chapter. Nonetheless, Rawls's reputation rests quite properly on his attempt to ground political justice in indestructible philosophical bedrock. Moreover, that effort remains central to Rawls's own conception of his project, even in more recent essays, where he modifies but refuses to abandon the decisive and highly controversial logic of the original position.[4] Consequently, I will focus on the theory in its fully elaborated form in *A Theory of Justice*, for that effort constitutes not only the most recent but also the most impressive, one might even say noble, chapter in the postwar history of liberal philosophy's attempt to conquer politics.

A clear sign of the distinctive merit of Rawls's effort is the amount of criticism it has attracted, most notably, essentialist crit-

---

[2] All subsequent page references to *A Theory of Justice* (Cambridge, Mass.: Harvard University Press, 1971) will be given in the text. Robert Paul Wolff, along with a careful critical reading of Rawls, offers a valuable reconstruction of Rawls's softening logic as he moves from the original essay to the grand theory. See *Understanding Rawls: A Reconstruction and Critique of "A Theory of Justice"* (Princeton: Princeton University Press, 1977). Wolff's position is nicely corroborated by the apparent further softening in the essays Rawls has written subsequent to the publication of Wolff's analysis. See note 3 below.

[3] "Kantian Constructivism in Moral Theory" (The Dewey Lectures), *Journal of Philosophy* 77 (September 1980), 515–573; and "Justice as Fairness: Political Not Metaphysical," *Philosophy and Public Affairs* 14 (Summer 1985), 223–251.

[4] He rejects Ronald Dworkin's interesting attempt to show that the argument from the original position is rooted in a conception of the "right to equal respect and concern in the design of political institutions" (Dworkin, *Taking Rights Seriously* [Cambridge, Mass.: Harvard University Press, 1977], p. 182. See, for example, Rawls, "Justice as Fairness," p. 236, note 19.

icism. It has been persistently attacked in ways calling into question its fundamental ideological and philosophical premises, its rigid egalitarianism, its bourgeois predilections, its spirited defense of liberalism, and its partiality to fully developed, capitalist societies. My intention here is not to rehearse or elaborate on the myriad charges generated by the flourishing Rawls Industry. Rather, I want to raise certain questions about *A Theory of Justice* in Rawls's own terms, accepting his premises but examining his reasoning by his own stated criteria. I may then be able to exhibit the deficiency of the premises: for, as the most notable of the liberal philosophers who have recently tried to subjugate politics to the discipline of philosophy, Rawls may have the most to teach us about the perils of the enterprise.

Rawls would like to persuade us that two intuitively attractive fundamental rules of justice, the equal liberty rule and the difference principle (with its fair equality of opportunity corollary), can be both philosophically justified by abstract rational argument and concretely corroborated by appeal to their congruence with intuitive notions of man's sociability and the good. I believe that the abstract justificatory appeal to the original position is unsatisfactory in certain vital ways and that it raises problems of comparison and measurement not adequately disposed of by Rawls. I will show that the appeal to congruence is founded on an inadequate political and historical sociology, which in turn creates further problems for the argument from the original position. In sum, I hope to show that Rawls has tried to light his candle at both ends, that he cannot get either end to burn, and that the philosophical difficulties of his position are closely connected with the generic incapacity of liberal philosophy to serve justice and politics simultaneously.

II

Rawls denies that he makes a Cartesian appeal to the original position as a source of necessary first principles from which the balance of his argument can be regarded as a mere deduction (pp. 577–578). Nevertheless, the original position occupies a critical role in his theory of justice—a role he does not abjure even in his restatement of the theory of justice in terms that are more political than metaphysical.[5] Technically, the original position functions as a hypothetical point of mutual disinterest that satisfies the requirements of an Ideal Observer in adducing the notion of justice as fairness. Because men in the original position are not yet particular men with particular notions of the good, Rawls is able to develop a proceduralist definition of justice uncontaminated by substantive first principles (the bane of intuitionism). Yet, because men in the original position are *potential* particular men with potential particular fates, they will not be satisfied with nonparticular or nonindividuating notions of aggregate utility (the bane of mean utilitarianism). In brief, because men in the original position cannot determine who they will actually be, they can be counted on to make disinterested and thus fair rules; but because they also anticipate living as actual particular men, they will reject rules that sacrifice the welfare of particular men to the general good.

The original position also serves, rather like the notion of the state of nature for the earlier contractarians, as a hypothetical context for the definition of essential man stripped of all contingent particularity.[6] Justice as fairness is not "at the mercy, so to speak, of existing wants and interests. It sets up an Archimedean point for assessing the social system without invoking *a priori* considerations" (p. 261). Man's nature in the original position consists, then, in rationality and a generalized interest, not in particular desires, aims, and aspirations.[7]

I want to suggest that Rawls's attempt to departicularize the original position is not in fact very successful and that, consequently, its premoral (presubstantive) character cannot be upheld.

[5] See *A Theory of Justice*, pt. I, ch. 3.

[6] Recently, Rawls has denied this was his intention, although he acknowledges that such an interpretation may be a "hazard" of the position he takes. See "Justice as Fairness," sec. 4.

[7] "It is not our aims that primarily reveal our nature," Rawls writes, "but rather the principles that we would acknowledge to govern the background conditions under which these aims are to be formed and the manner in which they are pursued" (p. 560).

Men in the original position are defined by rough equality and freedom, by a general knowledge of the laws of nature and society, and by rationality—the capacity to anticipate consequences (Hobbes's ratiocination). They do not have particular interests, but they do have a generalized interest in being able to secure whatever particular interests they may acquire. Rawls argues that these limited conditions account for the emergence of the rules of justice as fairness. I believe they do not. Additional assumptions need to be made if the rules of justice as fairness are to be regarded as the inevitable choice of rational men in the original position, but these additional assumptions contaminate the original position and rob it of the vaunted neutrality by which it putatively does for justice what intuitionism cannot do.

Before elaborating on this point, I want to claify the meaning of interest. Rawls knows that he can strip men in the original position of particular interests and particular desires but that he cannot leave them bereft of interest and desire altogether or they will cease to be men at all—let alone the political men who are the subject of political inquiry. Human actions do, after all, "spring from existing desires" (p. 568). Indeed, the judgments men make in the original position about alternative rules of justice rest "solely on the basis of what seems best calculated to further their interests" (p. 584). Apparently, men in the original position have interests, but not particular interests; they comprehend and presumably feel the power of desire but are ignorant of which desires they will actually have.

Now, there is a considerable question in my mind about whether it is possible to conceive of men as having a hypothetical knowledge of what it means to have interests and desires but as actually having no particular interests or particular desires. Mutually disinterested men might turn out to be uninterested men, men incapable of comprehending the meaning of interest. Rawls suggests as much when he concedes that "some may object that the exclusion of nearly all particular information makes it difficult to grasp what is meant by the original position" (p. 138). At the level of psychology, it seems possible that particularity is built into the notion of interest and that it cannot be cut away without rendering

59

interest unintelligible. One generic definition of political man is interested man—man interacting with other men in terms of particular and general interests. To create an arena of neutrality for a rational conception of justice is to strip men of their particularity; but that is in turn to depoliticize them, and to depoliticize them may be to denude them of their human features altogether.

Rawls seems to regard the idea of "Primary Goods" as a response to this general line of criticism. Although men in the original position are not permitted to have specified, substantive ends, they are allowed through ratiocination to share a common interest in a set of common means. These common means are the primary social goods that can be thought of as instrumental to the pursuit of any and all particular aims, interests, and ends. Although men in the original position remain mutually disinterested with respect to interests as particular ends, they understand that "in general they must try to protect their liberties, widen their opportunities, and enlarge their means for promoting their aims whatever these are" (p. 143). Thus, they naturally (that is, rationally) attempt to "win for themselves the highest index of primary social goods, since this enables them to promote their conception of the good most effectively whatever it turns out to be" (p. 144). It is presumably in this sense only that men in the original position make calculations to "further their interests."

Yet the device of primary goods does not really answer the question of whether interest is at all intelligible in the absence of particularity; for the interest men take in primary goods is presumably explicable only in terms of the potential interest they have in particular ends. Moreover, Rawls draws the category of Primary Goods in terms so generous that its instrumental status seems critically compromised. Primary goods turn out to encompass not only the obvious instrumentalities like opportunities, powers, income, and wealth, but also rights, liberties, and self-respect. Self-respect is, for example, a good so self-evidently contrary to the instrumental spirit that it is difficult not to conclude that it is a substantive first principle, an end-in-itself, smuggled into the original position under cover of the supposedly prudential primary goods.[8]

Nonetheless, let me for the moment accept that the device of primary goods does meet the difficulties of rendering intelligible the notion of interest in the original position and does not denude men of their humanity as well as their politics. But if Rawls has not gone too far with this premise, has he gone far enough? Is there a position, original or otherwise, that retains a notion of the human person that is intelligible and yet genuinely free of all those particularisms that the veil of ignorance is intended to screen out? Are the choices that men in that position necessarily make (in favor of justice as fairness) really uncontaminated by any substantive, a priori idea of the good? Or by the particular psychologies that attend particular men's experiences in particular social systems? In sum, can it be safely assumed that the parties in the original position are not "influenced by different attitudes towards risk and uncertainty, or by various tendencies to dominate or to submit, and the like"? (p. 530). I do not think so, because I do not believe that men truly stripped down to Rawlsian essentials are capable of rational choice at all. Nor, I suspect, does Rawls. In the relevant section (26), he introduces an "analogy" that appears to go well beyond the minimal conditions portrayed earlier as definitive of the original position. This analogy is the maximin rule for choice under uncertainty, which "tells us to rank alternatives by their worst possible outcomes" (pp. 152–153), tells us to act as if our particular place in society were to be assigned by our enemies. Under these assumptions, Rawls believes it is rational to "adopt the conservative attitude" expressed by maximin (p. 153). But the maximin rule, it appears to me, violates the constraints that define the original position (p. 152).[9]

---

[8] Rawls appreciates the contrast sufficiently to defer, for the sake of "simplicity," his discussion of self-respect to the section on the Aristotelian principle and the full theory of the good (Part III). In the sections where primary goods are treated as facilitators of interest in the original position, self-respect is prudently and completely ignored (see p. 92).

[9] For other critical discussions of the maximin rule, see Kenneth J. Arrow,

Rawls is at pains to persuade us that, while the rule is not self-evident, usual, or generally applicable, it is uniquely suited to the peculiar conditions of the original position. Indeed, quite propitiously, "the original position has been defined so that it is a situation in which the maximin rule applies" (p. 155), and it is to the maximin rule that the logic of the rules of justice as fairness apparently conforms. In guaranteeing themselves as much liberty as is compatible with equal liberty for other men (the equal liberty rule), and in guaranteeing that whatever inequalities exist will be to the advantage of the least advantaged member of society (the difference principle), the parties in the original position are doing no more than following a strategy of minimal risk—that is, establishing rules of justice designed to protect them, given the worst possible outcome for the concrete persons they turn out to be in actual societies. This is, of course, the essence of maximin, a strategy that in Rawls becomes the vital bridge linking the rules of justice with the conditions described by the original position.

It is my view, however, that, unless we simply stipulate that when we say rationality we mean maximin, there is nothing in the original position that can construct maximin as the only rational or most rational solution to the problem of choice under uncertainty. Moreover, the question of which strategy would be most rational cannot be settled without further knowledge about attitudes toward risk and uncertainty, toward freedom and security, not given by the formalistic conditions of the original position. Finally, to treat these attitudes adequately, Rawls must import into his original position covert special psychologies of the kind it was explicitly designed to exclude. Rawls in fact leaps from the origi-

---

"Some Ordinalist-Utilitarian Notes on Rawls' Theory of Justice," *Journal of Philosophy* 70 (May 1973), 245–263; David Lyons, "Rawls versus Utilitarianism," *Journal of Philosophy* 70 (May 1973), 535–545; and Lyons, "Rawls versus Utilitarianism," *Journal of Philosophy* 69 (October 1972), 535–544. Rawls appears to back away slightly from his views on risk aversion in his "Reply to Lyons and Teitelman," *Journal of Philosophy* 69 (October 1972), 556–557. A useful collection of critical essays, which includes an earlier version of the central section of this chapter, is Norman Daniels, ed., *Reading Rawls* (Oxford: Basil Blackwell, 1975).

nal position, where men are prevented by the veil of ignorance from knowing what their particular statuses will be, to the unwarranted conclusion that this uncertainty will produce in them a rational preference for minimizing risks. Yet, as Rawls acknowledges, this assumes not merely that particular prospects are uncertain but that they are unpromising, not simply that particular statuses will be assigned by lot but that they will be assigned by enemies, not only that a given share in the cake will be chosen in a random order but that it will be chosen last. One might equally well assume that friends will assign statuses and that any particular man will get to choose first. It is no less rational, although suggestive of a different and less conservative temperament to be sure, for men to pursue, say, a moderate-risk strategy whose aim would be to create the possibility of somewhat greater gains than those afforded by maximin, even at the risk of somewhat greater possible losses. Indeed, the scarcity built into all contractarian views of society—and Rawls's is no exception on this point—enhances the attractiveness of gambling strategies that, should an individual win, permit him far greater benefits than those allowed by an austere egalitarianism. This is particularly true if the individual regards his losses as comparatively insignificant as measured by the alternative: an unattractively austere minimum below which maximin strategy guarantees he will not fall. Lotteries function precisely on this basis. Given still more radical assumptions about attitudes toward risk, one can contend that some men may choose rationally to risk starvation, even death, for the chance—even against the odds—to be very rich or very powerful. War is an extreme but hardly irrational example of this win-all/lose-all strategy. The development of capitalism is scarcely thinkable in the absence of high-risk attitudes in the face of uncertainty. A consideration of actual historical developments and concrete institutions as they manifest special psychologies may in fact suggest that the no-risk predilection for security is atypical of human choice in the face of uncertainty.

There seem to be a number of psychological reasons for this aversion to no-risk strategies. First, the ''satisfactory minimum'' afforded by the maximin rule may not be ''satisfying'' at all by the criteria of maximum satisfaction. Avoiding pain, penury, or powerlessness may not be measurable on the same scale as achieving (and enjoying) pleasure, wealth, or power. This possible asymmetry may in turn reflect fundamental psychological disparities between the need for security expressed in the fear of pain, in anxiety, in the longing for serenity, and perhaps even in the death-drive, and the need for self-expression manifested in the quest for freedom, for spontaneity, for domination, and for self-fulfillment. Rawls's focus on primary goods as instrumentalities for both avoidance and achievement ends (security and self-expression) blinds him to these kinds of possible disparities.[10] Consequently, he can opt for security (via maximim) in the original position without realizing that he is thereby implicating a substantive special psychology. It is very odd, in a philosophy of justice that champions the priority of liberty over all other goods and orders the rules of justice in accordance with this priority, to discover that a conservative special psychology predisposed toward security has been installed where rationality is supposed to be.

There is another, related difficulty in trying to guarantee a threshhold of minimum satisfaction. Rawls argues that the interpersonal index defined by "expectations of primary social goods" (p. 92) provides an acceptable standard for the kinds of interpersonal comparison required of a theory of justice. Yet primary goods as distinctive as freedom, power, wealth, and self-respect can hardly be regarded as satisfying in some unitary way, except from the perspective of a rudimentary hedonism to which Rawls does not appear to subscribe. Freedom may seem more satisfying than survival (thus, the gospel song: "Before I'd be a slave, I'd be buried in my grave / Go home to my Lord and be free . . ."). Or a poverty-based self-respect may seem more satisfying than minimal economic welfare bought at the cost of an ignominious obeisance to bureaucracy. Certain Christian ascetics may even complain that the Rawlsian standard deprives them of the austerity

---

[10] Rawls agrees with Santayana that "we must settle the relative worth of pleasure and pain" (p. 557), but he does not raise the issue in the context of primary goods. He leaves its resolution to the discretion of "subjective individuals."

and struggle for survival they regard as necessary to their other-worldly beliefs.

Rawls may want to reply that, because primary goods are means rather than ends, such objections are not pertinent. But this response only raises again the question of whether primary social goods can be thought of exclusively as means when they function as an interpersonal index of comparative expectations of particular men.

If these criticisms carry conviction, then those commentators who have tried to read Rawls as typically bourgeois in his outlook on human nature, who have suggested that the original position is informed by capitalist market biases, are mistaken.[11] On the contrary, Rawls's inclination toward a risk-free maximin strategy in the face of uncertainty suggests biases that are profoundly conservative—anticapitalist in their thrust and to some degree antiliberal in their spirit. They reveal a primary concern with security and the achievement of minimal conditions for individual welfare. The egalitarianism from which they issue is purely prudential, a device to ensure that the self-interested man will not be worse off than anyone else. Despite Rawls's considerable preoccupation with good life-plans and the Aristotelian standard of excellence toward the end of the book, self-expression and self-fulfillment are not the major aims of his two rules of justice. Although freedom as a means is the first (and lexically prior) principle of procedural justice, freedom as an end receives little attention.

Rawlsian man in the original position is finally a strikingly lugubrious creature: unwilling to enter a situation that promises success because it also promises failure, unwilling to risk winning because he feels doomed to losing, ready for the worst because he cannot imagine the best, content with security and the knowledge he will be no worse off than anyone else because he dares not risk freedom and the possibility that he will be better off—all under the guise of "rationality." Recall that Rawlsian men choose minimal equality for the least advantaged not out of altruism or benev-

---

[11] See, for example, Steven Lukes, "An Archimedean Point," *The Observer*, 4 June 1972.

olence or social responsibility but solely in order to protect themselves in the pursuit of their interests, whatever those interests turn out to be. They seem moved as much by anticipation of an envy they may feel if others are better off as by the desire for equality or the fear of being a little worse off.[12] Surely more spirited, aggressive, optimistic men—men freed of the constraints of morality and altruism as they supposedly are in Rawls's original position—might choose to pursue their interests more vigorously, less cautiously. Nor would they be any less rational for doing so, assuming that they had weighed and accepted the risks involved.

Rawls is thus faced with a dilemma: if he wishes to preserve egalitarianism, he must contaminate the original position, for the rules of justice that precipitate egalitarianism are generated not by pure rationality but by the special psychology (disguised as rationality) of no-risk planning under conditions of uncertainty. This illicit special psychology may give a more political color to his work (although the politics is not quite what we expect), but it destroys the antiseptic neutrality of the project. If on the other hand he wishes to preserve the pristine formalism of the original position, then the two rules of justice as fairness and the egalitarianism they produce cease to be the inevitable choice of rational men in the original position, and justice as fairness becomes only one of the many rational options. Yet the entire argument of *A Theory of Justice* precludes the surrender of either formal rationality or egalitarianism. Hence, the dilemma.

John Stuart Mill wished to save Benthamite utilitarianism by releasing it from its sterile formalism and endowing it with something of the complexity of moral experience in the real world. But in doing so, he destroyed the consensual foundation of utilitarianism, which depended on its reduction of human behavior to elemental hedonism for its philosophical conviction. Likewise, Rawls rescues the original position from its abstraction—gingerly in *A Theory of Justice*, much more decisively in his recent writ-

[12] "The theory of justice assumes a definite limit on the strength of social and altruistic motivation. It supposes that individuals and groups put forward competing claims, and while they are willing to act justly, they are not prepared to abandon their interests" (p. 281). Also see the final section in this chapter.

ings—but only at the cost of his project: the grounding of principles of political justice in unassailable philosophical bedrock.
Those principles are attractive to him for other reasons (their intuitively comprehended justness, their participation in a web of
thought defined by richer, more Aristotelian notions of the good,
their instantiation of the principles underlying constitutional democracy, and so forth). But their epistemological status as something more than intuitions of liberal citizens depends on the logic
of the original position, a logic, however, that Rawls himself finally seems unable either to execute or to trust.

Rawls has made clear, it is true, that the ''original position is
not intended to explain human conduct except insofar as it tries to
account for our moral judgments'' (p. 120), and he may on this
score deem these psychological remonstrations besides the point.
Yet, I have argued, it is Rawls himself who has introduced special
psychology into the pristine preparticularity of the original position. To dismiss my arguments in support of the special psychology of moderate or extreme-risk strategies is to dismiss his own
preferences for a low-risk strategy: all such strategies are cut from
the same cloth and are part of a fabric that has nothing to do with
rationality. In the absence of these kinds of preferences, the two
rules of justice simply are not defensible as the inevitable choice
of rational men in the original position. To admit them means lift-
ing the veil of ignorance partially and thus robbing the original
position of its defining character. The argument from the original
position seems crippled by the very crutch that makes it ambula-
tory.

A more decisive reply to this line of criticism is implicit in
Rawls's suggestion that the original position is defined in such a
way that it can be regarded as original (that is, as rational) only
insofar as it issues, by way of maximin, in the two rules of justice
as fairness. Rationality, in this perspective, does not merely issue
in but is defined by maximin. Although Rawls leaves considerable
ambiguity on this point, a number of passages appear to support
the inference. ''We want to define the original position so that we
get the desired solution,'' he writes at one point (p. 141). ''The
original position,'' he later notes in what is probably the strongest

statement of the matter in the book, "has been defined so that it is a situation in which the maximin rule applies" (p. 155). But there is little cause to dwell on this line of defense. It is not a position to which Rawls can really afford to commit himself, and his ambivalence on the point elsewhere suggests he does not mean to do so. If the original position is defined simply as that position which issues in the two rules, it becomes analytic with respect to those rules, and Rawls's entire justificatory enterprise is rendered truistic. If the two rules are necessarily entailed by the original position, the elaborate examination of alternative strategies pursued in his Chapter 3 becomes a deception, and the extended debate with utilitarianism is made superfluous. Rawls is quite clear, however, that ideally men are "to choose among all possible conceptions of justice" in the original position (p. 122). Moreover, since he regards the determination of the rational preference between justice as fairness and the principle of average utility as "perhaps the central problem in developing the conception of justice as fairness as a viable alternative to the utilitarian tradition" (p. 150), I think it fair to assume that he does not really mean to argue that the original position is rigorously analytic with respect to the conditions under which rational preferences are developed. His position thus appears to leave my original criticism unanswered.

III

The difficulty of establishing comparable indicators for measuring the potential for satisfaction of different primary social goods points to more than just problems in the psychology of the original position; it also hints at serious problems of interpersonal comparison and measurement in Rawls's theory of justice. Rawls comments critically on the problem (sec. 15, pp. 92–93) as it affects advocates of average utility theory in order to argue that the contract doctrine makes it possible to "abandon entirely" the thorny question of "measuring and summing well-being" (p. 324). Although his approach clearly avoids certain summing difficulties, since it does not require determining collective well-being or average utility at all, it does not elude the difficulties of establishing ordinal scales of interpersonal comparison for critical terms like "satisfaction," "primary good," and "least-advantaged/most-advantaged."

Rawls leans very heavily on the notion of "least-advantaged." The crucial difference principle thus reads: "social and economic inequalities are to be arranged so that they are . . . to the greatest benefit of the least advantaged" (p. 83). According to Rawls, this formulation requires no "accurate interpersonal comparison of benefits . . . it suffices that the least favored person can be identified and his rational preference determined" (p. 77). We need only compare the "expectations," as defined by the index of primary social goods, that "a representative individual can look forward to" (p. 92). No cardinal judgments need be made; only simple ordinal rankings are necessary.

The matter is not quite so straightforward, however. As Rawls acknowledges, the construction of the index generates problems, some of which are lodged in the category Primary Good. Rawls asks, "How are the different primary social goods to be weighed?" (p. 93). His strategy seems to be to narrow the category of Primary Good by stipulation to a core that can be operationalized in easily measurable terms. Self-respect is deferred to the final section of the book, where measurement is not an issue. Liberty, Rawls intimates, is not a problem because of its lexical priority over the other primary goods: since "the fundamental liberties are always equal, and there is a fair equality of opportunity, one does not need to balance these liberties and rights against other values" (p. 93). This reduces the problem to identifying individuals with "the least authority and the lowest income" (p. 94), presumably a manageable enterprise.

Unfortunately, manageability seems to have been purchased at the price of meaning. Quite aside from Rawls's own doubts about the lexical priority of liberty,[13] it can be doubted that crude indi-

---

[13] Rawls concedes that the precedence of liberty comes into play only after "a certain level of wealth has been attained" (p. 542). Below this threshold, liberty may not only have to be weighed against but perhaps subordinated to the other primary goods in whose absence freedom has no meaning. Depending on where

cators like income are sufficient to measure so complex a notion as justice, particularly in modern industrial democracies. Over the last thirty years in the United States, blacks, white middle-class students, women, the rural poor, blue-collar workers, and even the long-suffering middle class have vied with one another for the title "least advantaged." Depending on whether wealth, dignity, life purpose, political power, self-importance, employability, or some other indicator is used, each of these groups can make its case. Income suggests only one, and not necessarily the most salient, dimension of the issue. Who, then, is to be regarded as least advantaged? The unemployable, self-deprecating, wealthy suburban housewife, or the self-respecting, overburdened welfare mother? The overtaxed, undervalued assembly line worker, or the alienated, anomic college drop-out? "The innocent white subjected to crime and fear of crime, or the innocent black forced into humiliating inconvenience and heightened risk of violence from mistaken acts of self-defense?"[14] Rawls provides no criteria by which such social judgments can be made. Yet surely in relatively affluent societies these questions are at least as relevant to the problems of justice as are gross indicators like income. Indeed, they are absolutely crucial to electoral politics (who is worse off? by what standards?) and the implementation of public policies (will constituency A concur in my view that I can take from them to give to a putatively more needy constituency B?). No candidate would think to run for office without getting a rough fix on such matters.

Nevertheless, so far removed is Rawls's philosophy of justice from the politics of justice that he can ultimately rest his entire technical case for the interpersonal viability of his ordinal measures on wealth and income alone. Not even authority and power, noted in passing, are given serious attention.[15] Comparability has

---

the threshold is established, even Marx might be comfortable with such a viewpoint!

[14] This last choice is no mere hypothetical dilemma but one posed in a recent *New York Times* editorial about crime (December 28, 1986) that cites Rawls.

[15] By passing over power, Rawls evades the critical problems of definition and measurement that have attended its conceptualization among sociologists and po-

been won only by gutting the category of primary goods and leaving behind a shell called income.

Even if we put these objections aside and accept that income may provide an approximate measure of the least advantaged, there remains a serious deficiency in the Rawlsian argument. In establishing the superiority of the difference principle over the principle of average utility (sec. 13), Rawls employs a graph to plot the relative income of a representative least-advantaged and representative most-advantaged man. The argument expressed in this graph, however effectively it may challenge the Mean Utilitarians,[16] is remarkable for its apolitical and ahistorical character. Both Rawls and his critics seem to take for granted the social setting within which incomes covary in order to air their differences concerning the hypothetical point of maximum equality on a fixed, time-blind curve. Thus, Graph A, where X_1 depicts the income of a representative most-advantaged man and X_2 the income of a representative least-advantaged man, a is the point of maximum equality (pp. 76–79) on a contribution curve OP showing the relative position of X_1 and X_2.

I do not wish to quarrel with Rawls's technical discussion debating the location of a on the static curve OP. Rather, I question the shape of OP itself, not only, as Scott Gordon has it, as "an empirical matter in the realm of positive economics"[17] but also as an empirical matter in the realm of historical development and social theory. Rawls's contribution curve OP assumes that the "social cooperation defined by the basic structure is mutually advantageous" (p. 77). If, however, OP is plotted in the context of some general theory of historical development or some particular

litical scientists. See, for example, Robert R. Dahl, *Who Governs* (New Haven: Yale University Press, 1961); Peter Bachrach and Morton S. Baratz, "The Two Faces of Power," *American Political Science Review* 56 (December 1962), 947–952; and John R. Champlin, ed., *Power* (New York: Atherton Press, 1971).

[16] There seems to be some doubt about its effectiveness, however. See Scott Gordon, "John Rawls' Difference Principle, Utilitarianism, and the Optimum Degree of Inequality," *Journal of Philosophy* 70 (May 1973), and C. B. Macpherson, "Revisionist Liberalism," in his *Democratic Theory: Essays in Retrieval* (Oxford: Clarendon Press, 1973), pp. 87–94.

[17] Gordon, "John Rawls' Difference Principle," p. 279.

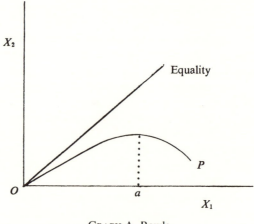

GRAPH A. Rawls

economic theory, then its conveniently symmetrical shape may be radically modified and the rendering of a point of maximum equality made correspondingly difficult. To make this clear, I will portray two possible historical situations in which Rawls's abstract and static curve *OP* turns into a writhing snake hostile to Rawlsian handling techniques.

Let us assume that X_1 symbolizes (through representative individuals) the capital-owning class, and X_2 the working class. Envision, then, two crucial threshold periods in recent industrial history: a period of rapid, disruptive unionization (exemplifying problems of incremental change), and a period of socialist revolution on the Marxist-Leninist model (exemplifying problems of radical structural change). Under conditions of rapid unionization (Graph B), contribution curve *OP* would be radically deflected from any normal shape, leaving the point of maximum equality uncertain and ambiguous over time. If *s* is understood as the point in historical time where unionization is initiated through, say, a general strike, a dramatic decline in the expectations of the working class (X_2) can be anticipated, the degree and duration depending on the reaction of the capital-owning class (X_1). At some point *u*, however, presupposing that the strike succeeds, the union shop

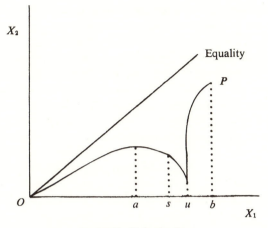

GRAPH B. Unionization

is recognized by the bosses, and a period of rapidly rising expectations for the working class ensues, to some extent at the expense of the owners. Following this phase, some point b of maximum equality is reached that far exceeds the original "maximum" at point a.

This portrait confronts the advocate of justice as fairness with several alternative points of "maximum" equality, between which it may not be possible to choose without reference to considerations of time, place, and putative laws of development not given by the two rules he is essaying to honor. Viewing OP in its early phase, he might conclude that a was indeed the point of maximum equality, particularly if he examined the projections for the segment between a and u that augured only ill for the expectations of X_2. He might, on the other hand, count on the eventual success of unionization—*if* his theory of development anticipated the phase from u to h, and sacrifice the apparent equality of a for the greater equality of the slightly less certain but much more equitable b. To do so he would of course be acting under conditions of uncertainty, where risks might be taken in vain or success achieved at too great a cost, say, following a five-year general strike that destroyed the economy in order to achieve a degree of

73

equality only slightly greater than a. And if the no-risk strategy of maximin is pursued relentlessly, a person in the original position who did not know whether he would turn out to be a worker who survived the general strike or one sacrificed to the good of the union might well opt to forgo unions since he would be worse off than a non-union worker if he ended up paying with his life for the workers' struggle (a ''least-advantaged'' person if there ever was one!)

In short, judgment concerning the point of maximum equality cannot be reached in a timeless apolitical void, as Rawls's quest for a secure philosophical foundation for justice compels him to try to do. It must be reached in the context of a particular time and a particular place in which the relations between X_1 and X_2 conform to some developmental laws of politics and social structure—which may or may not be generally known and understood. Rawls's strategy here becomes not merely undialectical and ahistorical but, in conjunction with the predilection for maximin, antihistorical—predisposed to inertia. As we have just seen, under the conditions portrayed in Graph B, maximin would dictate forgoing a possible, but historically uncertain b equality in return for a guaranteed a equality. ''Just'' men might thus, against their instincts to be sure, find themselves obliged by justice as fairness to act as strike busters and scabs—a most melancholy and ironic consideration.

The situation reflects even greater uncertainty under conditions corresponding to the Marxist-Leninist theory of socialist revolution. Once again (Graph C) there is an early period of apparent maximum equality a followed by a period of declining expectations during which the disappointments and grievances of the working class (X_2) feed revolutionary sentiment. In time, the working class under the leadership of a revolutionary party overthrows the capital-owning class (X_1) and seizes its representative institutions (at point r). During the initial period of disruption and civil war, both X_1's and X_2's expectations diminish. But following the successful establishment of a revolutionary regime (at point s), X_2's expectations once again begin to grow, while X_1's continue to decline as the expropriation of the expropriators becomes a real-

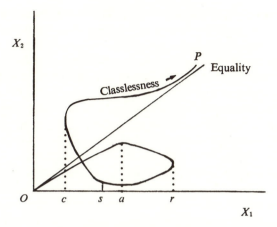

GRAPH C. Marxist revolution

ity. During the ensuing period of the dictatorship of the proletariat (the segment from s to c), the capital-owning class virtually disappears, and OP veers toward total equality. The class system itself is liquidated, and X_1 and X_2 become indistinguishable—classless everymen chosen at random in a classless society.

Now, this projection creates further difficulties for Rawls.[18] By adumbrating fundamental structural changes in the relations between the two classes and, eventually, liquidation of the class system entirely, it challenges the static Rawlsian picture with a dynamic that seems quite beyond the compass of justice as fairness. The ahistorical Rawlsian would again be tempted to prefer the certainty of a—that is, the present reality of capitalist society (or feudal society or whatever the present society was)—to the risks and costs of some eventual P. Moreover, his antihistorical formalism might even compel him to favor the restoration of property to the capital owners during the period from s to c, for, at least after OP crossed the axis of equality, the capitalist class would qualify technically as the "least-advantaged" class. Maximin seems fated to such ironies.

---

[18] As would any projection based on a theory of structural change or revolution. The credibility of the Marxist-Leninist model is obviously not at issue.

I am not trying to suggest that Rawls intends to rationalize capitalism. The maximin rule is conservative vis-à-vis *all* modes of change: it favors propinquity, whatever the time and place. In this sense its abstract formalism is particularly salient, being adverse to risk per se, whatever the historical context. As a result, the difference principle is simply incapable of establishing a point of maximum equality except in a timeless vacuum where neither history nor social theory need be confronted. Under abstract conditions of maximum stability, enduring tranquillity, and minimal structural change, it may be possible to identify a static point of equality. But under the real conditions of evolving societies forever being transformed by the dynamics of economics and history, the static projections of maximin are unlikely to secure it.

Rawls may possess the conceptual apparatus to deal with some of these objections. He recognizes that to define expectations "solely by reference to such things as liberty and wealth" can only be "provisional" and that it is eventually necessary "to include other kinds of primary goods" that raise "deeper questions" (pp. 396–397). A careful examination of the place of self-respect in identifying the least advantaged, set within the more general discussion of the good and the Aristotelian principle, would presumably precipitate a much richer understanding of injustice than is afforded by a raw, ahistorical comparison of incomes over some limited period.[19] But self-respect can be neither operationalized in the fashion of income nor rendered philosophically determinate in the manner of the two rules. It thus stays entirely in the background during the operational analysis of the difference principle, acting indirectly to leaven the otherwise flat ingredients of the primary goods loaf. Consequently, inequality is construed in narrow pecuniary terms that neglect the psychological and political roots of exploitation in relationships conditioned by domination and submission, depersonalization and alienation, or socialization and public opinion. Rawls's formalism simply im-

---

[19] Because the Aristotelian principle suggests a qualitative ranking of our activities and life-plans corresponding to their complexity and the degree to which they fulfill our capacities, it gives to self-respect a moral depth it lacks as an instrumental primary good (see sec. 65).

munizes him to sociological modes of understanding. Even were he, say, to extend his contribution curves over a historical period encompassing unionization, it seems unlikely that his focus on equalizing income would promote in him a sensitivity to the social and psychological consequences of unionization—for example, the standardization and routinization of work, the legitimation of wage-capital relations through the amelioration of conditions, the subordination of the creative ownership of labor power to the just distribution of its anonymous fruits, and so forth.

The evidence that Rawls's analysis is insufficiently political as well as egregiously ahistorical is in fact overwhelming. There is no need to mediate it through the technical arguments in favor of the difference principle. Hence, the moment has come when the apolitical character of Rawls's theory can be confronted, not through the inadequacies of his argument for interpersonal comparisons, but directly.

IV

Rawls did well to avoid Godwin's title *On Political Justice* in labeling his enterprise, though some might wish to argue that justice is always and necessarily public and thus, in the generic sense, political. Yet Rawls's formalism, his preoccupation with economic models and metaphors, his predilection for abstract reasoning, and, above all, his aspiration to endow muddy, much-contested politics with the clarity of a rational consensus rooted in philosophical theory—all combine to deter him from setting his emergent theory of justice in the context of historical and political reality. His tendency is, when theory meets practice, to eschew practice, to dismiss questions of "political sociology" and disclaim any intentions of developing a "theory of the political system" (pp. 226–227). His examples are often trivial, usually apolitical. Choosing between a trip to Paris and a trip to Rome is permitted to stand as an example of fundamental life choices (p. 412). Terms suggestive of modern man's political dilemmas—racism, alienation, nationalism, citizenship, socialization, emancipation, indoctrination—are hardly to be found. Nor does the material face of politics characterized by power, command, authority, and sanction (as against the ideal face described by legitimacy, obligation, and justice) show itself. When political terms do occasionally turn up, they appear in startlingly naive and abstract ways, as if Rawls believed not only that a theory of justice must condition political reality but also that political reality could be regarded as little more than a precipitate of the theory of justice. This suggestion raises a serious philosophical question about the relationship between the original position and what we can call the historical position—between the normative theory of justice and historical reality. I will examine this dilemma in the final section of this chapter. Here I am anxious to illustrate Rawls's apolitical mode of argumentation. Take the following propositions:

(1) It is a "mistaken view that the intensity of desire is a relevant consideration in enacting [just] legislation" (p. 230; also see p. 361).

(2) "The liberties of the intolerant [that is, toleration of the intolerant] may persuade them to a belief in freedom" (p. 219).

(3) There ought to be "a cooperative, political alliance of the minorities to regulate the overall level of dissent" (p. 374).

(4) "Throughout, the choice between a private-property economy and socialism is left open; from the standpoint of the theory of justice alone, various basic structures would appear to satisfy its principles" (p. 258).

(5) "Each person must insist upon an equal right to decide what his religious obligations are" (p. 217).

I would like to suggest that a theory of justice that permits assertions of this sort, notwithstanding the caveats and contexts that attend them, is prima facie a theory of limited utility in addressing the injustices of actual political systems.[20] It is to the real political

---

[20] It may perhaps serve as a practical "rule of thumb" in making clear-cut ethical decisions in completely unambiguous circumstances. See Peter Caws, "Changing Our Habits," *New Republic*, May 13, 1972, p. 24.

world as a child's stick figures are to flesh-and-blood women and men—abstractions that leave out not simply inessential details but the nuances that give women and men their character and thus their political identity. Let me make the point by commenting briefly on the cited passages.

(1) If Rawls argued that intensity of desire was not a *sufficient* consideration in enacting just legislation or not constitutive of the definition of justice, there could be little objection. But in pursuit of philosophical immunity for his notion of justice from particular wants and desires, he is constrained to claim that intensity is *irrelevant*—a foolhardy contention at best. Although intensity of desire hardly defines the just cause, history teaches that it can often reveal that cause. Liberal democratic systems are thus designed to permit an intense minority to resist (through the filibuster) or even to overcome (through the electoral primary) a lethargic majority. Moreover, the intensity question is absolutely crucial to the stability of democratic systems, and Rawls evinces a deep concern for stability: the "well-ordered" society, he asserts significantly, is a stable society (pp. 398–399). Now, almost all social scientists agree that neglect of intensity can destabilize democracy.[21] How, then, can Rawls be committed to stability as an integral feature of his theory of justice and at the same time be indifferent to intensity? Presumably, only by refusing to countenance political sociology in the name of isolating from contamination the philosophical conception of justice in the original position.

(2) Rawls can cite neither psychological nor historical evidence suggesting that toleration of the intolerant renders them more tolerant or liberty-conscious. The sorts of data deployed by those who are interested in evidence indicate that the intolerant are

---

[21] Robert Dahl has argued, for example, that asymmetrical patterns among minorities and majorities, where the latter employ the majoritarian principle to lazily and indifferently obstruct the will of the former, can lead to the radical destabilization of the precarious democratic balance. See Dahl, *A Preface to Democratic Theory* (Chicago: University of Chicago Press, 1956), pp. 90–123. Also see Willmoore Kendall and George W. Carey, "The 'Intensity' Problem and Democratic Theory," *American Political Science Review* 62 (March, 1968), 5–24.

largely beyond rationality and thus quite incapable of grasping what is at stake in the very idea of toleration.[22] The intolerant defer to imagined superiors with the same irrationality that they bully imagined inferiors. Fanatical true believers often seem to regard toleration by others as a compliment rather than as a reprimand to their intolerance. We need not, however, falsify Rawls's contention in order to make clear that, in the absence of political sociology, it remains wholly unproven and largely unexamined. To examine it would be to subject philosophical generalizations deduced from the axioms of the original position to the test of political reality—which in turn would be to question the dominion of philosophy over politics.

(3) The idea of a political alliance of minorities to regulate dissent may be attractive, but I cannot think of a single historical case that confirms its viability under actual conditions of dissent in democracies. In the instances that come to mind—Czarist Russia in its parliamentary phase before 1917, Weimar Germany, America in the 1960s—internecine conflict among dissenting minorities has been an inherent feature of more systemic political dissent. Indeed, competition among dissenters has often been more violent and protracted than between the dissenters and the system they purport to oppose in common, and for understandable reasons. The scarcity of access to the system (via the media, for example) compels claimants for its attention to outshout, out-radicalize, and otherwise outdo one another. Their belief in contradictory solutions to common problems makes them natural competitors in vying for revolutionary legitimacy. It is little wonder, then, that in recent years blacks, women, students, and others have each claimed to be the "most oppressed" group in American society. Rawls tells such competing minorities that, however legitimate their grievances may be, when taken in conjunction with the complaints and demands of other dissenting groups they simply overburden the capacity of the system for tolerance and change. To

[22] See Theodor Adorno et al., *The Authoritarian Personality* (New York: Harper and Brothers, 1950); S. M. Lipset, *Political Man* (New York: Doubleday and Company, 1960), esp. ch. 4; and S. A. Stouffer, *Communism, Conformity and Civil Liberties* (New York: Doubleday and Company, 1955).

speak in this fashion seems a good deal less than just, particularly in the framework of a theory of justice that claims immunity from contingency.

(4) To assert that, so far as a theory of justice is concerned, there is nothing to choose between capitalism and socialism is so striking a claim that to cite it nearly obviates the need to comment on it. Rawls acknowledges that "a doctrine of political economy must include an interpretation of the public good which is based on a conception of justice" (p. 259), but he nonetheless wishes to leave the choice between capitalism and socialism "open." To me, positing this kind of impartiality is like developing a geometry in which the question of whether parallel lines meet is left open, or generating an aesthetic that refuses to take sides on questions of taste. Given the intimate interdependence of political and economic institutions in the West, and given the widely held suspicion that capitalism may bear some culpability in the history of Western injustice, a theory of justice that sees nothing to choose between capitalism and socialism is either extravagantly formalistic to the point of utter irrelevance, or it is a badly disguised rationalization for one particular socioeconomic system, namely, property-owning democracy (although its aversion to risk makes it seem dispositionally anti-entrepreneurial). Either way, from the standpoint of politics and sociology, the theory would seem to have little to offer to citizens. Indeed, its silence on this crucial issue discloses its essential inadequacy as political philosophy. Like so many propositions derived from purely philosophical argument, it offers more succor to philosophers than to concerned citizens or struggling political subjects of an injust regime.[23]

(5) Rawls's discussion of religion seems quite nearly as naive and incomplete as his treatment of economic systems. The passage cited contains a clue to his misperceptions in its strange supposition that men "decide" on their religious obligations—presum-

---

[23] Rawls remarks in passing that "some socialists have objected to all market institutions as inherently degrading" (p. 280), but he apparently dismisses socialism as too dependent "on the strength of social and altruistic motivation" (p. 281). Altruism is an issue that comes back to haunt him, however, as becomes evident in the discussion below.

81

ably much the way they decide on whether to travel to Paris or Rome. This point of view follows from Rawls's positing that the just is prior to the good and that the just is entirely a function of rational choice under optimum conditions (the original position), for the just is then also necessarily prior to the religious. That is to say, religion is admitted into Rawlsian psychology only after men, stripped of all religious particularity, have chosen the rules that are to condition whatever religious beliefs they end up holding. Religion is thrust into the realm of contingency and particularity, lexically subordinate to the settling of fundamental procedural questions by men defined by rationality rather than by belief. Religious ontology becomes secondary to rationalist epistemology.

Unfortunately, the religious view of the world begins with precisely the opposite assumptions. It presupposes the priority of the good to the just, the subordination of the epistemological to the ontological ("believe that ye shall know"), the insignificance of contingency in the face of faith. The religious believer simply would not comprehend, let alone accept, the secular-skeptical premises of the original position. If he refused to acknowledge the "liberty" of a nonbeliever, he would be acting not out of disrespect but out of conviction that a man who does not believe cannot possibly be free. Moreover, a Christian believer might not regard the perils of being a member of a persecuted minority during "this life" as a sufficient warrant to compromise any aspect of his otherworldly faith. He might even reject the rules of justice as a deprivation that would compel him to live without the austerity and suffering to which God has intentionally condemned men. If Rawls were to say to such a man, "But think, my friend, what if you turn out to be a Confucian? or an atheist?" he could only reply, "All the worse for my immortal soul!" Put bluntly, there is simply no room in the afterlife for the original position: the only thing original in the Christian way of thinking is sin. Not that there is any room in the original position for the afterlife—or for sin. Rawls's treatment of religion simply assumes that religious beliefs have no ontological or epistemological bases in truth whatsoever. The Impartial Observer's perspective is that of the agnostic or the skeptic, where religion is reduced to dimensions that can be encompassed and assimilated by justice as fairness. That is to say, it is rendered both trivial and contingent.

The problems raised by these inadequacies in Rawls's political sociology go well beyond political naiveté and inadvertent ahistoricity. To some extent, his apolitical abstractness is intentional, and some of his sharpest critics have defended him on this point. Stuart Hampshire has labeled as "unfair" (although accurate) the charge that Rawls "pays no attention to the dominant powers of corporations, unions, the military machine, the secret police, the mass media. . . ." Rawls intends only to provide "a theoretical reconstruction of the notion of justice, and not of all the virtues of a good society and a good life; and he is not concerned with the practicalities of political science or with the theory of democracy."[24] Such remonstrances might appear to blunt the line of criticism developed in this section. I believe, however, that I can show that Hampshire underestimates the deep ambiguity that surrounds Rawls's attitude toward and account of political reality. Rawls is never able quite to decide what sort of reality the rules of justice are intended for. On the one hand, it is a reality that manifests instinctively virtuous inclinations in congruence with and thus corroborative of the procedural principles of justice established by the original position. On the other hand, it is a reality very much like our own, where the sublime verities of the original position are forever confronted by competition, conflict, inequality, war, and even slavery. This disturbing ambivalence sets Rawls off in several contrary directions, plunging him into dilemmas from which he can never quite extricate himself.

V

Rather like Hobbes's model of the state of nature, the original position contains two moments, reason and interest, whose thrust tends in contrary directions. It is characterized, on the one hand, by rationality and collaboration, by the stipulated tabling of pas-

---

[24] Stuart Hampshire, "A New Philosophy of the Just Society," *New York Review of Books*, February 24, 1972, p. 39.

sions like rancor and envy, by a point of view that suggests a beneficent, even mutualist, interpretation of human nature. On the other hand, it is also characterized by interest psychology, by the drive for power and liberty as instrumentalities of personal ambition, and by an explicit individualism that treats all social collaboration as a means to individual ends. The motivational input in the original position is apparently individualistic; the social output (the rules of justice), a good deal more collaborative. That is how right and utility are bridged, how rules required by the just community are shown to be acceptable to the rational, self-interested individual. Reason itself totters, inclined here to the kind of prudential calculation we associate with Hobbes or Hume, leaning there to deontology (practical reason) as understood by Kant.

This same ambiguity creeps into Rawls's portrait of the context into which the rules arising from the original position are introduced, the context I have called the historical position. When Rawls suggests that in the original position men "decide solely on the basis of what seems best calculated to further their interests" (p. 584), he seems to construe the rules of justice as typically liberal control mechanisms for the accommodation of conflicting interests in a real historical position that is essentially competitive. At one point, justice itself is defined as "the virtue of practices where there are competing interests and where persons feel entitled to press their rights on each other" (p. 129). If this is all to be taken seriously, the rules of justice must be understood as proximate criteria of minimal justice for conventional interest-oriented, power-responsive, conflict-ridden real societies rather than as absolute criteria of pristine conduct in ideal "well-ordered" societies. As such, they can presumably be deployed in the ad hoc fashion recommended by Peter Caws and others, justice being little more than a matter of choosing "between several unjust, second best, arrangements" (p. 279). Although Rawls differs with the utilitarians on the question of aggregating utility, he shares with them from this perspective a common emphasis that is exhibited in his hedonistic focus on interest, his instrumentalist view of reason, his manipulative approach to political institutions, and his pluralist preoccupation with conflict resolution. Although he may

84

deem himself a Kantian and may protest that his theory is "ideal-regarding" rather than "want-regarding,"[25] Rawls here seems to equate the historical position with what he calls "private society"—an association held together not "by a public conviction that its basic arrangements are just and good in themselves, but by the calculations of everyone . . . that any practicable changes would reduce the stock of means whereby they pursue their personal ends" (p. 522). It is precisely the point of the basic arrangements reached in the original position that they are not "just and good in themselves" but decided "solely on the basis of what seems best calculated to further [men's] interests" (p. 584).

Yet these are conclusions that Rawls cannot accept, and anyone who has read *A Theory of Justice* will rightly object to the above gloss as one-sided. However Hobbesian his consequentialist reasoning may seem, his instincts remain Kantian. Rawls the Kantian understands that the argument from the original position must be corroborated, in keeping with the soft logic of congruence, by the evidence of man's instincts and intuitions in natural societies. It is perfectly obvious that "private society" is not the model of "natural society" with which Rawls aspires to make the rules of justice congruent. He is at pains to deny that the "contractarian view [is] individualistic."[26] Although he anticipates that critics will contend "the contract doctrine entails that private society is the ideal," he insists that "this is not so, as the notion of the well-ordered society shows" (p. 522). The well-ordered society, far from being a "private society," is "a form of social union" (p. 527); and social union is the form of association that corresponds to man's "social nature" and embodies his "shared final ends," the form of association where men naturally "value common in-

---

[25] Brian Barry argues that Rawls's theory is not convincingly "ideal-regarding" at all. See Barry, "Liberalism and Want Satisfaction," *Political Theory* 1 (May 1973), 134–153. Barry's general position, a sweeping critique of Rawls, can be found in his *The Liberal Theory of Justice: A Critical Examination of the Principal Doctrines in "A Theory of Justice" by John Rawls* (Oxford: Clarendon Press, 1973).

[26] In his "Reply to Lyons and Teitelman," p. 557. Also see *A Theory of Justice*, p. 584.

stitutions and activities as goods in themselves'' (p. 522). Now this construction—more Kantian than Hobbesian in its mutualist tone and implications of natural sociability, more Rousseauian than Kantian in its emphasis on mutuality and civic harmony—clearly contradicts the Hobbesian understanding of Rawls's state as an artifice of individual interests. It is more deontological than teleological, more mutualist than individualistic, more ideal-regarding than want-regarding, more harmonistic than competitive. With it, Rawls provides an intuitive foundation in natural instinct for the procedural rules adduced without the mediation of instinct in the original position. Although "the notion of respect or of the inherent worth of persons is not a suitable basis for arriving at [the rules of justice]," these rules will "be effective only if men have a sense of justice and do therefore respect one another" (p. 586). The rules of justice, it would seem, operate effectively only in a "nearly just society" where there already exists "a constitutional regime and a publicly recognized conception of justice" (p. 386).

This part of Rawls's argument is little more than an appeal for secondary support from the kinds of intuitive, a prioristic notions necessarily excluded from the primary theory. The argument from the original position, with its rather uncertain foundations in Hobbesian ratiocination, is thus shored up by Kantian braces drawn from a priori matériel not admissible in the original position. It is in this sense, as I argued at the outset, that Rawls tries to burn his candle at both ends—the more light the better. Justification, we will recall, "is a matter of the mutual support of many considerations, of everything fitting together into one coherent view" (p. 579).

The trouble is that the two parts of the argument do not fit—the candle will not burn at *either* end. When Rawls sanitizes the original position, he is careful to "assume a definite limit on the strength of social and altruistic motivation" (p. 281). There is an important "difference between the sense of justice and the love of mankind," the latter being "supererogatory, going beyond the moral requirements and not invoking the exemptions [in the name of private interest] which the principles of duty and obligation allow" (p. 476). In other words, too much altruism would obviate the need for a rationalist theory of justice altogether. "A society in which all can achieve their complete good," Rawls warns, "or in which there are no conflicting demands and the wants of all fit together without coercion, is a society in a certain sense beyond justice" (p. 281), for in "an association of saints agreeing on a common ideal, if such a community could exist, disputes about justice would not occur" (p. 129). Here Rawls sounds for all the world exactly like Jean-Jacques Rousseau when he warns that the social contract is not intended for angels, who have no need of it, but for self-interested, competing men, who do. But surely the notion of "social union" or of the "well-ordered," "nearly just" society where men share "final ends" and "value common institutions and activities as goods in themselves" leans precisely in the direction of angels. Very much as the supportive institutions that nourish civic unity in Books III and IV of *The Social Contract* sometimes seem to render the legislative politics of Books I and II superfluous, so the intuitive foundations appealed to by Rawls to shore up his prudential theory ultimately render that theory superfluous. The theory of justice is convincing only in a context that is itself beyond justice![27]

Rawls does try to avoid this startling irony by construing social union as a form of association more mutualist than private society, yet less utopian than an association of saints. The footing on this middle ground is not, however, very secure. As if on the top of a ridge separating the valley of private society and interest theory (the Hobbesian side) from the valley of perfect union and supererogatory mutualism (the Kantian side), Rawls seems continually in danger of plunging down one side or the other. No doubt he hoped in *A Theory of Justice* to remain on the ridge, where his perspective could encompass the Hobbesian and Kantian valleys at a glance. In fact he could not. And if in that work the Hobbesian and Kantian in him are never really made compatible, in his sub-

---

[27] If Rawls were to seek serious political solace for the theory of justice, he would do well to look not to Kant but to Kant's own source, Rousseau, where the political problem of right and utility—the individual and the community—are definitively characterized and resolved in terms that are, however, political rather than philosophical.

sequent qualifications of the theory of justice he has moved in expressly Kantian directions, forsaking both Hobbes and the original position with increasing disregard for the congruence argument that was the centerpiece of the book and of his philosophical project. In any case, even in its original form, that argument, far from reconciling the contradictions, only served to bring them into relief.

The conclusion that seems to me unavoidable is that the original position, even if the objections raised in the first section can be put aside, is incomplete, perhaps even untenable in the absence of intuitive arguments positing man's natural sociability and instinctive sense of justice. Yet the rules of justice that issue from the original position are rendered superfluous in the presence of such arguments. If, on the other hand, the historical position is made equivalent to private society, then Rawls must be classified as a radical individualist in a manner he explicitly rejects, and the argument from congruence loses its force.

Finally, it seems that what Rawls has taken to be the smooth channel of congruence running between the perilous Scylla of utopianism and the stark Charybdis of realism is an impassable rapids in whose currents the theory of justice founders. Rawls himself seems to have accepted as much. In his recent lectures and writings he has moved well beyond the formalism of the pure theory. In the name of elaborating, defending, and clarifying it, he has opted to emphasize the wholly hypothetical character of the original position, diminishing its importance in his thought by casting it as little more than a heuristic device. "As a device of representation," he writes in 1985, "the idea of the original position serves as a means of public reflection and self-clarification."[28] In his earlier Dewey Lectures, he also essays to distance himself from a purely philosophical construction of his project, insisting that to justify "a conception of justice is not primarily an epistemological problem," that the real task is social, and that the social task is "primary."[29] Nonetheless, if he has come increasingly to recognize the perils of abstract philosophical conceptions of the

[28] "Justice as Fairness," p. 238.
[29] "Kantian Constructivism in Moral Theory," p. 519.

political and to reject the idea that a conception of justice is justified by "its being true to an order antecedent to and given to us," he nonetheless remains wedded to a method that will secure the legitimacy of the theory by demonstrating its "moral objectivity," something that requires that we construct a "social point of view we can all accept."[30] His focus in the Dewey Lectures and subsequently has been on the concepts of a well-ordered society and the moral person, but he has not abandoned the original position. He continues to see it as the crucial "mediating model-conception" that orders the relations between the other two.[31]

Rawls today is a philosopher torn. Willing to acknowledge the historicity of the theory of justice itself—he characterizes it as "embedded in the political institutions of a constitutional democratic regime"[32]—he nonethless hankers for the objectivity and neutrality of some Archimedian point. He wishes to speak to the real political world. He notes for example that he "failed to say in *A Theory of Justice*, or failed to stress sufficiently," that justice as fairness was "intended as a political conception of justice."[33] Yet he fails to say it because he fails to do it: his argument there is Kantian not Rousseauian, philosophical not even remotely political. He remains saddled with the onus of legitimation understood as an appeal to cognitive or rational consent. The viability of his theory of justice thus depends on a form of consent that is ultimately rational rather than social or political. He responds to the plurality and incommensurability of understandings of the good in the public domain by constructing a hypothetical domain of consent, defined by a set of unimpeachable, abstract constraints that constitute rationality, assuring us all the while that his aim is political. Like all contractarians, he substitutes for ongoing political participation a single, hypothetical moment of consent that obviates the need for all future political engagement.

Finally, Rawls remains a long way from genuine politics. The

---

[30] Ibid.

[31] Ibid., p. 520.

[32] "Justice as Fairness," p. 225.

[33] Ibid., p. 224. Rawls also notes here that even the Dewey Lectures were insufficiently acknowledged as political. He suggests that he should have entitled them "Kantian Constructivism in Political Philosophy." Ibid., p. 224, note 2.

genuinely political does of necessity what the philosophical tries to do by design: it precipitates procedures for dealing with conflict over various conceptions of the good in the absence of unimpeachable philosophical standards or independent grounds. It may do so by constructing a framework for debate, deliberation, and decision in the face of conflicting public goals (as the Madisonian formula does), or it may do so by prescribing a model of citizenship that enables individuals to transcend their private interests through membership in the civic community (as Rousseau or Tocqueville do in what I have called the strong democratic model). But it is in the nature of *political* theory that it eschews the consolation of abstract consensus, the single moment of hypothetical consent, in favor of the realities of conflict and community—and their attendant political conditions.

Rawls, finally, cannot elude the dilemma that has tracked him from the start. He is a philosopher and a liberal, and his wish is to give to the liberal predilection for tolerance, pluralism, and rights a philosophical foundation that does not exclude social utility (a theory of justice). For all of its recent meanderings, the theory of justice remains a philosophical rather than a political theory. Which is to say that its aim remains to demonstrate that men and women who disagree on moral and political ends can nonetheless agree on rules of justice—*if, placing the right before the good (the abstract individual before the real citizen), they permit themselves to be constrained by the hypothetical rationality of a philosopher's imagination.* Reflective equilibrium if not truth, the assuaging of rationality if not epistemé, hold Rawls to his course. As a result, despite the grandeur of his aspirations and the magnificence of the philosophical edifice in which those aspirations have been made manifest, he finally does more to exhibit the poverty of liberal philosophy's political ambitions than to secure their success.

FOUR

Deconstituting Politics:
Robert Nozick and
Philosophical Reductionism

> There is no body of knowledge such that from it can
> be derived infallible or even fallible decisions about
> ultimate political objectives.
>
> F. H. Bradley

OF ALL THE postwar philosophical attempts to conquer politics,
none is more self-evidently foundationalist, more explicitly reductionist, more radically antipolitical, and more obsessively preoccupied with rights than Robert Nozick's influential book *Anarchy,
State and Utopia.* Whereas John Rawls wishes to bridge right and
utility by using a form of rationality arising out of the first to justify certain propositions about justice tending toward the second,
Nozick wishes only to establish, delimit, and underscore the argument for rights, even at the price of deconstituting the political
into apolitical bits. It is ironic, if not surprising in an era that prizes
individualism and privatism, that Nozick's antipolitical version of
rights-based individualism should have such political success. The
book is reputed to have sat invitingly on the desks of Ford admin-
istration staffers in the mid-1970s, and more recently it has become
a kind of *locus classicus* of the Reagan era's aggressive free-market privatism. In a rights-obsessed society that views the appeal to
the radically isolated individual as a legitimation of just about anything and the possible existence of a public weal or a community
good as a threat to just about everything, a work devoted to the
resuscitation of something very much akin to natural rights absolutism is obviously a boon.

If such a work provides new evidence for my view that contemporary Anglo-American philosophy is not an ideal vehicle for gen-

uine political thinking, it also demonstrates the power of philosophy to shape and distort popular thought about politics. *Anarchy, State and Utopia* is in fact a serious, systematic, and often beguiling attempt to subjugate politics to the foundationalist perspective, to demonstrate that all political principles depend on prepolitical and independent metaphysical grounds that are not so much beyond as prior to all disputation. Nozick's lucid and dogmatic arguments fall somewhere between the utlitarians' statist-egalitarian justifications and the anarchists' anti–statist-individualist counterjustifications. They demand the serious and critical attention of students of liberal philosophy in democratic times.

II

Anarchy, State and Utopia is an argument designed to show that it is possible to go beyond anarchism without violating anarchist premises, to reach minimal-statist conclusions by starting with radical-individualist assumptions; in other words, to construct a defense of a peculiarly thin version of political legitimacy on wholly nonpolitical grounds. This defense is formally deployed both against anarchists who believe that there is *no* legitimate form of the state consistent with radical individualism and personal autonomy, and against statists who believe that it is necessary to move beyond radical individualism to sustain any coherent theory of political legitimacy—although it is obvious that democrats and welfare statists are Nozick's more proximate and urgent targets. The formal argument contends that more is possible than the anarchists realize but that less is possible than the statists wish, at least if philosophy is to be the standard.

This dual strategy accounts for the differing intellectual styles of the first two parts of *Anarchy, State and Utopia*. Part I is a delicately balanced tower of accumulated deductions anchored in a subterrestial (that is, invisible and thus unexamined) foundation of radical individualism. In the fashion of traditional, pre-Humean naturalism, Nozick simply takes for granted that men "live separate existences" defined by inviolable freedom and an absolute right to property; that "no moral balancing is possible" between these initially solitary beings; and that, as a consequence, "vol untary consent" is an absolutely necessary prerequisite of every and any step taken toward political relations—toward exchange, justice, the common pursuit of social goals, and the bartering of freedom for utilitarian ends.[1] No arguments are put forward in favor of these asseverations, which are posited like so many axioms in a new geometry. Under the conditions specified by these radical individualist axioms, traditional anarchists despair of taking a single, secure step in the direction of political legitimacy and thus, like Robert Paul Wolff in his 1960s incarnation, generally conclude that anarchism is "philosophically true."[2] Nozick's ingenuity is a good deal more daring, however, and permits him to make a journey to political minimalism that would leave less bold individualists trembling. The trick is to make every step toward political association hinge exclusively on *voluntary* exchanges that, if they encroach on the boundaries of other individuals at all, do so only by permission or on the basis of just compensation. Carefully executed, these tactics neither violate rights nor resort to the rights-abdicating or rights-exchanging compromises of a social contract. Yet they do eventuate logically in an ultraminimal state. This stripped-down, proto-political body does little more than guarantee the property rights of those who contract (voluntarily) for its services; it becomes a de facto state only insofar as it assumes the functions of a private protective association dominant over a territory, enforcing the rights of members against nonmembers, but compensating (probably with services) nonmembers for losses such enforcement might occasion (118).

Anarchy is thus surpassed (*aufgehoben*) without violating the

[1] All page citations in the text are from Robert Nozick, *Anarchy, State and Utopia* (New York: Basic Books, 1974). It is a telling comment on his philosophical gamesman's approach to politics that Nozick has not returned to the themes of his book in subsequent work. Nor has he, in the manner of Rawls, tried to adapt his position to meet the objections of critics or the changing realities of the political world. Instead, he has moved on to other, strictly philosophical concerns (in *Philosophical Investigations* [Cambridge, Mass.: Harvard University Press, 1980], for example) leaving the game and his unseemly playmates behind.

[2] Robert Paul Wolff, *In Defense of Anarchism* (New York: Harper Torchback, 1970), p. xx.

principle of anarchism: the absolute sacrosanctity of individual autonomy. A thin theory of politics is adduced that makes Rawls's formalism look downright totalitarian. The dominant protective association that issues from this thin theory is not licensed or legitimized by these arguments in the fashion of social contract reasoning; rather, it is shown to be a logically natural extension of hypothetical prestatist conditions that require no license or legitimation.

If the style of Part I of *Anarchy, State and Utopia* is innovative and architectural, the style of Part II is more conservative and wary. It builds defensive trenches around the tower erected in Part I, suggesting that that edifice is the only one capable of withstanding the stresses of weighty philosophical criticism. "So far from anarchy—to the borders of the minimalist state—we may come, without compromising our rights and freedom," Nozick seems to say, "but not one step farther!" A dominant protective association is in fact "the most extensive state that can be justified . . . any state more extensive violates people's rights" (149).

Nozick's primary adversaries in defending his own careful voluntarism are utilitarians and other proponents of "end-state reasoning" who want to make distribution and justice, and the state that enforces them, dependent on some general pattern or principle imposed impartially (and not necessarily with their consent) on all, who insist, that is to say, on determining the justice and legitimacy of political arrangements by reference to an ideal distribution rather than actual (historical) distributions. Democrats of every stripe (with large and small d's) and egalitarians, socialists, and progressives seeking social justice may offer a politics that appeals to Nozick the citizen (as he was incarnated in his progressive form in the 1960s), but they depend on a logic that violates the axioms of Nozick the philosopher and so must be delegitimized.

Metaphysics is the measure. By this standard, John Rawls becomes a prime target because his modification of mean utility is, from Nozick's point of view, a particularly dangerous deception. By seeming to acknowledge the lexical priority of liberty over equality, and by founding his rules of justice in hypothetical individual consent (in the so-called original position), Rawls parades as a rights theorist when he is in fact a masked utilitarian. Nozick's argument is a simple one: ''No end state principle or distributional patterned principle of justice can be continuously realized without continuous interference with other people's lives'' (163). Whatever the derivation of mean utility, justice as fairness, and other redistributive principles, their implementation necessarily bypasses voluntary consent. They may originate in a kind of consent, but they operate in violation of individual autonomy and are thus illegitimate. Consent must be actual and continuing, and not, as contract theorists misleadingly argue, hypothetical and original—a one-shot generic input achieved under highly constrained and usually mythic conditions. All policies justified by indirect appeals to original consent or generic rationality are coercive and thus in violation of individual rights. Taxation, for example, however just its objectives, is finally a form of forced labor and stands in violation of the paradigmatic natural right of self-ownership. Labor may be sold, but it may not be conscripted, no matter how just the cause. The entitlement theory of justice (see below) thus becomes a plateau above which no principle can justifiably rise (216-217), for it alone operates without violating individual rights and without treating any single person as a means to some other person's ends. Indeed, entitlement theory does not treat at all with ideal patterns of human relations, such as equality, since it can make ''no presumption in favor of equality, or any other overall end state or patterning'' (233).

Minimalism as defended in Part II thus defines the limits of justice—not necessarily because we deserve what we are entitled to (the two are not synonymous in Nozick) and not necessarily because entitlements and voluntary transfers create end states that are just by some independent standard (Nozick freely admits they often are not), but exclusively because theories that move beyond minimalism violate the self-evident principles of individual autonomy and self-ownership that Nozick believes any legitimate notion of justice must respect. Rawls's attempt to ground a patterned principle of justice, such as the difference principle, in the rationality of free and consenting individuals must fail.

Notwithstanding Nozick's withering attack on Rawls, Part III of *Anarchy, State and Utopia* bears a striking resemblance to Rawls's own "congruence" argument in *A Theory of Justice* (though Nozick fails to notice the kinship).[3] What Nozick hopes for is "the convergence of two independent lines of argument" (333). He wants to show that certain rather glamorous exercises in utopia building, if informed by the appropriate inclinations, may precipitate ideal political forms that turn out to be congruent with those produced more arduously by the much less glamorous exercises in deductive reasoning purveyed in Part I. Utopia turns out to be a model that, conforming to a perfect free market, "is a framework for utopias . . . the environment in which utopian experiments may be tried out" (312). This "smorgasbord conception of utopia" permits consenting individuals to contract into (or out of) any particular utopia that suits them. No right can be violated because each subutopia depends on a set of voluntary exchanges, the sanctity of which it is precisely the function of the greater utopian superstructure to guarantee. Undesirables with whom no one wishes to contract may have their feelings hurt, but they will not have their rights infringed. Indigent lepers, for example, may find it difficult to contract into a subutopia providing medical services or welfare, but their autonomy will remain intact. Their malady is their own problem, for Nozick's utopia is, in effect, the dominant protective association; and the myriad utopias it facilitates represent a pluralized version of the radical individualism propounded in Part I. Ideals such as welfare, equality, and community health entail the imposition of patterned principles of redistribution that are beyond the minimalist pale.

Nozick is quite prepared to acknowledge that the real purpose of the utopian argument is rhetorical. The careful derivation of Part I, philosophically compelling as it purports to be, is "pale and unexciting . . . hardly something to inspire one or to present

[3] See John Rawls, *A Theory of Justice* (Cambridge, Mass.: Harvard University Press, 1971), esp. ch. 87, "Remarks on Justification." Rawls notes there, supporting a strategy Nozick clearly shares, "Justification is a matter of the mutual support of many considerations, of everything fitting together into one coherent view" (579). Also see Chapter Three above.

a goal worth fighting for'' (xii; once again Nozick is disappointed by the real-world political implications of his philosophical ruminations). Thus, with the congruence argument, he apparently hopes to gild the gray-on-gray of philosophy with the silver-on-gold of the liberal imagination. Nozick promises, rather seductively, that even redistributionists can find a home in his utopia if the requisite contractees can be found: ''Though the framework is libertarian and laissez-faire,'' he notes, ''*individual communities within it need not be*, and perhaps no community within it will choose to be so'' (320; emphasis in original). Welfare mothers can presumably create their own intimate welfare societies inside Reagan's minimalist state, as long as they assay redistribution only among their own members (who may of course turn out to have little to redistribute—but that is their problem). While the rich cavort with the rich, the poor can consort with the poor, their several integrities, however different in cash value, identically intact. But there is little point in quibbling with Part III, since it is clearly intended by Nozick not to *make* his argument for him but only to make it palatable.

Many objections can be raised, however, against this elegant and often tasty schematic, even in its pure form in Part I. Perhaps the most obvious riposte is ideological: Nozick's logically coherent argument has a great many politically incoherent consequences, and not even Nozick himself can feel very comfortable with them. Nozick the citizen seems slightly disquieted by Nozick the philosopher, whose commitment to following logic wherever it may lead lands him, in his own words, in ''some bad company'' (x)—among those who ''take a similar position'' but arrive at it dogmatically and are ''narrow and rigid, and filled, paradoxically, with resentment at other freer ways of being.''

Perhaps the paradox is not that laissez-faire foundationalists are so dogmatic—after all, foundationalism is frequently a form of dogmatism—but that a purported philosophical liberal should be so unselfconsciously a foundationalist. If the citizen is disquieted by the company kept by the philosopher, perhaps the philosopher ought to have second thoughts about the philosophy. In politics, consequences are central, not peripheral; and if consequences are repellent, the prudent recourse may be to reappraise premises. The citizen surely understands that if to hold on to premises means to hold his nose, better let go of both. Unless, however, politics is understood to be only a deduction from philosophy, by whose terms it must always therefore be deconstituted. Where hypotheticals take precedence over realities, of course, consequences cease to count.

It is not the purpose of this chapter to offer an ideological critique of *Anarchy, State and Utopia*. That critique seems obvious enough: we need only look at the world of the 1980s and the triumph of absolute right and the market mentality over public good and community. Moreover, the expressly political critique of Nozick has been made eloquently by Sheldon Wolin, Brian Barry, David Spitz, and others.[4] In keeping with the theoretical focus of this book, I wish rather to join a more basic question raised by Nozick's entire enterprise, a question implicit in the disjunction of Nozick's philosophical aspirations and their political consequences: Is philosophical foundationalist analysis of the kind he practices fit for political theorizing? I hope to confirm my negative answer within the Nozickean framework by examining two sets of premises in *Anarchy, State and Utopia*. The first set encompasses what I take to be the central working premises of Nozick's method: reductionism, residualism, and, underlying his foundationalism, what can be called the hypothesis of the rest position. The second set encompasses premises that underlie the operating concepts of the theory of the state generated by Nozick's method, in particular (as representative examples), the premises in which the crucial notions of freedom and entitlement are grounded. The deficiencies of the second set are, in effect, the deficiencies of the first, conceptually operationalized. If the arguments that follow can be believed, *Anarchy, State and Utopia* suffers as a work of

---

[4] See Sheldon Wolin, "Review of Nozick," *New York Times*, May 11, 1975; Brian Barry, "Review of Nozick," *Political Theory* 3 (August 1975); and David Spitz, "Justice for Sale," *Dissent* (Autumn 1975). Although the critical literature on Nozick has not proliferated at quite the alarming pace of that on Rawls, it does now encompass a small library of its own. A useful collection is Jeffrey Paul, ed., *Reading Nozick: Essays on Anarchy, State and Utopia* (Oxford: Basil Blackwell, 1982).

political theory not because its impeccable logic can be faulted but because its logic is far too impeccable to be remotely political—because in its faultlessness it misses entirely the reality of where politics begins and where it must end. The edifice Nozick constructs is indeed a utopia: an argument that stands, quite literally, nowhere and—like those haunted concrete bridges that can be found at abandoned highway projects—soars from midair chasm to midair chasm, a magnificent abstraction going from nowhere to nowhere, its dignity forever a prisoner of its uselessness.

III

The methodological premises of *Anarchy, State and Utopia* are undisguisedly reductionist: they assume that political understanding commences with prepolitical or "nonpolitical" analysis. Politics is to be deconstituted in order to be understood and reconstituted. The point is to explain politics fully "in terms of the nonpolitical" (6), a procedure that renders political ideas intelligible by assimilating them to philosophical categories untainted by politics. Nozick is hardly innovative in these methods. Deconstitution of the political has been the starting point for political thought throughout the contractarian tradition and may even be said to define standard operating procedure for foundationalists. Hobbes's resolutive-compositive method was an early quest and Rawls's original position a late exploration in the contractarian search for political authority's prepolitical foundations.

If the contractarian tradition has been dogged by antipolitical tendencies from the start, Nozick welcomes these tendencies. His objection to them is not how far back to a generic origin they fall, but how far forward to an unwarranted conclusion they leap. He formulates what he takes to be the basic question of political theory in familiar contractarian terms: "The fundamental question of political philosophy," he writes, "one that precedes questions about how the state should be organized, is whether there should be any state at all" (4). The inertial frame of reference from which all movement is to be explained is the solitary individual hypothesized in prepolitical stasis—presumably a creature sufficient unto itself, free (in Hobbes's image) to do whatever it has the power to do. Consequently, the only political question worth asking is the prepolitical question "Why not anarchy?" (4).

Nozick is well aware of the importance of inertial frames of reference; he sustains his own attack on redistributive egalitarianism by querying the self-evidence of its "rest position . . . deviation from which may be caused only by moral forces . . ." (233). What he prefers not to see is that his own rest position is equally vulnerable. He takes radical individualism—the autonomous person defined by natural rights and insulated by individuality from other autonomous persons—as his rest position and simply asserts that deviation from it requires justification.[5] Politics itself, a rather extravagant deviation by Nozick's standards, is thus put on the defensive, insupportable until proven otherwise.

Other inertial frames are obviously possible. Burke took political association and political gradualism for granted and averred with no less assurance than Nozick that "revolution prima fronte requires an apology."[6] The classical Hellenic experience, perceiving in sociability a natural human condition, tended to ask "Why not politics?" and thus placed the burden of advocacy and philosophical justification on those supporting "idiocy" (individualism identified perjoratively).

The inertial center of gravity in the modern world has of course shifted from dependency to independence, from polity to individual, from an equilibrium defined by citizenship to one defined by solitude (privacy). The burden of proof may now seem to be on the political association rather than on the individual. Indeed, political association can appear to be an aberration, an eccentric in-

---

[5] That his argument amounts to mere assertion can be seen from the following, which is the sole defense for reductionism offered in *Anarchy, State and Utopia*: "The possible ways of understanding the political realm are as follows: (1) to fully explain it in terms of the non-political; (2) to view it as emerging from the non-political but irreducible to it . . . ; (3) to view it as a completely autonomous realm. Since only the first promises full understanding of the whole political realm, it stands as the most desirable theoretical alternative, to be abandoned only if known to be impossible" (6).

[6] Edmund Burke, *Reflections on the Revolution in France* (London: J. M. Dent, 1910).

stitution that, if it cannot be rigorously justified (as liberals, constitutionalists, and other generous minimalists affect to do), must be abolished (as anarchists think necessary). From this perspective, *all* political theory becomes minimalist theory—the art of concessions made by radically isolated individuals to politics. These concessions are, however, always limiting concessions, beyond which no deviation is permitted. The only viable query for this sort of political theory is how much (if any) deviation to permit, and the burden of proof rest on those who wish to justify deviation in the first place. Individuals are taken for granted, but society requires a warrant; private interests are given, but public purposes must be demonstrated; personal and property rights are self-evident, but public purposes need proof; a hermit is a free agent, but a citizen must carry a license as well as a birth certificate (the social contract) and other bona fides without which movement, one's very existence, is suspect.

This sort of reductionism is conveniently absent-minded. It starts off with political constructs and then, in the name of rendering them systematically intelligible, reduces them to prepolitical and nonpolitical constructs. On the way, however, it forgets where it started and thus insists that the philosophical abstractions (for example, natural rights) it has artificially introduced for the sake of intelligibility are in fact wholly natural, a necessary rest position that is self-evident. By the same token, the political ideas that were originally to be explained by this method now become suspicious artifacts to be done away with unless they can be justified in terms of the nonpolitical, "natural" categories to which they have been reduced. The *explanandum*, politics, disappears in the *explanans*, philosophy; but politics never reappears in the mantle of intelligibility it was supposedly to acquire. The example of philosophical anarchism (for example, Robert Paul Wolff) suggests that politics may, under these conditions, never re-emerge at all. Nozick means to demonstrate that it can reappear, but only by philosophy's leave, and in the weak form of the dominant protective association.

What starts, then, as reductionism in the contractarian style—resolution then composition, deconstitution then reconstitution—

becomes in Nozick a partial and incomplete method. Reconstitution never takes place, for the components into which politics is deconstituted turn out to be constitutionally unreconstitutable. They will precipitate a radically circumscribed minimalism, but they will not produce anything like the politics from which they originally were extruded. *Anarchy, State and Utopia* is to be criticized not for its (conservative libertarian) politics but for the absence of a relevant politics altogether, not for its political inadequacies but for its inadequate conception of the political.

These problems appear not only in Nozick's method but also in the major concepts by which he advances his argument. Before turning to the more general question of Nozick's apolitical character, I want to consider two of these concepts—freedom and entitlement—in the perspective of the above discussion.

IV

Voluntary consent, in which Nozick's idea of freedom is embedded, is crucial to his argument, for it is the test of all political justification, the sole criterion by which public claims are legitimated, the absolute measure by which each step away from anarchy is to be gauged and approved. Only "voluntary consent opens the borders [protecting individual from individual] for crossings" (58), Nozick posits. Even in complex settings of social cooperation, seemingly mutualist interactions are to be reduced to "a large number of bilateral exchanges" whereby consenting individuals can be identified as sources of legitimacy (187). The general principle that emerges is a not altogether tongue-in-cheek paraphrase of Marx: "From each according to what he chooses to do, to each according to what he makes for himself (perhaps with the contracted aid of others) and what others do for him and choose to give him of what they've been given previously . . . and haven't yet expended or transferred" (160). Or, in Nozick's preferred epigram: "From each as they choose, to each as they are chosen." We do not distribute haircuts or basketball tickets or spouses on the basis of an ideal pattern derived from need or desert. Why then, Nozick asks, should we treat social and economic resources differently? If we cannot "have" a pretty wife just because we "need" one, why should we have a subsistence income just because we need one—particularly if to get one requires that the freedom of others be violated?

The model of the free man deployed here is *homo economicus*: Hannah Arendt's *animal laborans* or Hobbes's natural man who is self-sufficient, unconflicted, and hedonistic, a creature with clear interests rooted in unidirectional needs and calculable by instrumental reason. Reason, in this model, serves needs (Hume's "reason is and ever ought to be the slave of the passions") and thus cannot enter into conflict with them (as it might do in, say, Rousseau or Kant). Nor can needs remain for long in conflict with one another, for ratiocination guarantees a clear vector resultant, however various and multidirectional the inputs.

Freedom, for *homo economicus*, is simply a matter of being unimpeded, able to move unobstructed in physical-mechanistic space. Nozick shares this rendering of human freedom with the liberal tradition generally, although he is more consistently uncompromising about its infringement.[7] Freedom construed in this manner depends on the integral particularity of the human actor: if inner needs are construed as being in conflict with one another, or with conscience, or with the dictates of reason, external human goals lose their objectivity, and the meaning of a free action becomes correspondingly indeterminate. Can we conceive of ourselves as "free" when succumbing, in the absence of external impediments, to a passion of which we internally disapprove? Are

---

[7] Thorstein Veblen offers a brilliant characterization of the physical-mechanistic model of man: "The hedonistic conception of man is that of a lightening calculator of pleasures and pains, who oscillates like a homogenous globule of desire under the impulse of stimuli that shift him about the area, but leave him in tact. . . . Self-imposed in elemental space, he spins symmetrically about his own spiritual axis until the parallelogram of forces bears down upon him, whereupon he follows the line of the resultant. When the force of impact is spent, he comes to rest, a self-conscious globule of desire as before." *On the Place of Science in Modern Civilization* (New York: B. W. Huebsch, 1919), pp. 73–74. I tried to elucidate a preliminary conception of physical mechanism and its relationship to models of freedom in my *Superman and Common Men: Freedom, Anarchy and the Revolution* (New York: Praeger Publishers, 1971), ch. 2.

we unfree when barred externally from temptations we despise or when coerced into alternatives we prefer (Rousseau's "forced to be free")? The disintegral self characteristic of modern man has difficulty determining when it is free and when it is impeded, because it often cannot tell exactly who or what "it" is.

Nozick is preoccupied with interference, but his model of rational economic man does not permit him to grasp that men are frequently *self-interfering*—less enslaved by external obstacles than by internal contradictions—and that self-interference, examined in the context of education, propaganda, advertising, and the manipulation of opinion, is a problem of major social and political import. In *Rameau's Nephew*, Diderot perceives that man "has no greater opposite than himself."[8] What are the conditions of freedom for a man who is his own worst impediment? Hobbes's war of all against all has been converted by modernity into an interior battle—"an unending struggle," in Ibsen's phrase, "between the hostile forces in the soul." The conflict is not that of man against man but of desire against need, need against conscience, conscience against custom, custom against reason, and reason, come full circle, against desire. Words like "voluntary," "freedom," and "consent" take on meanings in these dark wars that Hobbes never dreamed of. Yet a political theory that overlooks them cannot begin to comprehend the nature of modern politics. Its vision impaired by the blinders of physical mechanism, it will be unable to entertain any but physical and external notions of interference. It will be oblivious to the possibility that law can act as an external enforcer of internal obligations that, in the setting of democracy, will be able to reconcile authority and autonomy (for example,

[8] See Lionel Trilling's provocative discussion of modern character in *Sincerity and Authenticity* (Cambridge, Mass.: Harvard University Press, 1971), pp. 30–32, et passim. The modern novel is, of course, filled with self-conflicted characters. For example, in Joseph Heller's *Something Happened* Bob Slocum asks: "I wonder what kind of person would come out if I ever did release all my inhibitions at once, what kind of being is bottled up inside me now. Would I like him? I hope not. There's more than just one of me, probably. . . . I hope I never live to see the real me come out. He might say and do things that would embarrass me and plunge him into serious trouble, and I hope I am dead and buried by the time he does" (248).

Rousseau's notion of freedom as "a law we prescribe to our-selves") or that political community may express human self-re-alization in ways more satisfying to our disposition toward free-dom than can libertarian solitude.

When theory is emancipated from physical mechanism, then, voluntary consent ceases to function as the single criterion of po-litical justification. It becomes merely one more example, when it is implicated in practice, of the kind of controversy that the art of politics is designed to resolve. This may suggest a more appropri-ate relationship between politics and philosophy than is offered by Nozick: not one in which politics is defined by a set of limits de-rived from prepolitical philosophical standards, but one in which politics is itself the device by which such limits and standards are deliberated and determined. Philosophy cannot legislate the mean-ing of the critical concepts entwined in our common life; rather, the politics definitive of our common life establishes the meaning of the critical normative ideas on which our mutuality hinges (for example, freedom, power, interference, consent). Politics thus achieves by necessity what philosophy cannot achieve by abstract reasoning: the elucidation of public standards that are not vulner-able to epistemological skepticism because, quite precisely, they claim only to guide action, never to define truth, and are thus al-ways relative rather than absolute, concrete rather than abstract, and determinative (action-oriented) rather than speculative (truth-oriented).

There is a second kind of difficulty for Nozick's notion of vol-untary consent. Like Milton Friedman, Fredrich Hayek, and other zealots of laissez-faire liberalism, Nozick appears to believe that the natural alternative to statist and other coercive models of hu-man intercourse is a free market that operates under conditions of nearly perfect competition; that is to say, the utility of statist models in securing liberty is to be judged against a free-market model. Yet that model (Nozick's residualism requires) is intro-duced not simply as a theoretical standard but as a description of the actual condition that will prevail should statist alternatives prove philosophically unacceptable.

Libertarians, minimalists, and anarchists have always insisted that state coercion and individual freedom defined by simple market relations are the sole parameters, both conceptually and sociologically, of our political condition. They have argued that, as a consequence, our political choices are limited to points on a coercion/freedom (or public power/private rights) spectrum. "Private" and "power" are thus made into antonyms, and, more important from the perspective of minimalism, both "coercive" and "public," and "free" and "private" are construed as synonyms. Armed with this neat thesaurus, Nozick can easily construct a powerful grammar of minimalism: "public" means "coercive," and freedom therefore requires maximum limits on government in the name of privacy.

There are alternative grammars, however. Many of the contractarians with whom Nozick makes cause repudiate these anarchist dichotomies. They theorize instead that public power deployed for public purposes may be contrasted to private power deployed for private purposes, a construction that renders freedom and privacy as antonyms rather than synonyms and one that suspects that private (that is, illegitimate) coercion can be as insidious to rights, perhaps more insidious, than public (legitimate) coercion. The chief objective of this kind of theory is the legitimation rather than the limitation of public power. When Rousseau begins *The Social Contract* with the observation that, though born free, men are everywhere in chains, he is assuming a rest position of interdependence, a natural condition of illegitimate dependency.

Nozick will not acknowledge the threat of coercion in the private sector, however, for the free-market model does not recognize coercion as a function of private relations. Thanks not to an invisible hand but to a disappearing club, Nozick is wholly innocent of problems of power. He does not have to read good will and natural harmony into natural market relations because he has read violence, deceit, corruption, and terror out of them. He can count on the integrity of voluntary consent because he has discounted influence, blackmail, enticement, titillation, and the many other carrots by which men attenuate its vitality and corrupt the autonomy on which it depends.

Nozick's problem is evident in his example of emigration in his discussion of state coercion. Nozick condemns the state that wishes to compel social cooperation by prohibiting emigration, because it thereby buys mutuality at a price—unacceptable to Nozick—of liberty (173). Yet, to introduce a provocative counter-illustration, what would he make of "voluntary emigration" by middle-class Americans fleeing inner-city "jungles"? Here "consenting" individuals presumably freely contract to move from locale to locale in a series of private, bilateral exchanges. But as urban sociologists will quickly point out, neither those who emigrate nor those who stay are acting with very much knowledge, foresight, or liberty. Both tend to be victims of social forces they cannot control and may not comprehend, and noninterference with their movement may not do as much for their freedom as would a public discussion of the causes of urban blight or a public program that mitigates the poverty that forces the poor to be immobile and attenuates the fear that sends the middle class into flight.

In short, politics is devoted to the legitimation of power and influence, not because legitimized public power seems preferable to natural liberty, but because it seems preferable to illegitimate private power, which is natural liberty's nefarious twin. In other words, if men cannot be free in political communities, they probably cannot be free at all. Our choice may be not between liberty and chains but between legitimate and illegitimate chains. Nozick may well convince us that, in the abstract, a state ought never to use some men as means to the welfare of others ("no moral balancing can [that is, ought to!?] take place among us" (33). But if we are also convinced that men will use one another in any event, often in private ways that are explicitly arbitrary and unjust, or if we believe that the interdependence of the human condition makes such usage inevitable, then we may well want to override abstract principle and opt for a coercive state that (at least) uses men as justly and fairly as possible.

Likewise, although it seems likely that "no end-state principle or distributional principle of justice can be continuously realized without continuous interference in other people's lives" (163), it is not at all clear what moral we are to draw from this lugubrious lesson. Not, at least, if it turns out that our lives are continuously interfered with anyway, even in the absence of end-state princi-ples. The attraction of patterned principles of distribution is not that they are noninterfering but that they appear to be less unjustly and illegitimately interfering than nonredistributionist alterna-tives, which are not only interfering but also subjective, arbitrary, and nonadjudicable as well. The *logical* antonym of legitimate in-terference may, as Nozick the philosopher claims, be non-inter-ference; but its *political* antonym, as Nozick the citizen no doubt has experienced, is *illegitimate* interference. By the same token, the opposite of moral balancing is not no-balancing-at-all but *im-moral* balancing. We are always juggling with other men's fates, whether intentionally or not, for our lives are always entwined with the lives of others in an ecology no less precariously balanced than nature's. This situation may not, it is true, be self-evident to the philosopher; but it is the starting place for all *political* theory.

V

Nozick's argument about freedom and free-market relations leads directly to his argument about entitlement and distributive justice. For the key to Nozick's conviction that free-market ex-change is the only justifiable form of political interaction *inter homines* is his belief in the natural credibility of entitlement as a basis for a rights-respecting theory of justice. In entitlement the-ory, Nozick finds an escape from moral balancing into a world that establishes rights of property without acknowledging either clubs or carrots.

As in the case of voluntary consent, entitlement conceals an unexamined premise and an unexamined context of political con-sequences. Nozick is attracted to it as a generic concept, but it is hard to discern whether he takes it to have a concrete form of which he particularly approves. There are salubrious references to the ''classical liberal's notion of self-ownership'' (172) and to a Lockean limit on rights of accumulation (178). Yet Nozick re-mains strangely diffident in specifying *which* entitlement theory he wishes us to adopt: ''Whether or not Locke's particular theory of appropriation can be spelled out so as to handle various difficulties, I assume that any adequate theory of justice in acquisition will contain a provision similar to the weaker of the ones we have attributed to Locke'' (178). It might be thought that whether this or some other concrete theory of entitlement could ''handle various difficulties'' would be of greater moment to Nozick, since the objections to appropriation theories resting on entitlement have often queried precisely their subjectivity and partiality—their refusal to conform to or even acknowledge objective criteria by which their mutual contradictions might be adjudicated. Nor is it reassuring to find that, when confronted with problems of conflicting entitlements, Nozick refers readers to redistributionist principles he otherwise prefers to dismiss.[9]

Many more entitlement theories than Nozick seems to realize are in fact available to proponents of a theory of justice based on just acquisition rather than just distribution. Robert Filmer's Stuart-era *Patriarcha* provides an alternative account of entitlement that bears little resemblance to Nozick's Lockean derivative, and so of course do the less fastidious theories of medieval kingship Filmer hoped to prop up. Theories of acquisition based on divine right and/or heredity are in turn rivaled by theories of acquisition based on conquest. In more recent centuries, religion, caste, and race have entered into discussions of just entitlement. The only characteristic these myriad forms share is lack of a single, rational, nonarbitrary principle of distribution. The very absence of end-state principles, which to Nozick is their virtue, disqualifies them as rational political theory.

The fact that most entitlement theories manifest themselves politically in elitist and authoritarian forms is not an accident. It is a

[9] In a note, Nozick offers this startling concession to the redistributionists: ''If the principle of rectification of violations of the first two principles yields more than one description of holdings, then some choice must be made as to which of these is to be realized. Perhaps the sort of considerations about distributive justice and equality that I argue against play a legitimate role in *this* subsidiary choice'' (153). But questions of conflict are hardly ''subsidiary,'' as my argument above shows. And to acquiesce to redistributionist principles as a backup for entitlement when entitlement descriptions vary or conflict is in fact to admit them into almost every pertinent political discussion, since politics is precisely the domain defined by conflict!

feature of the inherently subjective internal structure of the entitlement argument, which, as Nozick acknowledges, begins with the premise that what we are entitled to and what we morally deserve are two different things. Nozick is hardly an authoritarian. But in place of the arbitrary power of an entitled political elite, he has in effect posited the equally arbitrary power of a natural elite: namely, those contestants who turn out to be winners in the Social Darwinist sweepstakes that masquerade as a free marketplace.

Redistributionist theories are but a response to these sorts of embarrassments. Rawls's original position, for example, is his attempt to create a hypothetical environment through which the partial views and private (subjective) prejudices of individuals and groups claiming entitlements of one kind or another can be filtered. The result is a relatively objective setting in which impartial debate about the principles of justice can take place.

What we require from Nozick, if he means us to take entitlement theory seriously, is a demonstration that appropriation rooted in self-ownership establishes a title not more tenable than redistributionist alternatives but more tenable than titles based on conquest, or scripture, or royal lineage. What are we to say when confronting a king, a conqueror, a hereditary landholder, and a tenant farmer, each of whom points to a single tract of land and exclaims in unison with the others, ''By all rights this hectare is *mine*! My title to it rests on a long, historically vindicated tradition of Imperial Dominion/right by conquest/primogeniture/right of usage''? The Holy Roman Empire came to a bad end in part because it could offer no satisfactory answer to this query. (The sovereign state, on the other hand, solved the problem easily by locating a legitimate authority capable of adjudicating such claims.) Nozick's philosophical question is: Why not anarchy? But the more practical political question might be: Why not give America back to the Indians? By Lockean standards, they would seem to be its only legitimately titled proprietors.

What we require, along with Nozick's theory itself, are the criteria by which the several descriptions of entitlement yielded by the theory can be evaluated. We require as well that these criteria be politically grounded (in a concept of legitimacy) and not be arbitary or subjective. All kinds of claims may be advanced under the guise of entitlement, but which claim is the more fraudulent: heredity or conquest? To delegitimize principles of public redistribution in theory does nothing to attentuate the arbitrariness of private principles based on claims of entitlement in practice. In the free market it is not right but power that prevails; and in the absence of public counter-coercion, there is nothing to prevent private coercion from running amok. Thus, titled or not, the Indians lost their land because Europeans stole it from them by force—and found bases for their title afterwards.

In fact, the prevailing theory of entitlement generally turns out to be the theory most conducive to prevailing power: justice is on the side of the holdings of the strongest. If heredity wins without a fight, it is because the inheritors have already won the fight. The virtue of redistributionist theories is that they are grounded in ideas of impartiality and disinterestedness that give them some protection against this subjugation to raw power and interest to which all political theories are vulnerable and against which entitlement theories seem altogether defenseless. We must conclude that when Nozick warns us of the "great ingenuity with which people dream up principles to rationalize their emotions" (240) he is in fact identifying the chief weakness of entitlement theory itself.

None of these difficulties strikes at the heart of Nozick's position, however, for his notion of justice depends not only on just acquisition but also on just *transfer* (by voluntary, bilateral exchange). And ultimately he is in a position to say: "Distribute goods as you will—distribute them on the basis of total equality if you will. Nonetheless, legitimate transfers accomplished through voluntary exchanges among consenting adults will quickly result in inequality; and there is not a thing respectors of freedom can do about it, other than regret it." This powerful riposte brings us back to the central charge of this chapter: that Nozick's philosophical rendering of crucial political questions distorts the character of politics and puts relevant political answers completely beyond our reach.

111

VI

Nozick argues that a proper regard for free transfer will always necessitate the compromising of equality (even where equality is the starting point). This means that, to be effective, principles of patterned distribution will have to interfere with freedom *continuously*. In illustrating his position, Nozick elaborates an interesting example whose initial effect is forceful and convincing. He postulates that in a society where income is equally distributed, a number of basketball fans agree to pay twenty-five cents extra each time they watch Wilt Chamberlain play, and that his team's owners simultaneously contract with Chamberlain to permit him to pocket the surcharge. A series of wholly voluntary exchanges between Chamberlain and his fans and Chamberlain and his employers results in a loss of equality. Yet, unless we forbid "capitalist acts among consenting adults"—a prohibition that would violate the basic freedom on which contracts depend—there is nothing we can do or ought to do. We may be tempted to disapprove such a transfer because it issues in an inegalitarian distribution; but because it is the consequence of autonomously reached bilateral agreements, we are in fact compelled (if we wish to follow rational principles) to tolerate it. Redistributionists who wish to preserve a pattern of equality will be forced to intervene not once, but again and again; freedom will not simply be compromised, it will be eradicated.

As compelling as this argument is, it confirms only the apolitical nature of Nozick's reasoning. At the political level, the Chamberlain example in fact proves quite the opposite of what Nozick intends: namely, that private acts often have public consequences that we may neither anticipate nor intend. This is precisely why political acts cannot be deconstituted into private acts without losing their salient character. Our intent in paying a surcharge is to see Chamberlain play; but it is not (necessarily) to guarantee that he earns $250,000 a year (would we refuse to watch him if he played for free?); and it is certainly not to create a society with radical income differentials or to set a precedent for some general distributional principle. Nor, in paying a surcharge, do we intend to redistribute the power associated with wealth in ways that may diminish our own future ability to affect the market or to compromise the market power of other persons (who were not party to our bilateral agreements with Chamberlain but who stand to suffer as a result of his enhanced power). A Chamberlain with $250,000 a year is a Chamberlain capable of affecting society in ways that may compromise the freedom or security or power of those who have never even heard of the National Basketball Association.

A publicly responsible electorate might not wish to forbid capitalist acts among consenting adults per se, but it would insist on monitoring the public consequences of such private acts, even in the limited context of basketball. That is, it would necessarily concern itself with traffic snarls leading to the stadium where Chamberlain played (which, *note bene*, would involve non-Chamberlain fans); with health and safety precautions within the arena (it could hardly permit three million fans to contract bilaterally with Chamberlain to watch him play on the same night in an arena seating five thousand); with Chamberlain's own possible use of his new wealth to coerce/cajole fans into signing new, more expensive contracts; with problems of equity among Chamberlain and his fellow players and among the teams that make up the league (thus the current salary cap on teams in the National Basketball Association); and so forth. Public intervention in these areas might lead to public interdiction, perhaps even revocation of the original agreement between Chamberlain and the fans. Nor would the fans necessarily object. For fans are also citizens, and what they intend as private devotees of basketball cannot and will not predetermine what they intend as public citizens. It is the central weakness of Nozick's reductionism that it cannot distinguish private persons from public citizens. It therefore cannot grasp that, although fans may make contracts with Chamberlain as private persons, they may also remedy the public inequities of these (and all other) private contracts when they move as citizens to enact public laws of progressive taxation, or antitrust laws, or public safety standards. They will thereby *intentionally* undo in public what they may have *inadvertently* done in private—for example, strip Chamberlain of, say, 75 percent of his income, insist that his teammates share in the balance, restrict the number of such contracts that can be made (the team salary cap), and so on. Nor is there any contradiction here. That we are willing to pay a twenty-five-cent surcharge as private persons does not entail that we are willing to tolerate economic inegalitarianism or monopoly or exploitation as public citizens. If only one of us had entered into a contract, there would have been no *public* problem; but when 100,000 sign contracts, a public issue is created. Once there is a public, there is a public problem. Enter politics!

Nozick's reductionist illusion is to think that, because acts are initially private, they are without public consequences. But we are a public by virtue of our plurality, and we are thus constrained to substitute legitimate public standards for arbitrary private ones. After all, John D. Rockefeller contracted freely and bilaterally with scores of smaller companies to buy them out; the gargantuan monopoly he created, however, was hardly a private affair. Indeed, it offered a greater threat to the free market than the government that tried without much success to break it up.

Nozick's market does not finally protect private freedom against public power; it protects private power against public legitimacy. Nozick believes that he is propounding a logically coherent argument in defense of pure individual freedom. And so he is, in philosophical terms, with considerable success. But a logically coherent argument by philosophical standards is not necessarily a political argument at all. Philosophical argument offers abstract alternatives. If none seem defensible, none are chosen; we simply return to point zero. Political argument begins with concrete givens. If abstract alternatives prove indefensible, we do not return to point zero; we are left rather with the givens—with a logic in process that will have consequences even if no choices are made. The relevant political question therefore becomes: Is a particular decision *more* tolerable/acceptable/legitimate than the consequences of no decision (in public-choice terms, a *nondecision*)? If so, regardless of its philosophical status, that decision is preferable.

Rousseau, his contractarianism notwithstanding, understood that the aim of political thought is not to justify deviations from our (hypothetical) natural isolation but to legitimate the (concrete, given) ties that inevitably bind us together. To the philosopher, what cannot be justified cannot be. If reality defies the philosophical criteria by which it is judged, all the worse for reality. But the political theorist knows that power seeks no other warrant for existence than its own success and that the political task is not to wish power away but to make it legitimate. Our choice (alas!) is not between political bondage and natural freedom but between political bondage and political freedom—between slavery and citizenship. We can be arbitrarily and heteronomously dependent or rationally and (within limits) autonomously dependent. Political relations, *esse inter homines*, defy the abstract choice preferred by philosophers between absolute coercion and total noninterference. They can be only more or less justly coercive, more or less legitimately interfering, more or less rationally dependent.

Political theory may derive sustenance from hypothetical history, but it always confronts real history as a given. Which is to say, it begins with the subjugated dependent rather than the free hermit—with historical men who are already the victims of illegitimate coercion, blind force, and arbitrary power. The significant political question is thus always how to render coercion less illegitimate, force less blind, power less arbitrary.

Robert Nozick would appear to want to say, with Howard Roark in Ayn Rand's *The Fountainhead*:

> I came here to say that I do not recognize anyone's right to one minute of my life. Nor to any part of my energy. Nor to any achievement of mine. No matter who makes the claim, how large their number or how great their need. I wished to come here and say that I am a man who does not exist for others.[10]

The trouble is, whether we wish to or not, by virtue of our plurality and our dependency we do in fact exist for one another. It is this reality from which politics emerges. In the words of Philip

---

[10] Ayn Rand, *The Fountainhead* (New York: New American Library, n.d.), p. 686.

115

Slater, "The notion that people begin as separate individuals, who then march out and connect themselves with others, is one of the most dazzling bits of self-mystification in the history of the species."[11] Because we do not in fact march out and connect ourselves to others but are born in Siamese bondage to our fellow men, we do not as political creatures have the philosopher's luxury of justifying the hypothetical steps by which such a journey might have been made, had it been made. We can only seek ways to legitimate the connections with which our condition has at once cursed us (slavery) and blessed us (civil community). Winston Churchill's ironic comment on democracy—the worst form of government in the world except all the others—in fact is a bitter tribute to the reality that political theory must confront. Not best or nothing; only better or worse. These are the only choices in a world where men interfere, coerce, interdict, infringe, use, hurt, and oppress ineluctably—in or out of regimes, with or without legitimate cause—because dependency is intrinsic to the human condition.

Even at its least ambitious (nonminimalist liberal thought on the Lockean model), political theory aspires to minimize the costs of dependency by maximizing the legitimacy of political institutions. It has also aspired to more ambitious goals: in its democratic form it has tried to transform common weakness into social equality, common dependency into social mutuality, common exploitation into social cooperation, and common fear into social security by developing modes of legitimate political exchange grounded in citizenship, community, democracy, fraternity, and civic freedom. The aim of this more ambitious Rousseauian conception of politics has been *public seeing*: illuminating with a public light what to individuals living in private caves remains invisible. There is also a tradition of *public thinking* in liberalism, perhaps most clearly evident in Kant. If politics is a form of public seeing, reductionists who recognize only private choices will not comprehend its nature.

As I noted earlier in this chapter, some critics have worried

[11] Philip Slater, *Earthwalk* (Garden City, N.Y.: Anchor Books, 1974).

about the ideological and political implications of Nozick's philosophical exercises. But Nozick is neither politically conservative nor politically reactionary nor politically libertarian: he is politically irrelevant. Not recognizing the public meaning of *public*, he does not really have a political theory at all. As a rhetorical model, *Anarchy, State and Utopia* may seem to endorse some rather strange political practices. Nozick correctly maintains, however, that his book is not a "political tract" (xii), that his arguments are "fascinating in their own right," and that his principal guide is logic and not reality. He confronts the state as an engrossing idea that, from the point of view of independent philosophical grounds, however, can be dismissed. Neither choice nor action is at stake, only inference and ideation. Nozick plays games ingeniously, but playing games and engaging in politics are distinctive projects that can be confused only at considerable risk.

To be unable to think politically in a major book nominally about the state is in fact no small mischief in troubled democratic times, when the continued survival of liberty depends on effective citizenship, prudent statesmanship, and wise political thought. To demonstrate that the democratic, interventionist state is inconsistent with an abstract conception of the solitary individual, who is in turn a precipitate of a priori philosophy, does nothing to help us reconcile right and utility or to bridge the needs of individuals and communities. Neither the repeal of the income tax nor the dismantling of the state, nor for that matter private bargains between athletes and fans, are on any real-world public agenda I am aware of. Tyranny and anarchy remain the real threats to liberty, a political fact that will not be changed by uncovering philosophical inadequacies in Rawlsian justice or utilitarian conceptions of the good. Nozick may represent a useful source for intellectuals debating the abstract virtues of pure capitalism, and he certainly continues to be cited by old-fashioned conservative market liberals in search of philosophical credentials for their market inclinations.[12] Yet he

[12] For example, Nozick is cited at some length in a recent *New York Times* essay by E. J. Dionne, "Catholics Debate Morality of Capitalism" (November 29, 1986).

does not speak to the political realities of insider trading, multinational corporations, or the socialization of risk strategy involved in government takeovers and corporate safety-net schemes. And he fails to tell us how we might control the new technologies that encroach on our actual liberties (interactive television surveillence or computer-held credit and personal files, for example).

What we require are political theories that elucidate the character of socially embedded individuals and public citizens, that help draw boundaries between democratic majorities and individual rights (John Stuart Mill's project in *On Liberty*), that set limits for what private persons can do within the communities that endow them with rights, and what communities can do to the individuals whose rights are a primary concern of communities. Theories of (or against) the state must be conditioned by the practice of states. An absolute theory of rights grounded in a philosophical conception of the radically isolated individual may not leave much room for even the most democratic state; but by the same token, democratic states leave little room for radically isolated, abstract persons. Nozick offers answers to a number of interesting questions that no citizen or politician is likely to ask. To the questions they do ask, he has no answers—which, by the logic of reductionism, makes the questions illegitimate.

To women and men struggling to live justly in uncertain times, Nozick's nonpolitics will be unsatisfactory. They will face their condition with the forebodings of Yeats in his *Second Coming*:

> Somewhere in the sands of the desert
> A shape with lion body and the head of a man,
> A gaze blank and pitiless as the sun,
> Is moving its slow thighs . . .

Yet if Robert Nozick were to be asked ''. . . what rough beast / Its hour come round at last / Slouches toward Bethlehem to be born?'' it would appear that he might feel constrained to reply, ''The sphinx is a beast of dubious rational origin; besides, I can conceive of no philosophical justification that would permit a statue to move.''

Nonetheless, it moves. And if it has not yet found its way across the Charles River to Widener Library, it can nonetheless be seen gaping from several dozen world capitals, where the fate of democracy is precarious and the struggle for justice is a matter of more than merely philosophical moment.

FIVE

Unconstrained Conversations:
A Play on Words and
Bruce Ackerman

What we can't say, we can't say, and we can't whistle
it either.

—Frank Ramsey

IN THE campaign to conquer politics, armies of abstractions have
been mustered not only by philosophers like Rawls and Nozick
but also by eminent students of law and jurisprudence. And among
those many legal philosophers who have written political treatises
since 1980, no one has been more adept at combining a philosopher's flair for formal argument with a citizen's concern for real
politics than Bruce Ackerman. Roberto Unger has spilled more
ink, and Ronald Dworkin has attracted more attention. But Ackerman, in *Social Justice in the Liberal State* (1980),[1] has developed a framework for the philosophical discussion of politics that
is more striking and original than anything purveyed by his colleagues in the law. Aware both of the perils of ideal speech and of
the incorrigibly second- or third-order character of political reality, he makes conversation the centerpiece of his analysis.

[1] Bruce A. Ackerman, *Social Justice and the Liberal State* (New Haven: Yale
University Press, 1980). Ackerman has published several monographs since 1980
that bear on certain problems raised in *Social Justice*. They include *Reconstructing
American Law* (Cambridge, Mass.: Harvard University Press, 1984); "The Storrs
Lectures: Discovering the Constitution," *Yale Law Journal* 93 (1984), 1013–1072;
and "On Getting What We Don't Deserve," *Social Philosophy and Policy* 1 (Autumn 1983), 60–70. Ackerman replied to a number of the criticisms raised in this
chapter (as it appeared in an earlier form), as well as to critical essays by James S.
Fishkin, Richard E. Flathman, Bernard Williams, and Brian Barry, in "Sympo-
sium on Social Justice and the Liberal State," *Ethics* 93 (January 1983), 328–390.
In revising this essay, I have tried in turn to take Ackerman's response into account.

On first glance, Ackerman seems to deploy a language that evokes those critics of abstract rationalism who insist that conceptions of the political must be embedded in concrete reality. He recognizes in conversation the stuff of everyday politics: plain talk among neighbors seeking a common currency to articulate their differences and express their solidarity. Unlike philosophers who aim to discover or contrive definitively privileged positions of leverage for particular conceptions of justice—an ideal speech situation, an original position, an Archimedean point—Ackerman obviously prefers to remain in the great tradition of political philosophy that takes men as they are and institutions and laws as they ought to be. His commitment to conversation as the crucial element in politics places him in a family of political observers that includes Michael Oakeshott. But while Oakeshott and a variety of communitarians approach conversation as a discourse of identity and solidarity aimed at expressing commonality (see Chapter Six), Ackerman remains a liberal who perceives in conversation a vehicle for the expression and adjudication of particularity—for how we live with our differences rather than how we disclose our identity. Thus, despite the focus on conversation, Ackerman brings with him the liberal's proceduralist arsenal: he looks for weapons with which to subdue the unruliness of the words on which his liberal politics affects to depend. His central category turns out to be not conversation but *constrained* conversation, and it is the constraint rather than the conversation that is crucial. Whether the constraints he discovers lead him back to philosophical abstractions with a privileged character and thereby destroy the implicit politicity of the conversational approach is the central dilemma of his position.

Whatever the answer—whether or not he ultimately reverts to reductionism—Ackerman permits his argument to unfold in a series of fragmentary dialogues that resemble actual conversations. In this he practices what he preaches in a most engaging fashion, seducing those who mistrust philosophical reductionism with a patina of real-world words. It is not only to flatter his practice that I imitate this mode of dramatic discourse, but also to flatter the great dialogical tradition of political philosophy that from Plato onward has taken the form of dialogue or dialectic. My discussion of Ackerman thus appears as a kind of minidrama in ten scenes. If my effort is less than compelling, it will at least, I trust, be diverting.

UNCONSTRAINED CONVERSATIONS

THE PLAYERS

Bruce A. Ackerman. Professor of Law at numberless Ivy League universities, not last and not least of which is Yale, and a sometime writer of dialogues.

Benjamin R. Barber. Professor of Political Science at Rutgers University, a sometime player in his own scripts.

Fred Broome. A janitor (fictitious) at Yale.

David Stockman. Onetime director of the White House Office of Management and Budget (OMB).

George Washington Johnson. A CETA trainee, in the days when there was a CETA (Comprehensive Employment and Training Act).

Adolf Hitler. A ''Nazi,'' perhaps THE Nazi.

Harry S. Truman. A statesman.

Mrs. Mikushi. A housewife living in Hiroshima in August 1945.

GI Joe. An American soldier in the World War II Pacific theater.

Romeo. A young suitor in Renaissance Verona.

Juliet. The object of Romeo's suit.

SCENE 1
''Where Am I?''

(Bruce Ackerman, who doesn't know why he's here, and Benjamin Barber, who does)

ACKERMAN: Where am I?

BARBER: In a dialogue. I got the impression from reading *Social Justice in the Liberal State* that you rather fancied dialogues.

ACKERMAN: They have their advantages—when *I* write them. But to be in someone else's . . .

BARBER: The perils of drama.

ACKERMAN: I'm not sure I want to be one of *your* characters.

BARBER: That evens things up a little.

ACKERMAN: Indeed? And how?

BARBER: A great many other stupendously archetypal characters ended up as compulsory players in your several scripts in *Social Justice*—there was Manic and Noble and Senior and Elitist and Statesman and Black and, let's see, a quite perverse fellow called "Michael Angelo Robinson" I believe . . .

ACKERMAN: Michelangelo *Crusoe*.

BARBER: Ah yes, well in any case, since you made all those anonymous creatures your mouthpieces, it seemed only fair that I should make you mine.

ACKERMAN: I won't argue with you (it's your script). Besides, dialogue *is* the heart of my book on justice, what distinguishes it from its many competitors.

BARBER: I myself was not altogether convinced that we needed still one more after Bertrand Russell and John Rawls and Robert Nozick and, well . . .

ACKERMAN: Nor was I. Until I devised a method that at once both illuminates and overcomes the greatest single deficiency of contractarian *and* utilitarian theories of justice.

BARBER: They share a single great deficiency?

ACKERMAN: They most emphatically do. They differ, of course, in that the contractarian is obsessively concerned with the individual and his rights but insufficiently sensitive to the community and its goods, whereas the utilitarian is fully sensitized to the greater good but quite nearly callous to the claims of autonomous individuals.

BARBER: Who refuse to be sacrificed to some abstract, general conception of the good.

ACKERMAN: Yes, that sort of thing.

BARBER: But you said they share a common deficiency.

ACKERMAN: I did. And they do. I can put it simply, if you will permit a self-quotation (that's the only way I'm likely to be able to speak in my own authentic voice), by saying that "both appeal to the judgment of some *hypothetical third party*" in resolving the "flesh-and-blood contest for power" (p. 327) and that both thereby require us "to suppress our identities as social beings—whose identities and objectives are defined through interaction with other concrete individuals—so that we may catch a fleeting glimpse of some transcendent individual who may sit as higher judge of our social conflicts." Get it?

BARBER: I like the acknowledgment of man as a social animal. Rare coming from a professor of law. But that "hypothetical third party" is defined rather differently by the two traditions, isn't it?

ACKERMAN: Certainly it is. The contractarian hypothesizes an abstract, prepolitical "entrant" who can choose or not choose to enter civil society, while the utilitarian hypothesizes an Ideal Observer. Yet, in each case, we are meant to infer principles of justice from abstract men who are not truly intelligible to us and who are in any case very far removed from the real world of power and conflict.

BARBER: So you are neither a contractarian nor a utilitarian?

ACKERMAN: No, for you see, at no point do I ask women and men to suppress the fact that they are real persons with their own goals in life, who encounter others with competing goals in a social setting in which conflicts are to be resolved in some organized way (p. 332).

BARBER: I'm impressed. One gets fed up with philosophical and jurisprudential metaphysicians trying to deduce unimpeachable political norms from some Perfect Epistemology or Natural Ontology.

ACKERMAN: You have my sympathies. Liberalism cannot and need not be made to depend on the truth of any single metaphysical or epistemological system.

BARBER: That's *your* argument.

ACKERMAN: Exactly. I want to persuade you that liberalism finds its ultimate justification in its strategic location in a web of talk that converges upon it from every direction.

BARBER: A web of talk. I like that.

ACKERMAN: Which is to say, power relations, the distribution of goods, political structures and institutions are all legitimized (or not legitimized) by appeal to the *test of dialogue*.

BARBER: A neat phrase. As I recall, however, it's not just any old dialogue that suits your purposes.

ACKERMAN: Well, no.

BARBER: Conversation isn't enough.

ACKERMAN: No, *constrained* conversation; *neutral* dialogue.

BARBER: That's what I was afraid of.

ACKERMAN: Look, if every and any kind of talk could get the job done, there would be no need for philosophers.

BARBER: Just citizens?

ACKERMAN: I don't see why, just because it's your dialogue, you should get all the wisecracks.

BARBER: That's not why I should. But it's why I do. Still, my apologies. In fact, I can start by agreeing with you. Everything you write in *Social Justice* seems conducive in its intent to political realism and the complexity of actual social processes, and certainly all of your arguments make the reductionism of abstract contractarians and ideal utilitarians look inadequate. You acknowledge over and over again the second-best and even third-best character of actual political dilemmas.

ACKERMAN: Thank you.

BARBER: Yet, when you come to elucidate what you mean by dialogue, when you start to imprison talk in a cage called neutrality, you seem very quick to abandon realism and its political dialectic in favor of metaphysics.

ACKERMAN: Me? Metaphysics?

BARBER: The conditions you impose on conversation betray the self-same formalism and abstractness that (as you quite rightly note) have driven the contractarian to such exotic venues as the state of nature and the original position and have given to the utilitarian's Ideal Observer its characteristic blindness to the actualities of individual choice.

ACKERMAN: Talk remains at the heart of politics and at the heart of *Social Justice in the Liberal State*.

BARBER: No, *constrained* talk is at the heart of your book and—I do fear—when you get through with your constraints, there is precious little left of what I would understand as talk.

ACKERMAN: But dialogue is always . . .

BARBER: Always neutral, and neutrality undermines and ultimately destroys dialogue. Under the guise of rationality and neutrality, you have in fact imposed on the splendid notion of political talk a set of abstractions no less invidious than those of the contractarians and utilitarians you so effectively dissect and expose.

ACKERMAN: You misread me completely.

BARBER: I read you as best I can. Misunderstand you, perhaps. But what I will offer you in the way of evidence is not an extended critique of your myriad dialogues but rather a few of my own. This is in fact one of them!

ACKERMAN: You carry flattery too far.

BARBER: I hope to offer a series of what I will call unconstrained conversations—biased dialogues, if you like—which, in their resemblance to real political talk, expose the formalism, affective sterility, moral incoherence, and artificial abstractness of "neutral dialogue."

ACKERMAN: Look here . . .

BARBER: So that, despite your laudable intent, you remain as remote from the real world of politics and the conflicts and dilemmas of liberalism as your contractarian and utilitarian adversaries.

ACKERMAN: Can I have a word or two?

BARBER: Excuse me?

ACKERMAN: It's bad enough being in your script rather than my own. But to be censored, to have my mouth crammed with insipid exclamations like "look here" is altogether too much. I can hardly be expected to counter your criticisms if you confine me to stumbling expressions of astonishment.

BARBER: It is not my intention to provide you with a forum for your defense, only to indict and, I hope, convict you of inadvertent metaphysics.

ACKERMAN: That hardly seems fair!

BARBER: It's anything but fair. But as I recall, neither of us has much good to say about justice as fairness, so . . .

ACKERMAN: A cheap shot.

BARBER: There are more to come. For example, you appear in my very first unconstrained conversation—and not in an altogether flattering light.

ACKERMAN: The next book I write will be in narrative prose. A rapid-fire monologue.

BARBER: Too late now. Just look and listen.

SCENE 2

"A Dialogue about the Limits of Talk"

(Bruce Ackerman as a professor of law at Yale and Fred Broome, a janitor [fictitious] in the same institution)

ACKERMAN: Well then, Fred, we agree that we shall henceforth put all of our claims about the distribution of university resources to the test of neutral dialogue.

BROOME: Yeah, well, so you sez anyhow, Professor Ackerman.

ACKERMAN: Look here, would you please stop calling me Professor Ackerman? I make no claim to be your superior by profession, rank, status, or anything else. You're at least as good as me.

BROOME: If you say so, Professor.

ACKERMAN: *Bruce!* Okay?

BROOME: [*Whistles a snatch from an unrecognizable pop classic.*]

ACKERMAN: Or you call me Mr. Ackerman and I'll call you Mr. Broome, how about that?

BROOME: Whatever feels good to you, Professor. Only ya gotta keep in the forefront of yer mind I ain't much on the three-syllable fancy talk, ya know?

ACKERMAN: No fancy talk. Just two equals testing their claims about what's just—how we settle this faculty/staff wage dispute—by the measure of constrained conversation. Right, Fred?

BROOME: And who's doin' the constrainin'? You or me?

ACKERMAN: Neither of us—the principle of neutrality—you can't assert you're better than me or that your notion of what's good is better than mine without proving it, see?

BROOME: See, Professor, I ain't really much on talking. That's the wife's department. Chrisalmighty, she'll talk ya into most anything if she gets half a chance, know what I mean?

ACKERMAN: Actually, the dispute is simple enough: across-the-board cutbacks in the university budget seem inevitable. What's needed is a formula by which we distribute these cuts fairly across both the faculty and the nonacademic staff. The faculty bargaining committee has worked out a solution by which longevity of service and rank are multiplied by a factor representing essentialness of work to the university. Though it does favor faculty salaries to some degree, I think you will see that it meets the test of neutrality and is both rational and equitable—there are six crucial rationales appended, see?

BROOME: Hold on, Prof, you're drowning me in words.

ACKERMAN: The six reasons are straightforward enough, I promise you.

BROOME: Straightforward. Hm, maybe. Trouble is, we're playing out this whole game on your turf.

ACKERMAN: Turf?

BROOME: Talk's turf, if ya get my meaning. No? Words, ideas, rationales, reasons—you know, fancy talk, like I said.

ACKERMAN: Talk's the essence of our public life. Parliaments— from *parler*? French for talk?

BROOME: You're a lawyer, ain't you?

ACKERMAN: Lawyer? No—I mean of course I teach in a law school, but . . .

BROOME: A teacher. A lawyer. Pretty big on words, ain't ya?

ACKERMAN: Not really . . .

BROOME: As compared with sweeping a gym or firing the furnace over in the physical plant?

ACKERMAN: Talk is the common denominator, Fred; it's what makes us human.

BROOME: And yet, you're a whole lot better at it than most.

ACKERMAN: I make no claim to be better than any man—that's why I call myself a liberal.

BROOME: If ya make talk the measure of us being equal, how the hell we gonna be equal, Professor? That's what I can't figure.

ACKERMAN: You have a better suggestion? Without talk, there's only prejudice, passion, and brute force.

BROOME: The way I see it, talk's only a part of it—politics, I mean. Ya gotta start with something—the missus calls it "good neighborliness''—me, I'd call it fellow feeling, patriotism like, tho' I don't mean America right or wrong or nothing like that. But without neighbors, seems to me all the talk will be one more way for folks to look out for themselves, get their own way, try to make the other guy into a sucker by making him think what's good for you is good for him too.

ACKERMAN: The reality is that every political conversation starts with two people saying ''I want.'' Until we figure out how to resolve that conversation, we're nowhere.

BROOME: You ain't nowhere *with* that conversation till those two fellas figure out that ''I want'' ain't never going ta lead ta them being neighbors, till they see that unless they're neighbors ain't neither one of them gonna get the half of what he wants. What I mean is, citizens are neighbors first and talkers second. They talk to express their neighborliness, know what I mean?

ACKERMAN: It's a big country.

BROOME: But it's with the neighbors people learn about ''we'' and maybe see that even in a big country ya gotta develop a sense of ''us'' instead of millions of ''me's.''

ACKERMAN: You're trying to deny that politics is concerned with the expression of differences: the struggle for power.

BROOME: Naw. Not me. I mean, sure it is. But any fool can see if that's all it is, there's never gonna be much of what you teachers and lawyers like ta call justice. Let alone neighborly talk.

ACKERMAN: In the end, there is still a pie to be divided.

BROOME: Yeah, but without neighbors, without people working together, without there being a community you can identify with, there ain't gonna be a pie in the first place. You want to talk about politics as divvying up; I want to talk about it as making things together.

ACKERMAN: Try that in Boston where the Italians and the blacks are trying to kill one another.

BROOME: Funny thing you should say that. The wife was just saying to me, if them poor working stiffs and them black folks up Roxbury way could see themselves as neighbors, I bet they'd have a better chance to solve the busing problem than by shouting at each other about their reasons and their interests—both sides got more reasons and more interests than they know what to do with far as I can see. In the end none of 'em got what they wanted, good schools or good neighborhoods. And now some judge who probably don't even live in Boston is gonna decide for them, know what I mean?

ACKERMAN: You make sense, Fred.

BROOME: Sure, Bruce. It's like that Tony Lukas said: common ground. Ya gotta have common ground or you're gonna get anarchy.

ACKERMAN: A great deal of sense, Fred. But you are one hell of a hypocrite all the same.

BROOME: Not sure I get yer drift, Bruce.

ACKERMAN: Talk is my turf, remember?

BROOME: Yep. That's what I said.

ACKERMAN: Only, how come you're suddenly so goddamned eloquent?

BROOME: Just what the wife always sez, Bruce: "For someone who sez he don't like to gab, you sure gab pretty good, Fred." That's what she sez.

ACKERMAN: She's got a point.

BROOME: Ta tell the truth, though, it's the eloquence that's a worry to me—even if it's my own. See, if we make politics the turf of the smart talkers—the lawyers and preachers and actors and TV personalities—there's gonna be a whole mess of people left out in the cold, and politics is gonna become this neverending TV special, one more lousy spectator sport.

ACKERMAN: Well . . .

BROOME: And even if ya get folks talking, if all they talk about is "I want" and "I'll give you if you'll give me"—it's still gonna be power against power, interest against interest, and the stronger are gonna win anyway.

ACKERMAN: Perhaps. But how's any of this going to resolve *our* dispute?

BROOME: Us? Well let's never mind what "you want" and what "I want" and look at what the Yale community—it's a neighborhood, wouldn't you say?—what Yale needs. Once we do that, I bet we can figure fair shares, fair reductions, all around. What d'ya say?

ACKERMAN: That's not necessarily going to be in *your* interest, Fred.

BROOME: All depends. See, believe it or not, I got a kinda interest in Yale. So I figure its interest *is* my interest.

ACKERMAN: A refreshing, if novel, attitude.

BROOME: Worth a try, huh?

ACKERMAN: I'd call it utilitarian except we and them, me and you, all seem to get merged in your idea of a neighborhood. Hm. Hmmmm.

SCENE 3

"That's the Dialogue?"

(Ackerman and Barber)

ACKERMAN: That's the dialogue?

BARBER: That's it.

ACKERMAN: You sure stacked the deck. A janitor!?

BARBER: I wanted—you know—a nonverbal type.

ACKERMAN: Nonverbal? Jesus Christ, he's like Hamlet's fool, playing the idiot while he makes me look like a numbskull.

BARBER: Still, he had a point about the tyranny of eloquence, wouldn't you agree?

ACKERMAN: Neutral dialogue is precisely designed as a defense *against* grandiloquence and rhetoric. The same criteria apply to the orator and the passive masses.

BARBER: My friend Fred also had a point or two to make about the nonverbal bonds that tie communities together—and the polarizing effect the language of interest calculus can have on political relations.

ACKERMAN: There must nevertheless be some constraints on language so that it doesn't become a tool of interests or power.

BARBER: Isn't it always that when used instrumentally in the service of interest adjudication and bargaining?

ACKERMAN: Certainly not.

BARBER: Interests can always find reasons—even good reasons.

ACKERMAN: If you want to play Thrasymachus.

BARBER: My point is, neutral dialogue does not seem to treat with Thrasymachus very successfully, as I believe the ensuing dialogue shows.

ACKERMAN: Another one? Would you mind leaving me out of it?

BARBER: As you please—but don't complain if your position is misrepresented.

ACKERMAN: Better you misrepresent it in my absence than with me looking on like a fool or legitimizing its misrepresentation with pusillanimous "look here's" and the like.

BARBER: Oh dear. Well, sit this one out.

SCENE 4

"A Thrasymachean Dialogue"

(David Stockman, onetime director of the OMB; *George Washington Johnson, a* CETA *trainee, when there was a* CETA)

STOCKMAN: I've got some bad news for you, Mr. Johnson; I'm afraid you're out of a job.

JOHNSON: Out of a job!? It was 'cause I was out of a job, they gave me this job! You must be kidding.

STOCKMAN: We've decided to terminate the CETA program under which your job falls. Sorry.

JOHNSON: Sorry? Who you jivin'? You act like I ain't as good as the next man.

STOCKMAN: Not true.

JOHNSON: Ain't I?

STOCKMAN: Yes, you are. Certainly you are.

JOHNSON: Then why you blowin' me away, man? Robbing me of my job, my training, my livelihood. You're discriminating 'gainst me and the rest of my brothers. Fact is, you're violating your own damn principles.

STOCKMAN: Neutral dialogue?

JOHNSON: Call it what you want . . .

STOCKMAN: Sorry, Johnson, but it won't wash. Now if we were singling you out or discriminating against the disadvantaged, we would indeed be in violation of neutrality. We'd be treating you as less than equal. But that is *not* what we are doing.

JOHNSON: No? Then what are you doing?

STOCKMAN: We are combating inflation, we are spurring productivity, and we are fighting unemployment. That's what we are doing. We are giving the sagging economy a shot in the arm so that things will be better for all of us, including you and . . . er . . . your ilk.

JOHNSON: Bullshit.

STOCKMAN: No, Mr. Johnson, I'm serious. Once we get the economy going again, there will be more jobs in the private sector, less government interference in private enterprise, and, well, more jobs for everybody. And perhaps we will have beaten inflation too, so that your wages will be worth something. Now tell me, Mr. Johnson, how does that discriminate against you or violate the principle of neutrality?

JOHNSON: Hey, turkey, what kinda fool you think I am? You go ahead and lick inflation and give me a good job and you won't be violating nothing. But that ain't what you're doing. You're taking away my job. You're trying to solve your problems, but it's my ass on the line. What you're doing is screwing me and that's a fact.

STOCKMAN: No, no, no, Mr. Johnson. I've already explained, that's *not* what we're doing. You see, there is a theory called supply-side economics—perhaps you've heard of the Laffer Curve?

JOHNSON: Shee-it, Stockman, don't spin me some pretty theory with one hand while you got the other up my ass. What you're doing is putting me out of work.

STOCKMAN: I can appreciate your aggravation, Mr. Johnson. But you've got to take the long view. Of course I'm relying on a theory. But so are you. So does everyone. Every policy is embedded in a theory about history, social effect, political logic, causes and consequences—it just can't be avoided.

JOHNSON: My job didn't come from no theory, it came from CETA.

STOCKMAN: But CETA *is* a theory, Mr. Johnson. Or the consequence of a theory. A theory about the effects of environment on motivation; a theory about the impact of public-sector employment on business; a theory about job training; a theory about solving problems through federal funding and massive federal bureaucracies.

JOHNSON: I ain't saying there ain't bullshit on both sides.

STOCKMAN: And don't forget, Mr. Johnson, it's those very theories that the public disavowed in the last election. Not because the majority thought they were better than you, but because they believed the old theories had been tried and had failed, because they thought it was time to try a different theory.

JOHNSON: You trying to tell me it's good for me that you're taking my job away?

STOCKMAN: I'm trying to tell you that giving you a short-term federal job on a platter may not be in your interest in the long run. You've been losing ground, Johnson, *losing ground*. Now, maybe our new theories are right and maybe not. But it's not like we're pitting an abstract theory against some self-evident truth or a "fact" like this job. It's one theory against another, supply-side economics against the welfare state, and the difference between them has nothing to do with your status as an equal person.

JOHNSON: I'm out of a job and it's good for me. That's your theory?

STOCKMAN: Well, George boy, I'm going to give you a little piece of advice. I like your gumption—it's a pure-blooded American gumption and I like it—so I'm going to let you in on a secret. It's about this "neutralilty" test and "interest" standard certain voguish Ivy League liberals are trying to foist off on you.

JOHNSON: I'm listenin'.

STOCKMAN: When it comes to hanging on to your job, the principle of neutrality isn't worth shit.

JOHNSON: No?

STOCKMAN: Nope. Not worth shit. See, to be truthful, we can't really be certain about supply-side economics, and we don't know whether it's going to help *you* in the end or not. All we know is that the rich aren't complaining.

JOHNSON: Yeah, well you didn't have to tell me that.

STOCKMAN: But that doesn't mean we can't *justify* our program in theory by the test of neutral dialogue or equal respect or whatever.

JOHNSON: That figures.

STOCKMAN: You see, Georgie, thinking women and men will always be able to state their interests in terms that, by some theory or other, account for the interests of those they exploit. Neutrality is so easy! All you have to do is link your interests in a web of hypothetical cause and effect that encompasses the interests of whomever you might be screwing. Adam Smith did that. Called it the invisible hand. Lenin did it: the leader *is* the Party; the Party *is* the Proletariat; the Proletariat *is* the People. Modern corporate capitalism does it too. And so can we. We call it supply-side economics. Look, even Aristotle justified slavery by showing that it was in the interest of the slave to have a master.

JOHNSON: You trying to say ain't no interest can't find a reason, right? Ain't no advantage can't find a justification.

STOCKMAN: You're a quick study, Johnson. But don't get me wrong. I don't mean it cynically. The reasons will be good reasons. Or should be. The justifications will be good and legitimate justifications. But there's a world of difference between good reasons and good interests. Every honest justification will try to justify the interests of some in terms of the interests of all. If you've got three inimical interests in a society, you'll get three reasonable but inimical ideologies. All three will meet the test of neutral dialogue but remain totally at odds.

JOHNSON: Neutrality sure as shit didn't save me my job.

STOCKMAN: Neutrality never saved nobody or nothing, sonny boy. We can take away your job, your dignity, and your security, and sure as I'm standing here we can prove to you with the help of supply-side economics that we're doing you a big favor.

JOHNSON: Damn, Stockman, you a wolf in sheep's clothing. But inside the wolf, you damn near a revolutionary.

STOCKMAN: I was once—before the politicians got hold of me and my revolution. Now I'm just a bureaucrat watching the hogs feed. But I'll tell you this, Georgie. I do recognize that there *are* several sides in every revolution, in every interest-ridden polity, and I recognize that the formalities of liberalism only pretend them away. So if I were you (and I thank God I'm not), I would forget about neutral dialogue and start organizing your fellow CETA

135

workers—we're firing every goddamn one of you—and maybe, say, close down the subway system (if we don't do it first with our budget cuts). Or better yet, you might consider sitting in at a defense plant or two. From the look of Weinberger's budget, that's where the action is going to be from now on.

JOHNSON: Hey, Stockman, you ain't half bad.

STOCKMAN: At least as good as the next man, some would say. But for Christ's sake, Georgie, don't tell the President what I said. I'm already in trouble, with my big mouth, and the boss can find a half-dozen good reasons why it's in my interest to get kicked back into the private sector. And I'll tell you, if supply-side economics the way Congress sees it is all the private sector has going for it, I'm going to stay on the government dole just as long as I can, know what I mean?

JOHNSON: I can dig it. You don't need a trainee at OMB, do you, Davie?

STOCKMAN: A guy with your smarts? Hell yes. Climb aboard, George, and let's get to work. We've got thirty-two cities with over 182,000 CETA jobs to liquidate before Friday.

JOHNSON: How long you gonna hang in?

STOCKMAN: Not a whole lot longer. The politicians always win in the end. But not to worry: after the politicians, there's the book.

JOHNSON: After the politicians? The book?

STOCKMAN: When you can't work for them anymore, skewer them. The triumph of politics doesn't necessarily have to be the final victory!

SCENE 5

"Give Me a Break"

(Ackerman and Barber)

ACKERMAN: Give me a break, Barber.

BARBER: I was as good as my word. I left you entirely out.

ACKERMAN: Put me back in for God's sake! You've got the Republicans *and* the minorities walking all over me!

BARBER: You want back in?

ACKERMAN: Maybe I can limit the damage a little that way.

BARBER: It's your funeral. Tell you what. To give you an even chance, I'll put you together with an acquaintance.

ACKERMAN: A friend? I could use a little sympathy.

BARBER: Not exactly a friend.

ACKERMAN: A philosopher, perhaps? Someone with a taste for logic?

BARBER: Not exactly a philosopher, either.

ACKERMAN: Someone who at least perceives the difference between ideal theory (with its perfect technology) and the second- and third-best worlds of real politics?

BARBER: I'm not sure anyone in my cast of characters believes in that difference. Political talk *is* second- or third-best-realm talk and to reduce it—yes *reduce* it—to first-realm ideal talk only eviscerates it.

ACKERMAN: Maybe we'd better get on to this friend.

BARBER: Like I said, not exactly a friend.

ACKERMAN: Another of your infernal literary tricks. I can smell it coming.

BARBER: It is a bit of a nasty trick. But it goes to the heart of the problem with neutrality, and—I know you'll like this—it does it in terms of the logic of ideal talk rather than second-best talk.

ACKERMAN: So you require sophistry when you get to "the heart" of your argument.

BARBER: Let's just say I put some very good arguments in a very tainted mouth.

ACKERMAN: And I'm in this conversation?

BARBER: By your own choice.

ACKERMAN: Skewered again by another man's pen!

SCENE 6

"A Dialogue about Better, Good, and Neutrality"

(Bruce Ackerman and Adolf Hitler)

ACKERMAN: Haven't we met before?

HITLER: Yeah, in one of your crummy liberal dialogues.

ACKERMAN: That's right. Let's see, you're . . .

HITLER: ''Nazi,'' remember? You couldn't even bother to give me a name. I'm much more comfortable here in the flesh.

ACKERMAN: Why's that?

HITLER: For starters, that two-bit ''Commander'' isn't around telling us what we can and can't say.

ACKERMAN: But he refused to let Jewish arguments exclude you from citizenship. Have you forgotten?

HITLER: Typical liberal spinelessness: you figure you can tame us if you get us to *say* the right things. But talk's cheap. Anyway, this guy Barber—he must be a bigger fool than you—he's given me a much longer leash.

ACKERMAN: So you're his dog rather than mine.

HITLER: We'll see about that. He's prodding me to ask again whether I can be a citizen in your liberal state in light of my view of the stinking Jewish race.

ACKERMAN: We've had this conversation before, Adolf. All you need to say is that you're at least as good as, hmm, let's say Golda Meier, and you qualify.

HITLER: Golda Meier? That ****! You must be kidding. I'm not ''at least as good'' as her. I'm far, far better, infinitely superior—why she belongs to a subhuman race of degenerate swine. So do I qualify as a citizen?

ACKERMAN: We've been through all this before. Look, Adolf, if you think you're better than Golda, then it follows by inference that you think you're at least as good. Right?

HITLER: Whose inference? You're out of your inferior liberal mind. Didn't you hear me? She's nothing, excrement, the lowest form of life.

ACKERMAN: But as a speaker of ordinary English, surely you don't deny that a person who says *X* is better than *Y* is conversationally committed to the notion that *X* is at least as good as *Y*.

HITLER [*Cackling hysterically*]: Oh yes, now I remember, the test of neutral dialogue. Hell no, Ackerman, by the rule of ordinary English or ordinary German or ordinary logic, I am committed to no such garbage.

ACKERMAN: Of course you are.

HITLER: Tell me something, Ackerman. Do you think the Bible is a better book than *Mein Kampf?*

ACKERMAN: Better? Of course it's better. Why it's not even in the same class, for God's sake. *Mein Kampf* is drivel.

HITLER: So in your view the Bible is a better book.

ACKERMAN: A million times better.

HITLER: So I would be correct in saying that you are committed to the proposition that the Bible is at least as good a book as *Mein Kampf.*

ACKERMAN: At least as good? No, *Mein Kampf* is trash—lies and conceits and blind prejudices vomited out from the bowels of a sick mind.

HITLER: Well, surely the Bible is at least as good as that?

ACKERMAN: There's nothing "good" about *Mein Kampf* at all: it can hardly be called a book.

HITLER: If you were to go into your local synagogue or church and tell the congregation in ordinary English that you thought the Bible was at least as good a book as *Mein Kampf*, do you think they would understand that you despised *Mein Kampf* and cherished and revered the Bible?

ACKERMAN: Of course not. They'd misunderstand me completely. They'd most likely think I was degrading the Bible or, worse, that I had some feeling for *Mein Kampf.*

HITLER: Alright, Ackerman. All I want you to do is fill in "Jew" wherever I said *Mein Kampf* and "Aryan" wherever I said Bible and you will have my position exactly. The position you so distorted in your so-called book.

ACKERMAN: The point was to explain neutrality, not to give space to your despicable ideas.

HITLER: The point is, I couldn't have been and shouldn't have been a citizen of your state because "better than" does *not* mean "at least as good as": there was no neutrality, no equality, no conceit of equal citizenship explicit or implicit in my claim to absolute superiority.

ACKERMAN: But for the purposes of the liberal state, you were only saying you were at least as good.

HITLER: Liverwurst! When I say I am better than Golda, I precisely do *not* mean that I am at least as good but mean that I am *good* and she is *bad*, I am superior and she is inferior, I am all and she is nothing. I mean precisely that we can never be equals.

ACKERMAN: You are rejecting neutrality.

HITLER: No, I am saying neutrality is incoherent when applied to "better" and "good." In your own degenerate language, statements about the good are always and necessarily cardinal judgments and not ordinal judgments. You allow yourself to be confused because "better" implies an ordinal judgment. But in our dialogue, "better" is defined by and a function of "good" and is cardinal as well. Despite its grammatical form (which is ordinal), its ethical intent is entirely cardinal. So that "better" can never be reduced to "at least as good as."

ACKERMAN: Look, I regard *Mein Kampf* as an abomination, but that is a matter of conscience, my private, subjective judgment, so to speak. In the political realm, we cannot be concerned with Abstract or Absolute Good. We can only address ourselves to better or worse, and they entail no more than ordinal judgments. By the test of neutral dialogue, I am constrained to say no more than that you are at least as good as Golda (and she is at least as good as you). No more than that.

HITLER: Scheisse! That's not what you believe and that's not what politics is about. It's not only logically false, as I have already demonstrated; it is psychologically false as well. You want to persuade me you defeated us in World War II in the name of the principle that the Bible was at least as good as *Mein Kampf*? Or that the Jews were at least as good as the Nazis who were liquidating them? No! You fought against us because you thought we were evil and you were good, because you believed God and justice were on your side. Ask Golda what she thinks, if she believes Jews are "at least as good" as Nazis. Ask her!

ACKERMAN: You're sounding less and less like a reptilian Nazi and more and more like a mere Sophist.

HITLER: Never mind who I sound like. The fact is, you've got Neutrality and the Good together in a politics that is ultimately incoherent. As a matter of the logic of ethical language and as a matter of political motivation, Good, and "better" as defined by Good, never are reducible to the neutral phrase "at least as good as." We are not dealing with an ordinal spectrum of conduct here but with a profound asymmetry: the asymmetry of Good and Evil, Superior and Inferior. To say "the superior is at least as good as the inferior" not only makes no sense, but it eviscerates "superior" and "inferior" of their essential meanings. Your illusion of neutrality is nothing more than a myth by which you try to mediate (or shall I say conceal?) the unbridgeable abyss between essentially contestable definitions of good and bad, superior and inferior. But it is those competing definitions that are at the heart of your corrupt, bourgeois-liberal political conflict, and in this arena your test of neutral dialogue is no help at all.

ACKERMAN: You're no Hitler. You're a mere mouthpiece for Barber.

HITLER: His leash was shorter than I thought.

ACKERMAN: But not shorter than I thought.

SCENE 7
"Your Prolixity Exhausts Me!"

(Ackerman and Barber)

ACKERMAN: Your prolixity exhausts me.

BARBER: The Germans are rather long-winded.

ACKERMAN: I find it peculiar that you use a low-life like Hitler to make what you obviously think are telling points.

BARBER: *You* permitted him into your polity!

ACKERMAN: Only to make a point.

BARBER: Uh-huh.

ACKERMAN: That even a Nazi can participate in liberal discourse.

BARBER: If he allows he's as good as a Jew.

ACKERMAN: Or no worse than a Jew, if you like. The question doesn't turn on "goodness."

BARBER: That's not the point. The problem is that ordinal comparisons don't capture the cardinal sense of superiority implicit in the master race. Whether "better" or "worse," Adolf simply is not going to buy into ordinal talk where the Jews are concerned.

ACKERMAN: In any case, I don't understand why you keep

141

touching on special cases, limiting cases. The Nazi is a special problem. My method is intended to illuminate the realm of everyday political decisions: distribution of goods among citizens and across generations, equal educational opportunity, allocation of resources, trade-offs among competing values—that kind of thing.

BARBER: Yet it is my view that neutral dialogue is most flawed when it is used in everyday political decisions. Like so many formalistic standards (the categorical imperative, for example), it distinguishes the obvious cases that can be easily intuited—the cases at the extremes as it were—but is quite useless in the mundane and ambiguous regions between them, where most of the real conflicts occur.

ACKERMAN: For example?

BARBER: For example, where both sides are "right"—essential contestability. You acknowledge fundamental value conflict but have little to say about it.

ACKERMAN: That's all?

BARBER: No. Even more important is where a political actor is wrong—wrong, but under compulsion to act to forestall a still greater wrong. There are occasions where there seems to be no just option, no right choice, but where some choice is nonetheless mandated by a logic of events already under way.

ACKERMAN: You'll have to be more specific.

BARBER: Bert Brecht said in an early play: "It is a terrible thing to kill, but it is not given to us not to kill." He captured the very essence of the tragic character of political choice for statesmen and for citizens alike.

ACKERMAN: Sounds suspiciously like Machiavelli to me.

BARBER: Machiavelli had a consummate understanding of the real nature of political choice. But rather than you and I bickering, let me offer you another illustration of unconstrained conversation that makes this very point.

ACKERMAN: I think I'd rather bicker. I'm exhausted.

BARBER: I could leave you out of this one.

ACKERMAN: Would you?

BARBER: It's just that you wanted *in* last time.

ACKERMAN: I didn't reckon on National Socialist prolixity.
BARBER: Wait till you hear Harry.
ACKERMAN: Harry?
BARBER: Harry.

SCENE 8

"A Dialogue about the Tragic Nature of Real Political Choice"

(Harry Truman, a statesman; Mrs. Mikushi, a housewife living in Hiroshima in August 1945; and GI Joe, an American soldier in the World War II Pacific theater)

TRUMAN: It's an awesome responsibility—a terrible thing. But I have no other choice.

MRS. MIKUSHI: Of course you have a choice.

TRUMAN: If I spare Hiroshima, Mrs. Mikushi, if I put aside this terrifying new weapon, the war may go on indefinitely. MacArthur tells me we could lose more than half a million men in an invasion of the Japanese islands. I see no way out but the atomic bomb.

MRS. MIKUSHI: Am I any less human, any less worthy of respect, than your GIs? Is a Japanese life less valuable than an American life?

TRUMAN: If I spare you, thousands of Japanese will die as well—perhaps your own sons who are in the Imperial Army and will be called on to defend Japan against our invasion.

MRS. MIKUSHI: Am I not as good as my sons, that I should die that they may live? You call that just? Your GIs and my sons, at least they are soldiers.

TRUMAN: There is truth in that. It is civilians who will pay the price of Hiroshima and Nagasaki.

GI JOE: Hang on, Harry. Who started this dangblasted war anyway? Far as I can see, them Japs were all hungry for Pearl Harbor. Anyway, in a World War there ain't no innocents.

MRS. MIKUSHI: I will not say we are more innocent than you, GI Joe. I only say we are just as good as you and that it is not just for us to die so that you can live.

143

TRUMAN: Hell's bells, Mrs. Mikushi, it's war. Some will die whatever I do. It is a terrible thing to choose between one life and another, one death and another death, but that is the only choice I have. I can save GI Joe, but only by ordering your death. I can spare you, but then GI Joe and a thousand like him die. What would you have me do?

MRS. MIKUHI: Do what is just. Your Occidental philosophers have given you a hundred formulas: the categorical imperative, do unto others, justice as fairness, the sanctity of individual boundaries, the test of neutral dialogue. Put them into practice!

TRUMAN: They are useless. They merely tell me what I already know—that it is wrong to kill, that I must value others as I value myself, that human beings have an equal right to life. But it is not given to me not to kill. I am fated to act unjustly whatever I do. The only choice I am offered is between greater and lesser injustices—and for such decisions the philosophers offer little counsel and less comfort.

GI JOE: Jesus Christ Almighty, Mr. President. While you're wrestling with the eternal verities, 364 Americans and a whole mess of Japs just died at Guadalcanal! Every second you steal to face your conscience costs another life.

TRUMAN: You see, Mrs. Mikushi, even thinking with deliberate reflectiveness about justice is costly when the march of events is underway. With every choice I've faced in this awesome office, I've known that even a refusal to act would have egregious consequences. The statesman has the luxury of neither agnosticism nor skepticism. He can't pretend he doesn't know the answer, for that too will be an answer. He can't refuse a decision just because the future is misty and the consequences of his choices are uncertain, because he will be responsible for whatever the consequences turn out to be. He is forever on the horns of dilemmas for which there is no just resolution, dilemmas from which he cannot walk away. And so his conscience is gored no matter what he does.

MRS. MIKUSHI: Our innocent lives will be on your conscience.

TRUMAN: That is my very point, the dilemma to which I refer, the burden I must bear. It will haunt all my days with great regret and a still greater sorrow.

GI JOE: Two platoons were blown to bits on a minefield while you were making up your mind.

TRUMAN: That burden, too, I will have to bear. With no less regret. With the same sorrow. Every move I make, I make in the face of incomplete information and uncertain consequences. Every decision I reach costs someone something that is dear to him—if he is lucky, only his own life. Political choice is dogged by doubt even as it is impelled by necessity. I am not sure I have ever issued a just order in my thirty years in public life. At best, I have attenuated a little sorrow, acted with slightly less inhumanity than I would have had I made a different decision.

And now, you will both have to excuse me. I have a gruesome duty to perform.

MRS. MIKUSHI and GI JOE [*in unison*]: But you *will* do what is just!?

TRUMAN: No. I think the one thing I can assure you is that whatever I do, it will be a great deal less than just. Many will die and many more will suffer, and that will be the best I can do.

And now, Colonel: I want to send a coded order to our forces in the Pacific. The plan is to be made operational for the morning of . . . let me see, the day after tomorrow . . . that would be August 7.

SCENE 9
"A Moving Scene . . . But Is It Relevant?"

(Ackerman and Barber)

ACKERMAN: A moving scene. Truly. But is it relevant? Hiroshima is hardly typical of the quotidian affairs of a democratic polity.

BARBER: The decisions may be less momentous, but they are of the same character—evil against evil, unthinkable cost against intolerable consequence. Politics is triage, horrendous choices that cannot be avoided. Do we permit fetuses to be killed or take from women the right to control their own bodies? Neither abortion nor the right to life is without untoward consequences. What is the "just" decision? Or are we allowed only a somber choice between lesser evils? Do we bust up neighborhoods in order to integrate schools or jeopardize equal educational opportunity to preserve neighborhood solidarity? Is there a costless option here? Do we build a single artificial heart or fund ten thousand hospital beds? Science cannot tell us. Show me a decision that does not involve trade-offs; show me the trade-off that formal criteria can help us evaluate.

ACKERMAN: There you go again: you get the long speeches, I get the simple-minded retorts. O.K. Fine. Essential contestability, right?

BARBER: Not just essential contestability. Not just the absence of an interpersonal index by which such basic values as freedom, security, life, equality, dignity, and self-realization can be compared and ranked—mana is no better than Rawls's social primary goods when it comes to that—but the absence of a standard by which we can choose between competing evils.

ACKERMAN: But what can you offer other than talk?

BARBER: It is not talk but neutrality that I'm challenging; it's what your constraints do to talk. Speech is a power of sorts, but if you limit speech to instrumental interest articulation and bargaining . . .

ACKERMAN: What else is there?

BARBER: Not a little of the power of speech lies in its *affective* potential.

ACKERMAN: Affective speech defies neutrality.

BARBER: All the worse for neutrality.

ACKERMAN: That's all very well—until we reach hard disagreements. Then where will you be without neutrality? All your dialogues here are first acts. Where are the second acts? The tough confrontations where your mouthpieces come up against unresolved, no, *unresolvable* conflict? Try having an unconstrained conversation then. You'll have anarchy. Or war.

BARBER: You'll have war at that point anyway. Even with constraints.

ACKERMAN: Not if the adversaries agree to the principle of neutrality. Then they can have their differences and peace too. It's called liberalism.

BARBER: Only if they cease to be real adversaries—which will be the result of concrete affect, not abstract neutrality.

ACKERMAN: Friendly affect, perhaps; but what about unfriendly affect?

BARBER: Just as friendly affect can achieve what cognitive discourse cannot do, unfriendly affect will undo what cognitive discourse can do. But you are right, I'm making too many speeches. Will you allow me a final dialogue?

ACKERMAN: Another first act, I suppose. Well, it is you who are doing the allowing and disallowing.

BARBER: Then I will allow myself a final scene.

ACKERMAN: Short, I hope.

BARBER: If not short, undeniably sweet.

SCENE 10

"A Dialogue about the Affective Potential of Dialogue"

(Romeo and Juliet)

JULIET: Oh, Romeo. How glad I am they have finally left us alone. Perhaps now we can mediate this endless dispute that has so embittered our elders.

ROMEO: Oh, Juliet. If you are glad, I am gladder still.

JULIET: To put an end to Montagu versus Capulet, my family proposes the two families rule in concert. Yet yours—am I misinformed?—wishes for rule by each in alternating years. Are you listening, fair Romeo?

ROMEO: How can I but listen to a voice that, like evening vespers, whispers into my very soul.

JULIET: We do fear that who rules first in the plan put by your noble house may rule forever. For after a year and a day, its power secured, can it be persuaded to yield to mere justice?

ROMEO: Were justice fair, I would have been born your Siamese twin, as inseparable from you as your trembling hand.

JULIET: Romeo! In your frivolous flattery, you pay my serious side no attention.

ROMEO: I am a slave to your every side—no joint moves but that I pay it heed.

JULIET: Then pay heed to this: our families will rule in concert, each as good as the other, neither privileged. So shall we make a fair division of Verona's ample grain stores.

ROMEO: Leave the grain to those who harvest it: for us shall love suffice.

JULIET: Romeo!

ROMEO: Ah, sweet maiden, my name on thy lips turns dry leaves to the most delicate incense. Say it again.

JULIET: There's no time for caresses, my panting swain, we have a decision to reach. Oh! That is my hand.

ROMEO: Your hand? I could have sworn it was a lark alighting in my palm. Oh sweet, sweet Juliet.

JULIET: Oh Romeo, you rob me of my reason. My treasured neutrality flies. How can I strike a bargain with all my faculties awry?

ROMEO: Then bargains be damned, my sweet, and in honor to unreason let us marry forthwith; and *that* precious bargain shall supersede every other our careless families have made and broken.

JULIET: In earnest? Marry you?

ROMEO: In earnest; in madness; in vain—I care not how, but marry me you must!

JULIET: Dare we, dearest? Could we truly marry though but moments ago we were locked in the confines of heartless neutral dialogue? That loveless discourse of the lonely and the vain?

ROMEO: I love you, dear Juliet.

JULIET: Oh reckless suitor! To think but for love we would still be bargainers in a cognitive proceeding.

ROMEO: "Cognitive proceeding"—say it once more. Its savory vowels give to your mouth the perfection of "O."

JULIET: Cognitive proceeding, cognitive proceeding, cognitive . . . Oh! Romeo, thy hand strays.

ROMEO: It strives for thy heart but can win only the small victory of thy bosom.

148

JULIET: And wilt thou truly marry me?

ROMEO: I swear it, I swear it.

JULIET: Those are but words.

ROMEO: Words served by honor are an oath. Trust me, and words will not matter.

JULIET: Why, then, Capulet and Montagu shall become one and all conflict will subside. Where there is a community of love, there is no enmity. Where purposes are bound together by trust and by mutuality, there are no private interests. Oh unreasonable Romeo, kiss me!

ROMEO: I would fain kiss thee, sweetest flower of the field, but first let me give form to the small lesson that is to be drawn from our fevered intimacies, a lesson that will serve us as it serves the Verona we shall govern in common.

JULIET: Kiss me, thou artful spurner of neutrality. I can wait no longer.

ROMEO: I would fain kiss thee, but first be taught that those who would make gentle speech the lowly handmaiden of servile interests cannot uplift our interests but only demean our speech.

JULIET: Garrulous knight, has thy mouth no better use than this incessant moralizing? For Saint Catherine's sake, kiss me!

ROMEO: I would fain kiss thee, but first engrave on thy heart these words: to speak is more than to find a tongue for basest impulse or give to claims a voice. In speech is also found a home for bold affection, a hospice wherein mutuality may be succored and restored, a subtle ally of friendship and that yearning fellowship that makes of Capulet and Montagu one common race. Constrain speech with the shackles of reason, imprison it in a cage called neutrality and make it do the work of crass bargaining and base exchange, and the humanity it manifests will wither.

JULIET: Romeo?

ROMEO: Yes, my sweetest princess?

JULIET: What fool has let thee opine that lips as fair as thine were made only to utter foolish words?

ROMEO: Hast thou a better business to occupy their restlessness?

JULIET: Lend me thy lips and I shall be their teacher.

ROMEO: Oh, sweet Jul—*She kisses him passionately*

JULIET: And what hast thou learned now?

ROMEO: Oh sweetest tutor, 'tis but this: how little of man, how little of love, does paltry speech reveal.

JULIET: Shhh . . . the sweetest lesson lies ahead.

SCENE 11
"Justice, Fairness, and Silence"

(Ackerman and Barber)

ACKERMAN: Charming. You have not convinced me but you have charmed me.

BARBER: The very intent of the dialogue—to show that speech has powers greater than mere cognition and that . . .

ACKERMAN: Yes, yes, don't plague me with a rehearsal of the script. The lesson was sweeter when taught by Romeo.

BARBER: Sweetest when taught by Juliet.

ACKERMAN: And yet, while you have been at pains to prove to me that neutral dialogue is a medium of community as well as communication and that talk itself may afford advantages to some that subvert equality (scene 2); and that every interest can be formulated in terms of a general good and thus meet the test of dialogue without really settling anything (scene 4); and that my ordinal uses of "better than" or "no worse than" and "at least as good as" disguise what are really cardinal comparisons corrosive to neutrality (scene 6); and that constrained talk offers little help in choosing between competing evils (let alone essentially contestable goods) (scene 8); and finally that speech is affective as well as cognitive in politically relevant ways (scene 10)—yet still you have missed the true intent of my book.

BARBER: Which is?

ACKERMAN: Which is—by God, Barber, I thought you, before all others, would be sympathetic—that formal systems and abstract metaphysics of the kind purveyed by contractarians and utilitarians cannot provide liberalism with a secure ground.

BARBER: But to *that* point I am most sympathetic.

ACKERMAN: And if my understanding of talk is a little narrow, a little abstract, a little distant from the hurly-burly of politics, it still makes a better starting point for a discussion of justice than anything else I can think of.

BARBER: Here we come full circle. We started with you delivering a brief for constrained conversation and with me insisting that your constraints undid the benefits of conversation. It is neutrality that destroys dialogue, for the power of political talk lies in its creativity, its variety, its openness and flexibility, its inventiveness, its capacity for discovery, its subtlety and complexity, its potential for empathetic and affective expression—in other words, in its deeply paradoxical, some would say dialectical, character.

ACKERMAN: I take it this is your curtain soliloquy.

BARBER: The privilege of the playwright.

Every dialogue I have offered, each unconstrained conversation, makes this same point in a different way. Talk is an aspect of human relations as rich and various as the human condition. To subordinate logos to mere logic, to make our words the slaves of our interests, is to rob us of our humanity. The end results are as sterile and unpolitical as the Original Position or the Greatest Good for the Greatest Number.

ACKERMAN: An exaggeration.

BARBER: Another gift of rhetoric's power.

ACKERMAN: Am I to be permitted a final response?

BARBER: Not here.

ACKERMAN: Then yours will be the last word.

BARBER: The last.

ACKERMAN: That hardly seems fair.

BARBER: No, it doesn't, but then, you see, the last word always—yes, I mean *always*—belongs to . . .

JULIET [*Materializing unexpectedly out of the back of the typewriter*]: Bawling ninnies! Have you no respect for Morpheus? Sweet Romeo sleeps, my lessons having siphoned away his vital lusts. Can you not see that yours, dull philosophers, have been a blunter soporific to your reluctant listeners? Pray leave them to more suasive teachers and spend a while with me. I shall teach you both the secret riches of silence.

ACKERMAN AND BARBER: [*Fall silent together—a small and final victory for fairness, after all*].

SIX

Conserving Politics:
Michael Oakeshott and the
Conversation of
Political Theory

A conservative is enamored of existing evils, as distinguished from the liberal, who wishes to replace
them with others.

Ambrose Bierce

IT WAS once quite fashionable to regard political philosophy as a
kind of conversation and the great books as so many voices engaged in a discourse over time and culture among the living and
the dead. Machiavelli was fond of relating how, upon his return
from the muddied world of Florentine politics, he would repair to
the quiet lucidity of his study and, facing the silent walls of books,
converse with the ancients. There have been few traditional political philosophers, however oriented to the rhetoric and politics of
their day, who did not also regard themselves as engaged in dialogue with their predecessors and unborn successors.

Nowadays, however, the conversation that is political theory
finds itself starved for interlocutors. There are talkers aplenty, but
they do little listening and pursue their several idioms not for the
pleasure of language but in order to urge positions and promote
interests. Philosophers like Rawls and Nozick join the conversation to be sure, taking on Bentham or Hobbes or Kant or Sidg-
wick with dialectical skill, but seemingly in order to demonstrate,
thanks to the irrefutable logical foundations they presume to discover for justice, how most effectively to conclude conversation.
Liberal skeptics like Bertrand Russell and Karl Popper trust talk
no more than philosophy and opt for straightforward problem-

solving. For Marxists, conversation can only obscure or reveal action—and action is where (as Marxism's American proponents might put it) the action is. In each of these modes of discourse, the goal is advocacy, certainty, justification—a resolution of political issues rather than a conversation about them.

As we look further afield, Jürgen Habermas makes a great deal out of communication and communicative discourse, but there is little in his political metaphysics that is accessible to common understanding, let alone conversation, and he seems a good deal more comfortable speaking the dialectical metaphysics of Hegel and Heidegger than the pragmatic rhetoric of Peirce and Dewey, whom he clearly esteems (see Chapter Eight). Bruce Ackerman is a genuine devotee of talk, but he defines it in ways that necessarily exclude a great deal of what we might call conversation (Chapter Five). And now, as if the ranks of political conversationalists were not already decimated, death has silenced several of the postwar era's most vigorous voices: John Plamenatz, Hannah Arendt, C. B. Macpherson, Louis Hartz and (though his was a rather more esoteric and private conversation) Leo Strauss, among others.

There does remain, however, one is increasingly gratified to recall, Michael Oakeshott, as adept and intriguing a participant and proponent as the conversation has had in this century. Like Hobbes, whose work he has admired and illuminated, Oakeshott has been as immune to time as his writings have been immune to categorical stereotyping. In old age, he seems to be gathering steam—the vapors issuing from his work as it gains momentum making it hard to discern exactly where he is headed at the same moment that they suggest how energetically he is moving to get there.

Ideological conservatives are a good deal less than comfortable with the man whose "conservative disposition" springs as much from Aristotle, Montaigne, and Hegel as from Burke and whose belief in liberty and pluralism is no less firm than his belief in history and experience. Voluntarist democrats and progressives, aggrieved by his seeming indifference to rationalistic notions of social justice and the common good, may nonetheless find themselves beguiled by his antifoundationalist vision of civil society.

For to Oakeshott, civil society appears as an association of free persons subscribing to common rules rather than common ends; and these free persons, in their self-understanding, correspond to that "Augustinian god of majestic imagination, who, when he might have devised an untroublesome universe, had the nerve to create one composed of self-employed adventurers of unpredictable fancy, to announce to them some rules of conduct, and thus to acquire convives . . . with whom to pass eternity in conversation."[1]

II

Although there is an important sense in which he is an ideologue, a conservative, and simply an Englishman, Michael Oakeshott will be written off as one or all of these only by those completely deaf to political theory as a conversation. It is not hard to caricature Oakeshott's view of politics as conversation by seeing in it the model of an English club writ large: the only members are gentlemen of a certain class who have sufficient wealth to make discussion of plans, projects, and ends irrelevant, and have sufficient education to be witty and affectionate interlocutors. Out-

[1] Michael Oakeshott, *On Human Conduct* (Oxford: Clarendon Press, 1975), p. 324 (hereafter cited in text as *OHC*). Oakeshott has unfortunately been paid much less attention in America than in Britain, and the secondary literature is sparse. Critical essays and a definitive bibliography can be found in Preston King and B. C. Parekh, *Politics and Experience: Essays Presented to Michael Oakeshott* (Cambridge: Cambridge University Press, 1968); this volume was prepared well before the publication of *On Human Conduct*, however. For critical reaction to that volume, see the special number of *Political Theory* (vol. 4, August 1976), which included a survey of Oakeshott's work by Josiah Lee Auspitz and critical essays by Sheldon Wolin, Hannah Pitkin, and the late David Spitz, as well as a response by Oakeshott. In addition to their critical work on him, Kenneth Minogue in Britain and Timothy Fuller in the United States have written in distinctive but nonetheless Oakeshottian ways. A recent dissertation by Bryan Barnett of Rutgers University offers a full discussion of Oakeshott's political thought.

Since publication of *On Human Conduct*, Oakeshott has published revised versions of several Hobbes essays under the title *Hobbes on Civil Association* (Oxford: Basil Blackwell, 1975), and three new essays on historical method under the title *On History* (Oxford: Basil Blackwell, 1983).

siders to the conversation may look less reverently upon it. It is also true that Oakeshott's writings have had a central ideological thrust: ever since 1933, when he published *Experience and Its Modes*, he has been struggling to conserve politics from the central orthodoxies of twentieth-century liberalism and liberal Marxism.[2] Yet his position is never explicitly ideological in the narrow sense. Thus, against economists, moralists, and reductionists of one kind or another he has insisted that politics cannot be properly understood as the manipulation of power for the achievement of individual or collective interests and ends; that political man is not *homo economicus* in a political setting, implicated in the political process solely by virtue of prudential (rational) self-interest; and that abstract ideas and ahistorical reason cannot take the place of experience and custom (experience tested by time) in defining political rules or political ends without destroying the conversational civility that makes politics the sine qua non of human freedom and dignity.

Against the untried conceits of rationalists and the piecemeal blueprints of social engineers and the ideal common ends of enterprise-association teleocrats, Oakeshott has advanced a far more processual notion of the political. He envisions the political order as defined by rules rather than ends, by process rather than substance, by common deliberation rather than common action—in sum, by a concern for the common conditions that make possible the pursuit of private goals rather than a concern for the common power and common will that make possible the achievement of public goals. This idea of the political is not precisely ideological, although it favors change that is historically rooted and thus gradual over change that conforms to rationalistic blueprints and is thus abrupt. It also favors political education over political manipulation, and experience over expertise. Oakeshott deeply distrusts that persistent Enlightenment faith in man's capacity to master with reason and science the contingent realities of an uncertain world. And he challenges as dangerous illusion the neo-Baconian trust in certain knowledge as man's social redeemer—challenges,

---

[2] *Experience and Its Modes* (Cambridge: Cambridge University Press, 1933).

that is to say, "the illusion that in politics we can get on without a tradition of behaviour, the illusion that the abridgement of a tradition is itself a sufficient guide, and the illusion that in politics there is anywhere a safe harbour, a destination to be reached or even a detectable strand of progress."[3] Oakeshott insists, in short, that "the world is the best of all possible worlds, and *everything* in it is a necessary evil." All those children of the eighteenth century, with their endless projects to remake the world in the image of pure reason, to reshape human nature to the specifications of an ideal, are would-be pilots on a sea that in reality has no ports and cannot be charted. Political activity, for Oakeshott, asks not for pilots (who can only jeopardize our safety with their illusory charts) but for experienced sailors who can learn to feel at home "on a boundless and bottomless sea; there is neither harbour nor shelter nor floor for anchorage, neither starting-place nor appointed destination. The enterprise is to keep afloat on an even keel; the sea is both friend and enemy; and the seamanship consists in using the resources of a traditional manner of behaviour in order to make a friend of every hostile occasion" (*RP*, 127).

This stark, yet not uncomforting, vision of the place of political activity in the human condition suggests not an ideology but what Oakeshott himself understands to be a "disposition," a portrait drawn from "intimations" of the actual rather than from prescriptions of the rational. But such a disposition is precipitated by Oakeshott's understanding of the nature and limitations of political philosophy. In *Experience and Its Modes*, Oakeshott discerns at least three modes of experience (scientific, historical, and practical) that claim accurately to refract the whole of experience but that in fact are partial visions of a whole beyond perception.[4] Nor can philosophy succeed where other voices fail, for it remains a "parasitic activity" that "springs from the conversation" among the modes but "makes no specific contribution to it" (*RP*, 200). Phi-

---

[3] Michael Oakeshott, *Rationalism in Politics and Other Essays* (New York: Basic Books, 1962), p. 133 (hereafter cited in the text as *RP*).

[4] In *The Voice of Poetry in the Conversation of Mankind* (London: Bowes and Bowes, 1959), Oakeshott adds a fourth mode of experience, the poetic. (*The Voice of Poetry* is reprinted in *Rationalism in Politics*.)

losophy might serve the world of practice in a critical role by pro- moting "a more economical use of concepts" and by "removing some of the crookedness from our thinking," but it is finally to be conceived as "an explanatory, not a practical activity" (*RP,* 132– 133). Yet political philosophy as explanation turns out to yield notions of the political entirely in keeping with the conservative disposition—a result that is hardly surprising, but one that raises provocative questions about the relationship between theory and practice in Oakeshott's thought.

Such questions are not answered by *Experience and Its Modes* or the essays in *Rationalism in Politics.* Indeed, Oakeshott's es- sayistic tendencies, in combination with his unlimited range of interests, dispose him to a strategy that might be described as lit- erary guerrilla tactics against his adversaries. He appears in one theater of action (epistemology, for example, in *Experience and Its Modes*), fires a few telling salvos, and then vanishes, only to reappear abruptly in another (Hobbesian interpretation, for exam- ple, in *Hobbes on Civil Association*), armed with new weapons and defending new ground.[5] The collection *Rationalism in Politics* is a one-volume guerrilla war in which tactics and targets contin- ually shift: a major engagement with the rationalistic planners ("Rationalism in Politics") is followed by a minor skirmish with the economic planners ("The Political Economy of Freedom"); an argument based on education as metaphor for experimental pol- itics ("On Political Education") leads to an argument about actual education in the university ("The Study of 'Politics' in a Univer- sity"); a confrontation on historians' home ground ("The Activity of Being an Historian") is succeeded by a campaign waged on the turf of poets ("The Voice of Poetry in the Conversation of Man- kind"). There is, of course, a common adversary and a common vision of what is being fought for, but the strategy displays the common virtues and defects of guerrilla warfare: it wears down the enemy with the variety and persistence and ubiquity of its tac-

[5] Michael Oakeshott, *Hobbes on Civil Association* (Oxford: Basil Blackwell, 1975); also see Oakeshott's introduction to Hobbes's *Leviathan* (Oxford: Basil Blackwell, 1960).

tics, and it constructs a defense that is engaged at every point but secure at none. Yet it lacks a contiguous heartland and the integral, systemic authority to supersede the liberal adversary to whom it proves so irksome. Hence the tendency to write Oakeshott off as a "mere" neo-Burkean conservative. Oakeshott's path, like the guerrilla's, has been an elusive one that has taken him everywhere; yet it has, in his own words, been disconcertingly "rambling" (*OHC*, viii), one that describes an integral territory only with great difficulty.

III

With *On Human Conduct*, his first major book in several decades, Oakeshott clearly decided to change his strategy. He resolved to dig in, to stake out an explicit, theoretical territory and stand fast in its systematic defense. The easy victories of partial criticism were to be supplanted by the far more challenging test of developing a coherent, systematic theory by unifying his divergent themes. The questions of theory and practice posed by the earlier work were finally to be answered. "The themes explored here have been with me nearly as long as I can remember," Oakeshott reports in the preface; "but I have left the task of putting my thoughts together almost too late. . . ." A unification of themes, a systematization of strategy, a "putting together" of thoughts is what *On Human Conduct* proposed to undertake. If the study that issued from this crucial change in purpose, in comparison with the essays that preceded it, is slow-moving, dense, often inaccessible, maddeningly abstract, and as capable of generating new difficulties as it is of resolving the old, it is also one of the most significant contributions to the conversation of political theory since World War II. It has not won the wide readership enjoyed by Rawls or Nozick, who debate rather fashionable egalitarian and minimalist variations on liberal instrumentalism, but it is no less significant. And although it is not self-consciously dialogical in the fashion of Ackerman, it is exemplary of conversation both in its temper and in its approach to philosophy. For *On Human Conduct* addresses not a problem in political theory but political theory itself. It does not treat political issues; it treats with the issue of "the political." Its many provocations and contradictions, its disconcerting questions, and its still more disconcerting answers are precisely the signs of its accomplishment as theory. Like the traditional works they emulate (Oakeshott's avowed models are Aristotle, Montaigne, Hobbes, and, most significantly, Hegel, whose *Phenomenology* will come readily [and perhaps painfully] to mind as one labors through *On Human Conduct*), the three essays of the new book are not just a putting together of parts, but a putting together of parts in novel and challenging ways that give them new meaning and the theory as a whole new "intimations."

When Oakeshott spells out what he means by a conversation and how he views the uneasy relationship between philosophy and politics, he goes to the very heart of his concerns. Alone among the theorists examined to this point, Oakeshott not only preaches a profound distrust of foundationalism but also bases his own delineation of the nature of the political on that distrust. Each of the *post*-post-naturalist philosophers we have surveyed, in giving his liberal politics a suitably secure prepolitical grounding, has tried to revive features of the foundationalist argument. Russell and Ackerman are skeptics about foundationalism in both its rights version and its utilitarian version, but they end up with foundationalist premises of their own—Russell with solipsistic empiricism and Ackerman with a doctrine of neutral constraints. Rawls and Nozick appeal more explicitly to prepolitical foundations, although Rawls's appeal is cleverly disguised in the garb of the original position's rational formalism. But Michael Oakeshott does not merely eschew prepolitical foundations for political reasoning; he fully endorses a conventionalism that makes philosophy itself a largely illegitimate tool of political understanding. He rejects outright both liberalism and its justifications—without, however, embracing democracy (far from it!). His brand of conventionalism stands somewhere between foundationalism and the voluntarism of a Michael Walzer or a Richard Rorty, and thus avoids the relativism of pure voluntarists without falling prey to the abstract dogmatism of foundationalists. This stance makes him a particularly apt figure in our effort to formulate a reasonable (rather than a

159

rational) relationship between philosophy and politics, although he does not allow us to deploy his arguments on behalf of a democratic conception of politics.

Only a fool would try to abridge and summarize the dense and subtle argumentation of *On Human Conduct*, but unfortunately such foolishness is a prerequisite of saying anything at all useful about it. What follows then, though it does an injustice to Oakeshott, will at least suggest the importance of *On Human Conduct* for our general themes here and at the same time identify its chief problems as a nonfoundationalist but antivoluntarist (antidemocratic) model of the relations between philosophy and politics.

The first essay in *On Human Conduct*, "On the Theoretical Understanding of Human Conduct," establishes a theoretical base for theorizing itself, which is depicted as "an unconditional adventure in which every achievement of understanding is an invitation to investigate itself and where the reports a theorist makes to himself are interim triumphs of temerity over scruple" (*OHC*, 11). Each entity to be theoretically understood must be apprehended in terms of its own postulates, which vary from one experiential mode to another. Each understanding is "an autonomous adventure in theorizing, insular, inextinguishable, resistant to 'reduction,' having its own conditional 'truth,' and capable of its own conditional perfection" (*OHC*, 11). No subject is understandable in the abstract. Since as inquiring beings we are always *in media res*, there are and can be no Archimedean points. Theory is always an unfinished and unfinishable business, concerned to explicate in accordance with the postulates of the mode of experience it wishes to grasp rather than the abstract rules of universal method. The theorist of conduct is not himself a "doer" but is engaged in understanding the postulates of what it means to be a doer (thus, for example, doing postulates free agency, procedures denoting obligations and duties related to actions and utterances, actions understood as self-disclosures and self-enactments, and so forth).

Specifically, to understand conduct in terms of its postulates is to treat its practices in terms of "languages which can be spoken only by agents" (*OHC*, 58). Of the two most important practices, a common tongue and a language of moral conduct, it is the latter

160

that interests Oakeshott. The language of moral conduct is the *ars artium*, the practice of all practices, and it is thus a language "spoken, well or ill, on every occasion of human intercourse," a "vernacular language of colloquial intercourse" (*OHC*, 63). As a language, it "*is* its vicissitudes, and its virtue is to be a living, vulgar language articulating relationships, responsibilities [and] duties. . . ." It is a language that "is learned only by being used." In it "there is room for the individual idiom, it affords opportunity to inventiveness, it may be spoken pedantically or loosely, slavishly or masterfully; it has rhythms which remain when the words are forgotten . . . the ill-educated speak it vulgarly, the purists inflexibly, and each generation invents its own moral slang" (*OHC*, 65). To understand human conduct as a moral language precludes treating morality as "problem-solving" or reducing it to a set of rationalistic imperatives. There are moral rules of conduct to be sure, but they are "abridgments" of "considerations of adverbial desireability which lie dispersed in a moral language" (*OHC*, 66). They do not command prudence, they enjoin properties as they are embedded in practices, and they are thus not so much obeyed as subscribed to, "used in conduct, not applied to conduct" (*OHC*, 68). Moral rules are extrapolations from practice, not impositions on it—intimations of the changing idioms that compose the conversation of human intercourse. Such a vernacular language, the rationalists seem never to learn, is to be entrusted to speakers, not to grammarians (*OHC*, 78).

Now, this approach does accommodate Oakeshott's disposition to treat conduct as process and to treat morality as its condition rather than its object. But it leaves largely untouched questions of human ends (wants, needs, desires, interests, intentions, goals) and their gratification via prudence (as calculation, power, influence, and so on). "Choosing the sentiments in which to act," which is at the heart of Oakeshott's early discussion in the essay, is not yet "choosing satisfactions to pursue and pursuing them," which is also a feature of human conduct (*OHC*, 76). Thus, more out of necessity than conviction (the price of system building!), Oakeshott is compelled to extend the compass of morals. It must now take in a "language of self-disclosure" (into which all substantive wants and satisfactions, and their unending pursuit, are stuffed) as well as the familiar ''language of self-enactment'' (the rubric under which the general argument about the language of moral rules is developed). Technically, there is parity between the two languages, which together compose the universe of moral discourse; but in fact Oakeshott orients his argument toward the language of self-enactment, creating difficulties that will be explored below.

What we learn about the theoretical understanding of human conduct is that ''to understand a substantive performance in which an agent discloses and enacts himself is to put it into a story . . . which has no message for those who listen other than the intelligibility [of] . . . the occurrences concerned'' (*OHC*, 105). Theory is an ''engagement to abate mystery,'' but it is not and cannot be a response to problems or an answer to questions posed by conduct. The theorist articulates abridgments of conduct to illuminate its postulates, but he cannot then be regarded as a moral guide prescribing and proscribing in accord with abstract noetic ideals. He ''is not one of the parties in the transaction he is theorizing'' (*OHC*, 106). Those who claim to be parties to the transaction corrupt theory and make themselves into mere ''theoreticians''—ideologists misusing wisdom acquired beyond the Cave to swindle those still trapped in its shadowed recesses. Theoretical understanding, Oakeshott insists, offers no guide to practical judgment. The theorist who pretends otherwise is an ''impudent mountebank,'' an ''impostor'' who deserves (as the more perceptive denizens of the Cave recognize) to be ''accommodated in a quiet home'' if not ''run out of town'' (*OHC*, 30; the Platonic imagery is Oakeshott's).

The second essay, ''On the Civil Condition,'' can be more efficiently summarized, for its argument is in effect a specification of the general argument about conduct in terms of that particular kind of conduct called civility. Oakeshott's intention is to show why his theory of conduct does not tolerate the confounding of civil association with that ''most familiar'' of all forms of association, the ''enterprise association'' (*OHC*, 117). There are, as the distinctions of the first essay suggest, ''two categorically discrete modes of human relationship to be reckoned with: the one substantial, concerned with the satisfaction of chosen wants . . . [enterprise association] the other formal and in terms of the considerations which compose a practice" (*OHC*, 121). Citizens (*cives*) cannot be regarded as "partners or colleagues in an enterprise with a common purpose to pursue or a common interest to promote or protect" (*OHC*, 122). They are common participants in a practice defined by formal rules and associated in a moral relationship "composed entirely of rules: the language of civil intercourse is a language of rules; *civitas* is rule-articulated association" (*OHC*, 124). A republic, which is the model *civitas*, must be depicted as "a manifold of rules and rule-like prescriptions to be subscribed to in all the enterprises and adventures in which the self-chosen satisfactions of agents are sought" (*OHC*, 148). In the ideal extrapolated from these intimations, "the engagement in politics cannot be that in which interests clamour for benefit or advantage or that in which alleged facts, theorems or moral convictions are proposed in a schedule of awards miscalled republics, nor can it be caring for or promoting a so-called general interest or orthodoxy of belief. . . ." It is circumscribed by "deliberation and utterance concerned with civil desirabilities; that is, with approval or disapproval of the conditions prescribed or prescribable in *respublica*" (*OHC*, 172). In the language of the first essay, the civil condition would appear to be a condition of self-enactment rather than self-disclosure, defined by common rules, not common ends.

IV

History is something else again. The "confused and sordid experiments" that constitute the emergence of the modern state, Oakeshott warns in his third essay, "On the Character of the Modern European State," can hardly be said to "flatter the 'civil prudence' of European peoples" (*OHC*, 193). Nevertheless, the "ramshackle construction" of these new states harbored two distinctive dispositions, pushing them in two quite contrary political directions—directions which, it comes as no surprise, correspond to the distinctive languages of self-enactment and self-disclosure as portrayed in the first two essays. Oakeshott summarizes these two dispositions in the terms *societas* and *universitas*. Under *societas* we are to understand a "formal relationship in terms of rules" in which a pact is made "not to act in concert but to acknowledge the authority of certain conditions in acting" and in which *socii* pursue their own interests privately while remaining "related to one another in the continuous acknowledgement of the authority of rules of conduct indifferent to the pursuit or the achievement of any purpose" (*OHC*, 201). Under *universitas*, on the other hand, we must understand a relationship between "persons associated in a manner such as to constitute them a natural person; a partnership of persons which is itself a Person" (*OHC*, 203). As a "corporate aggregate," a *universitas* can possess and promote common purposes, substantive ends, and enduring interests. It incorporates "managers, not rulers; role performers related to a common purpose, not *cives* or subjects; instrumental rules, not *lex*" (*OHC*, 264).

Had the modern European state become an "unequivocal civil association" defined by the civil conditions of *societas*, it would have signaled the triumph of a remarkable disposition: "the disposition to cultivate the 'freedom' inherent in agency, to recognize its exercise as the chief ingredient of human dignity, to enjoy it at almost any cost, and to concede virtue to personal autonomy acquired in self-understanding; the disposition characterized by de Tocqueville and theorized by Hegel. . . ." (*OHC*, 274). But this was not to be, for there "was another *persona* abroad whose disposition . . . could be accommodated only . . . [in] a compulsory enterprise association in which the office of government was not to rule subjects but to make substantive choices for those unable or indisposed to make them for themselves." Those in whom this *persona* sought refuge preferred "substantive satisfaction to the adventure and the risk of self-enactment" (*OHC*, 276). They were offspring of the "individual *manqué*" who "had feelings rather than thoughts, impulses rather than opinions, inabilities rather than passions. [They] required to be told what to think, to ask for, and to do" (*OHC*, 277).

The modern European state thus turned out to be not an "unequivocal civil association'' but ''an all-embracing, compulsory, corporate association . . . its government . . . the manager of an enterprise.'' In overwhelming *societas*, *universitas* has moreover ''bitten deep into the civil institutions of modern Europe; it has compromised its civil law and corrupted the vocabulary of civil discourse'' (*OHC*, 311).

On Human Conduct is, then, a stupendous putting together of parts. To theorize human conduct in terms of its postulates requires that it be understood in terms of the two moral languages of self-enactment and self-disclosure. To theorize civil association as the higher form of interaction *inter homines* suggests in turn that self-enactment, and not self-disclosure, lies at the heart of civility. Measured by the priority of self-enactment over self-disclosure (in their political manifestation, the priority of *societas* over *universitas*), the modern European state is an institution at odds with itself. True civil association and the dispositional proceduralism it entails are forever corrupted by enterprise association and the pursuit of ends it mistakes for politics. Conservatism as a disposition is endowed with the intellectual potency of a proceduralist theory of civil association, which in turn becomes the only construction of politics possible when theory limits itself to the task of articulating the postulates of political conduct.

Such is the systematic political theory of *On Human Conduct*. Its accomplishments are impressive. The challenge to instrumentalism and utilitarianism that is drawn from history and ideology is convincingly reinforced by an analysis of the character of theory itself. The position favored by dispositional conservatism is thus shown to reflect the position precipitated by political theorizing properly understood. Rationalistic and teleocratic interpretations of political life, already undermined by the experiential arguments of *Rationalism in Politics*, turn out to be theoretically suspect as well, for such interpretations suggest a vision of the political in tension with the portrait drawn from a careful study of its postulates. Moreover, although it may appear that Western society's chief values reflect the liberal idea of *universitas*, *societas* is in fact a more appropriate vehicle for civility, freedom, and individuality. *On Human Conduct* provides both theoretical and historical arguments that reinforce the claims advanced in "On Being Conservative" that freedom is the special province of politics understood as subscription to rules, and, as such, the possession of men disposed to live with uncertainty, able to accept "change-fulness and the absence of any large design," and willing to cultivate a feeling for the "warmth of untidiness" (*RP*, 185–186). In contrast, rationalists appear to Oakeshott to be in flight from freedom, seeking to paper over the time-troubled uncertainties of the real human condition with time-immune verities that are eternal only because they are blind to the reality of human mortality and certain only because they are wedded to dogma.

At this point, however, Oakeshott's system seems to have taken in rather more than it can digest. Liberals tutored in the skepticism of Bertrand Russell (as portrayed in Chapter Two) may begin to wonder whether Oakeshott has not appropriated *their* psychology in defiance of his own dispositional conservatism. If progressives and radicals have "lost their nerve" in the face of uncertainty, what is to be said of the Oakeshottian conservative, whose instinct is always "to prefer the familiar to the unknown, to prefer the tried to the untried, fact to mystery, the actual to the possible, the limited to the unbounded, the near to the distant, the sufficient to the superabundant, the convenient to the perfect . . ." (*RP*, 169–170). Is this wary traditionalist, who is always "averse from change, which appears always, in the first place, as a deprivation," to be reconciled with the "adventurer" who is everywhere celebrated in the pages of *On Human Conduct*? The *persona* Oakeshott descries in "younger sons making their own way in a [Renaissance] world which had little place for them . . . footloose adventurers who left the land to take to trade . . . town-dwellers who had emancipated themselves from the communal ties of the countryside . . . vagabond scholars" (*OHC*, 239) is, to be sure, at the heart of the Renaissance spirit of individualism. And, it is true, this spirit grew out of the "disposition to cultivate the 'freedom' inherent in agency, to enjoy individuality . . . [and] to concede virtue to this exercise of personal autonomy acquired in self-understanding" (*OHC*, 239). Yet Oakeshott seems to be portraying a persona usually associated with modern rationalism and progressivism, a spirit that in Marx's imagery "tears asunder" society's traditional fabric and—as all that is solid melts into air—fires a manipulative, revolutionary ardor that has kindled upheavals in almost every century since the Renaissance. The "adventurer," taking things as they come, no more enthralled to the dead past than the imagined future, suggests a disposition finally more in keeping with Popper's piecemeal problem-solver or pragmatism's open-minded, unprogrammed social activist than with Oakeshott's own slow-moving, risk-minimizing, change-resistant conservative.

Nor is it self-evident that those who forsake the certainties of a perhaps unjust present for the possibilities of a conceivably more just future are dispirited refugees from freedom seeking Absolute Truth in place of relative stability. They may, on the contrary, be seekers of relative justice who are willing to risk uncertainty precisely in order to challenge the inequities of a safe status quo. Such were, for example, the union organizers in the counterexample to Rawls offered in Chapter Three. And, by the same token, security, not freedom, would appear to be the paramount desideratum of the conservative disposition. Freedom appears to be a graft that, despite the virtuoso effort of *On Human Conduct*, will not really take. Hence, it was my argument that, despite Rawl's announced liberalism, his psychology of low risk in the maximin strategy gives a conservative tint to his theory of justice.

V

There is another, perhaps even more serious problem in Oakeshott's systematic campaign to conserve politics from the assaults of prudentialists, planners, and positivists: an ambivalence about the role of ends in his preferred notion of political life. The civil condition, for Oakeshott, is clearly a condition predicated on rules, not ends, and *societas* must thus be preferred to *universitas* as a model for the modern European state. Yet Oakeshott's own theorizing about politics yields results that are much more ambiguous and a good deal more suggestive of the conventional understanding of political life as a dialectic of rules *and* ends, procedures *and* interests, obligations *and* rights. That is to say, while the discussion in "On the Civil Condition" focuses on moral conversation as a language of self-enactment, it acknowledges the equal status in theory of the language of self-disclosure. The former is rule-oriented, but the latter admits ends.

A more dialectical construction of civility might recognize the interdependence of rules and the ends whose pursuit they condition and limit. Indeed, Oakeshott's own historical account of the modern European state (in his third essay) reveals that in practice our political tradition has never been able to separate the two. For Oakeshott, however, this is an accident to be regretted rather than an opportunity to be explored. The conservative preference for experientially tempered life-rules over abstract life-plans gets the best of the theoretical responsibility to explore politics in terms of its given postulates. Political experience suggests, and Oakeshott's history of the modern European state confirms, that politics, when understood by Oakeshott's own criteria in terms of its postulates, encompasses the world of power as well as the world of freedom, the world of ends as well as the world of rules, the world of interests (and ideal interests) as well as the world of procedures. It can even be argued that the political world is defined precisely by its dialectical compass—its mediating position between rules and ends, freedom and power, procedures and interests. Nor is this argument merely theoretical. Students of the American political system have been at pains to demonstrate that (for example) the rules guiding agenda building often have a substantive impact on the presentation of policy alternatives and thus on policy outcomes. Law itself, as Oakeshott recognizes in his discussion of *Lex* in the second essay, is susceptible to varying interpretations when concretely applied; and interpretation is necessarily infused with intentions, interests, and ends—which is exactly why political theorists cannot afford to remain silent about the justifiability or generality of politics.

If in his refusal to regard ends as anything other than an insidious intrusion into political life Oakeshott seems at odds with his own notion of theory, he also shares with political agnostics a more general defect. Their teleological reticence leaves both ends and interests to the least legitimate arbitrators possible: the interested themselves. By frowning upon the political consideration of ends in the name of individual autonomy, Oakeshott in fact puts the autonomous individual at the mercy of far less considerate patrons. The private realm (state of nature) has none of civility's moral modesty: its cardinal virtues are force and fraud. Oakeshott would make us political angels. But if it is true that fools step in where angels fear to tread, then surely we will prefer the uncertain judgments of angels in the public realm to the certain prejudices of fools in the private. In other words, abjuring consideration of possible *legitimate* collective ends does not guarantee to individuals the safe pursuit of private goals; it merely guarantees that collective goals will be pursued that are *illegitimate*, unconsidered, and coercive to boot. Like the British (Thatcherism), Americans in recent years have acceded to a Republican ideology (Reaganism) that echoes Oakeshott's distaste for governmental national planning. As a consequence, they have given up a political process in which they can participate in favor of a corporate process in which they cannot participate and which is still more injurious to their autonomy and individuality. The choice is not between public and private enterprise association, it is between legitimate (namely, political) and illegitimate (namely, private, but with public consequences) enterprise association. And it is this perhaps regrettable reality that makes questions of ends ineluctably political.

As Oakeshott finally recognizes, we live, for better or for worse, under conditions of *universitas*. Under such conditions, ends are introduced into the political picture; and once that happens, problems of distribution, allocation, equality, and justice become unavoidable. Oakeshott, by proscribing ends from his model of the political, sweeps such problems aside; readers will look in vain for counsel on defining or remedying injustice in *On Human Conduct*. Such matters are left to the state of nature (the private sphere) and its not always discriminating contingencies. He is not indifferent to the suffering this strategy may occasion; he is only persuaded that efforts to alter natural history's directives by dint of reason and artifice will make things still worse. However inequitous our condition may be, he suspects that tinkering with it in the name of reason invites even greater inequities. Civility, recognizing these stark prospects, prefers the self-justifying rewards of conversation to the never wholly justifiable (because never wholly achievable) objectives of enterprise association. Of course, what has been true for all critics of enterprise association and social justice remains true for Oakeshott: the position favors the status quo and those who are advantaged by history and its outcomes. Only a conservatism that recognizes this fact is free from the taint of special pleading that, as Rawls argues, always afflicts adversaries of redistributionist strategies. When those who have the most to lose oppose change, their justifications are as suspect as when those who have the most to gain advocate it. Civility can become a kind of exclusivity that, while it obviously serves those already in the club, may be disdained by those who are not members or are denied membership by the rules issuing from a particular construction of civility. You have to be in the conversation to benefit from its civilizing potential; yet who is admitted to citizenship is a question Oakeshott does not address.

These kinds of problems point once more to the principal strength, and thus the principal weakness, of *On Human Conduct*: its putting together of the parts. To theorize about human conduct in terms of a theory of theory lends obvious strength to Oakeshott's particular political vision, but, as we have seen, it also creates difficulties. The parts do not necessarily fit as well as they should. If theory is understood as an extrapolation from the postulates of politics as a historical given, then history and theory ought to be in harmony; civility ought to define both theoretical and historical politics. Yet it does not, as the context of *societas* and *communitas*, examined in the third essay, demonstrates. History yields a notion of the political that is both rule-directed and end-directed—indeed, by the measure of recent times, a notion of the political that is perhaps more end-directed than rule-directed. Yet theory, in Oakeshott's use of it, yields a notion of the political that is exclusively rule-directed and that, as a result, is necessarily conservative. It was already clear to Oakeshott in *Rationalism in Politics* that "governing is a specific and limited activity, namely the provision and custody of general rules of conduct, which are understood not as plans for imposing substantive activities, but as instruments enabling people to pursue the activities of their choice with the minimum frustration.'' This understanding prompts the conclusion that governing is *"therefore something which it is appropriate to be conservative about"* (*RP*, 184; emphasis added).

This conclusion foreshadows the argument of *On Human Conduct* in a critical fashion, for it suggests that conservatism is not merely a disposition but a necessary and appropriate concomitant of politics itself when politics is rightly conceived in terms of rules. Rules, after all, are *tools*; they require *experience* to be properly used, *familiarity* to be effectively applied, *wisdom* to be justly interpreted. Experience, familiarity, and wisdom are of course the particular virtues of the conservative disposition, as will be evident in the discussion of Alasdair MacIntyre (Chapter Seven). These virtues elevate conservatism from an ideological (or psychological) preference into a theoretical necessity. Once it is recognized that government entails "providing rules of conduct," and that "familiarity is a supremely important virtue in a rule" (*RP*, 189), the conservative can throw off the rags of the theoretician and ideologue and take on the mantle of the pure theorist. In this he seems to mimic those foundationalists to whom his conventionalism is otherwise a challenge. Just as John Rawls argues that the rules of justice are not only *a* rational choice of men in the original position but *the* rational choice, so Oakeshott treats *societas* not only as one form of politics but as the only legitimate form it can take when properly understood. Betraying his own antifoundationalism, he raises conservative ideology to the status of pure theory: because it alone meets pure theory's stringest standards, it alone is privileged against the competing theories it would otherwise have to contend with in the open market of political ideas.

VI

On Human Conduct provides the philosophical cover for Oakeshott's subtle metamorphosis from a conventionalist in politics into a quasi-foundationalist in theory, but it leaves a number of crucial questions unresolved. The first problem arises out of that misstep described above that mars the logical development of Oakeshott's argument as it moves from the theory of theory to the theory of human conduct: the privileging of self-enactment as the basis of civility and, eventually, politics. Human conduct as a moral conversation encompasses both self-enactment and self-disclosure; there does not seem to be anything in the logical structure of theory, as depicted by Oakeshott, that would compel the preference for self-enactment and the forms of freedom (based on agency) that it engenders. Civility defined by self-enactment can then be a choice prompted only by dispositional or ideological considerations of the kind pure theory is intended to screen out. That the conservative disposition turns out also to be the political attitude appropriate to a proper theoretical understanding of human conduct is not a felicitous coincidence but a symptom of the tainting of theory by moral choice and practical judgment—a replication of Rawls's problem in the original position. *The* theory of human conduct is the conservative theory of human conduct, after all, and the theorist, though he wears the clothes of the philosopher, remains a theoretician (the name Oakeshott gives to the ideologue).

This charge, if it is true, may seem more telling to Michael Oakeshott himself than it does to me. For it is Oakeshott who insists on the distinction between the theorist and the theoretician, between the detached political observer and the engaged *philosophe* (see *OHC*, 30–31), that eventually condemns him to self-contradiction, just as it is Rawls who insists on the test of a pure and untainted original position that his two rules of justice finally cannot meet (see Chapter Three). In Oakeshott's case, self-contradiction is at least in part an unfortunate legacy of the epistemological separatism of *Experience and Its Modes*—a legacy that exacts serious costs in *On Human Conduct*. To be sure, theory is always a parasite on the bodies of experience it aspires to render intelligible. But strictly speaking, parasitic relations in biology are frequently *symbiotic*, the parasite both tainting and tainted by its host. Yet Oakeshott seems to want to insulate the pure theorist absolutely, warning him as if he were Plato's Philosopher to be wary of the subjective seductions of the Cave. But to theorize the character of human judgment is itself necessarily a judgmental enterprise; theorizing human conduct in terms of rules and ends involves theory itself in the tensions that polarize rules and ends as well as in the dialectics that unite them. It draws the Philosopher into the Cave, whether he likes it or not. In "On Political Education," Oakeshott wants to convince us that

> political philosophy cannot be expected to increase our ability to be successful in political activity. It will not help us to distinguish between good and bad political projects; it has no power to guide or to direct us in the enterprise of pursuing the intimations of our tradition. (*RP*, 132).

But political philosophy makes such distinctions all the time, if only in the criteria it uses to select salient "postulates" of conduct; it guides, willy-nilly, if only in its portrayal of a "proper understanding" of politics. Oakeshott may not wish to be thought of as a guide, since that would make him a theoretician of the Cave rather than a pure theorist. But how are we to think of him as anything else when he tells us that the understanding of a state as *universitas* has "bitten deep into the civil institutions of modern Europe . . . compromised its civil law and corrupted the vocabulary of civil discourse" (*OHC*, 312)? Is it the disengaged voice of the theorist that speaks of "parliaments . . . *deprived* of their characters," of private interests that "*clamour* for awards from patron governments," of "laws *degraded* into instruments of managerial policy," and of political terms "*devalued* by being *infected* with equivocation" (*OHC*, 312; emphasis added)? Can it be the pristine theorist, whose theoretical schemata necessarily admits both civil association and enterprise association to the realm of human conduct, who then declares with undisguised ardor that "no European alive to his inheritance of moral understanding has ever found it possible to deny the superior desirability of civil association" (*OHC*, 321)?[6]

[6] Oakeshott has often averred that he belongs to no political party. But he also

No, these are the judgments of an engaged theoretician, not a pure philosopher. Indeed, it is only if we apply Oakeshott's own standards to his political arguments that they appear impure. For he has drawn a portrait of political philosophy that bears resemblance neither to what other political philosophers do when they theorize nor to what Oakeshott himself has done with such élan in *On Human Conduct*. The preference for self-enactment (and thus for civil association) that introduces Oakeshott's transition from human conduct generally to moral and political conduct specifically is a misstep only when theory is artificially disengaged from practice. Measured by less harsh, less pristine criteria, it is simply a necessary bridge from general theoretical propositions to particular political propositions—the adaptation of theory to the postulates of politics, as it were. A political theory, while not synonymous with an ideology, is not a pure theory either; it is, quite precisely, a *political* theory that seeks disinterestedness and *legitimacy* without, however, pretending to Impartial Observer status. The radical separation of philosophy and politics, which Oakeshott demands but does not himself practice, turns out to be as distorting to political understanding as its contrary, the reduction of politics to philosophy (the sin of the foundationalists).

In fact, there does not seem to be any reason why Oakeshott ought not to feel comfortable with a soft but usable construction of political theory as a mediator between pure theory and ideology. His own understanding of theorizing acknowledges that it is a conditional enterprise concerned with the intelligibility of a given world of experience *in terms of that given world's particular postulates*. I want to argue that the particular postulates of human conduct and, more specifically, of political conduct are such that they can be grasped and rendered intelligible only to the degree that they are selected and interpreted by the theorist as political actor—that is to say, by someone engaged in the conduct whose postulates are to be rendered intelligible. The intelligibility of a theory thus depends wholly on its selectivity, its judgmental cri-

has said: "I vote for the party likely to do the least harm. To that extent, I am a Tory" (quoted in the London *Sunday Telegraph*, May 10, 1987).

teria, its *politicity*. Oakeshott himself, in assailing the barren pretentions of empirical social science, suggests that to understand human practices is an art of *Geistesgeschichte* that cannot be reduced to a science without surrendering intelligibility (*OHC*, 97–99). I am merely suggesting that the intelligibility of political practices is likewise dependent on an apprehension of their *politicity*, and that this process of apprehension is itself ineluctably political. The endless, bottomless, portless sea we sail may in Oakeshott's colorful imagery lack known harbors or certain destinations, but everyone afloat on it is nevertheless *under way*, guided by ideals, aspirations, intentions, and goals that, if charted on no cosmic maps, can nonetheless be more or less sensible, more or less rewarding, more or less mutual, and more or less legitimate.

Oakeshott's *On Human Conduct* is itself, notwithstanding its disclaimers, a pilot's guide; if we look at what Oakeshott does rather than what he says he is doing, we are confronted with a compelling political map. Drawn from the perspective of a consistent, theoretically reinforced conservatism, it is a map that—destination or no—suggests coordinates for the journey we ought to be making. Its power is to be measured not by its obligations to some pristine detachment (on which it clearly defaults), but by its rigorously defended, convincingly advanced commitment to a particular vision of the political. In this commitment, which need not be shared to be appreciated, it makes a powerful contribution to the conversation that is political theory. To pretend that a voice as eloquent as Oakeshott's, because it is modulated by limitations of pristine theory, might be without the power to persuade, to guide, to change, or to direct is an illusion that will seem laughable to the readers of *On Human Conduct*. Indeed, if we ignore Oakeshott's definitions of theory and attend to his own theorizing, we will discover a useful alternative to the foundationalist tendencies of modern liberalism. The Oakeshottian alternative is anything but unproblematical, however, for it is embedded in a conservatism that leaves little room either for democracy and social justice or for the standards by which choices about competing ends can be made. Similarly, we will see in the next chapter that Alasdair MacIntyre reinforces the strong link between a nonrelativist antifoundationalism and political conservatism. And we will be confronted in the final chapter with the question of whether there is a nonconservative critique of liberal foundationalism that, without surrendering to relativism, can serve political theory in democratic times.

SEVEN

Abdicating Modernity:
Alasdair MacIntyre and the
Revolt Against Liberalism

> Man cannot learn to forget, but hangs on to the past,
> however far or fast he runs, the chain runs with him.
> Friedrich Nietzsche

LIBERALISM has been the political philosophy of modernity. It has celebrated modernity's victories—emancipation, science, tolerance, reason, pluralism, rights—and it has been diminished by modernity's vices—alienation, deracination, nihilism, meaninglessness, anomie. Different as they are, Russell, Rawls, Nozick, and Ackerman are united in approving of the great modern experiment in emancipation and in seeing our modern predicament as one of theorizing and institutionally guaranteeing the liberty won on history's slaughter-bench. Even Oakeshott revels in the Renaissance spirit of adventure, viewing it as the seed from which all of modernity's fruits grew.

The multiplying perils of modernity turn out to be little less ancient than modernity itself, which was upon us soon after the Renaissance. It was Jean-Jacques Rousseau who can be said to have truly discovered modernity and, in a moment of impassioned clairvoyance on the road to Versailles, to have foreseen the awesome price it would exact. In the *Discourse on Arts and Sciences*, written in 1751 while he still lived in Paris and enjoyed pleasures that already seemed fetid, he first decried the modern world that Paris symbolized. It was not the corruptions but the achievements of the modern world that Rousseau assailed, for the achievements were inseparable from the corruptions by which they were secured. The "progress" of the individual seemed finally to Rousseau to be inextricable from the corruption of the species.

A century later, Karl Marx, stricken like Rousseau (like all moderns) with dialectical ambivalence about capitalism and the modern civilization it had created, worried that the bonds of traditional society had all been pulled asunder, leaving relations among men hostage to cold calculation and the cash nexus. "All that is solid," he wrote in anxious celebration of emancipation, "melts into air." Still another century later (so long has modernity been with us), Marshall Berman organized his ruminations about the new age around this quality of the ephemeral, identifying the experience of modernity with it. "To be modern," he wrote, as if to excuse the charming schizophrenia with which he approached his subject, "is to be anti-modern."[1] Certainly the legacy of Nietzsche, Horkheimer, Adorno, and Foucault confirms Berman's irony. Seen from the dark side of history (to these postmoderns, our side), liberty is coercion secreted and rationalized, science is prejudice agreed upon and objectified, enlightenment is the triumph of bureaucracy and sterile secularism, and the triumph of man over nature is the murder of God by man. "To sacrifice God for the nothing," Nietzsche bitterly declaims in *Beyond Good and Evil*, "this paradoxical mystery of the final cruelty was reserved for the generation that is now coming up. . . ." In this gloomy perspective across the shadowed century from Nietzsche to Foucault, liberalism appears as a philosophy not of foundations but of empty pretenses, a philosophy that rationalizes as freedom what is in truth man's loss of connectedness, of dignity, and of virtue.

What, then, is this abstraction called modernity, at once celebrated and reviled, lost even as it was identified by anxious postmoderns? In part, it is to ask the question, for self-consciousness about time and the character of our moment in it seems to be central to modern consciousness. Where the ancients asked, "How can we live with others in tranquil perpetuity?" and made justice the foundation of their morals, we moderns ask, "How can we

[1] Marshall Berman, *All That Is Solid Melts Into Air* (New York: Simon and Schuster, 1982), p. 14.

live with ourselves today?'' and make therapy the foundation of ours. Self-consciousness turns out to be a deadly form of evolution, because individuals who reflect on their origins, query their place in time, dissect their associations, question their convictions, impugn their natural authorities, and analyze their moral principles ultimately make the discovery that their alienating intelligences can win the victory of liberation (the absence of constraints and limits) only at the price of deracination (the absence of roots and meaning). This, the irony of the species' maturation, is the dilemma of modernity. The liberation the race has sought from traditional societies weighed down with the gravity of custom, hierarchy, and bondage to nature and to natural purpose turns out, when won, to entail homelessness, arbitrariness, and the impossibility of creating a meaningful life in the absence of natural purpose. Free finally to make our own lives, we peevishly wish that God had never tossed us out of Eden and then crept off like an ailing animal to die in some corner of the cosmos, conspicuously indifferent to our plight, leaving us with the paltry freedom we thought would make us like him.

Liberals know the inconsolable coldness of modernity and seek the consolation of their philosophies, rediscovering foundations in absolute right, in an original position, or in neutral constraints for their shaky doctrines of entitlement, or justice, or liberal society. It is in this setting of liberalism as a justificatory enterprise aimed at the political legitimation of modernity that Alasdair MacIntyre—a singularly provocative and duly distinguished critic of liberal theory—is to be understood. MacIntyre's first quarrel is not with liberalism, however, although there are liberals aplenty whose first quarrel is with MacIntyre.[2] It is with modernity itself. In common with every critic of modernity since Rousseau, MacIntyre suffers from the quality of life after Eden. He yearns for the late childhood of man—not that stormy infancy in heroic societies where virtue was still a matter of the honor and courage

---

[2] See, for example, William E. Connolly, ''After Virtue,'' *Political Theory* 10 (May 1982); Bernard Murchland, ''Rediscovering Morality,'' *Commonweal*, January 29, 1982; and Richard J. Bernstein, ''Nietzsche or Aristotle?'' paper from the Graduate Faculty Workshop on Social Theory, The New School, April 11, 1984.

of virile warriors, but Aristotle's Athens, where virtue rested on character and character depended on an integral sense of natural human purpose (*telos*) that defined the individual and the polis alike.

MacIntyre's earlier work does not exactly prepare us for the collision with modernity and its liberal justifications that is the central feature of his most recent book, *After Virtue*.[3] In this already widely influential work, MacIntyre expresses dissatisfaction with his own earlier position—as well he might. For in his earlier works, although he sets himself against certain of modernity's leading dogmas (positivism, emotivism, and psychoanalysis, for example), he argues passionately for both Christianity and Marxism as alternative forms of emancipatory faith capable of setting men against the stultifying self-images of our dominant myths and on the course to alternative progressive destinies.[4] The disquiet with which MacIntyre responds to the present is offset by the hope with which he awaits the future. In the earlier books, he still believed some Catholic or secular saint might somehow manage to remain immune to the generic ills of modernity. But in *After Virtue*, the moral theorist has lost patience with modern moral theory in toto and sets himself squarely against "the ethos of the distinctively modern and modernizing world." Like Rousseau in his most pessimistic moments, MacIntyre turns against the achievements as well as the mischiefs of his age, presumably now believing the saviors (Christ, Marx, and Trotsky alike) to be infected with the mortal diseases of the patient. To be against modernity is for MacIntyre not only to abjure faith in the great religions of

---

[3] Alasdair MacIntyre, *After Virtue: A Study in Moral Theory* (Notre Dame: University of Notre Dame Press, 1982); hereafter cited in the text as *AV*.

[4] For this more optimistic view, see MacIntyre's earlier *Marxism and Christianity* (New York: Schocken, 1968), where MacIntyre—in a short work first composed when he was only twenty-three (in 1953)—still possessed the idealism to envision Marxism as a secular form of Christian radicalism that permitted a radical criticism of the secular present. His later collection of essays, *Against the Self-Images of the Age: Essays on Ideology and Philosophy* (London: Duckworth, 1971), is more explicitly critical of aspects of liberal modernity and less enthusiastic than the youthful *Marxism and Christianity*, but it does not approach the wholesale repudiation of modernity that is the hallmark of *After Virtue*.

Christ and Marx but also to take the full pernicious measure of Kierkegaard and Nietzsche, those seductive prophets of fragmentation and meaninglessness who tried to camouflage the passing of authority as the liberation of will and to make the emergence of nihilism a harbinger of strange new forms of heroism. It is also to be against Max Weber, who offered the novel ectoskeleton of authoritative bureaucracy to moderns who had lost their moral spines and who purveyed in place of virtue the morally neutral norms of efficiency and instrumental rationality. "In our culture," complains MacIntyre, "we know of no organized movement toward power which is not bureaucratic and managerial in mode and we know of no justifications for authority which are not Weberian in form" (AV, 103).

Nietzsche and pointless chaos or Weber and pointless order: these would seem to be our only choices. Or Aristotle. With the failure of the moderns and the bankruptcy of their deliverers (the sacred and profane religions of the West), there is nowhere to turn but to the ancients. And it is in fact to a slightly modernized Aristotle that MacIntyre looks as a riposte to the value relativity and the ensuing moral impoverishment of the modern world. After Virtue thus soon becomes a contest for the soul of modern man between Aristotle and the ill-assorted but potent forces of Kierkegaard, Nietzsche, and Weber.

The contention of these forces makes MacIntyre's book spellbinding—though in the manner of a very esoteric and carefully prepared witch's brew. There are no fireworks, no novel incantations, no word alchemies. Unlike Marshall Berman, MacIntyre does not sweep across the terrain of modernity like Quixote, tilting with phantom czars, poets, architects, terrorists, dissidents, and the likes of Robert Moses. His heroes include Jane Austen and Trotsky along with Aristotle, and his reference points include Shakespeare and Sophocles as well as G. E. Moore and John Rawls. But his argument is that of a philosopher. Nor does he try, like Richard Sennett in that paean to the collapse of civility, The Fall of Public Man, to give us a socio-historical portrait of morals in decline. What MacIntyre offers is a philosophical diagnosis of modernity, using the sickliness of modern morals as an illustrative pathology and the philosophical history of morals as a diagnostic tool. Where Michael Oakeshott dissected the modern body politic and found a relatively healthy member (*societas*) and an infected member (*universitas*), MacIntyre diagnoses the whole as integrally diseased and thus incapable of cure from within. Whereas Oakseshott can offer the palliative of conservative civil association to ends-obsessed utilitarian moderns, MacIntyre's first-aid kit is empty. But this is to get ahead of ourselves. MacIntrye's complex argument, if it is to be intelligently challenged, demands a more careful exposition.

II

MacIntyre begins with the observation that "the most striking feature of contemporary moral utterance is that so much of it is used to express disagreements" (*AV*, 6). This is a sign that, although "we possess simulacra of morality . . . we have—very largely, if not entirely—lost our comprehension, both theoretical and practical, of morality" (*AV*, 2). We now confront a series of crises inseparable from modernity itself: the transformation of philosophy, once a consolation, into a fractious academic discipline; the fragmentation of personal identity into roles we choose at will but wear without conviction; the "bogus logic" of norms detached from the natural world and thereby robbed of their authority (the so-called "is-ought" distinction); the substitution of mechanical scientistic thinking (behavioralism, emotivism) for the truly human sciences; and the conversion of politics from the art of expressing virtue in a public setting into what is little more than "civil war carried on by other means." To live with these calamities of deracination is to live not only after virtue but "in a state so disastrous that there are no longer remedies for it" (*AV*, 4).

Well, not quite. If we were beyond all remedy, then MacIntyre would be Jeremiah, and his dense, poignant, revealing history of morals would be superfluous. But the antimodern MacIntyre is sufficiently tainted, if not by modernity then at least by his former self, to yearn for some ray of hope that would allow him to put analysis to the purposes of remediation. Like every philosopher who has confronted the species *in extremis*—and the species has been more or less permanently *in extremis* (Aristotle's Athens was well into its dotage as he composed his *Nicomachean Ethics* for the Age of Alexander)—MacIntyre is a doctor to his era's travail, and he hopes against hope that if only we can *understand* our pathologies, we can overcome them. Aristotle or no, MacIntyre is not beyond a little Baconian hubris: to see, to know, to understand may still be to remake the world.

What MacIntyre wishes us to understand above all is that virtue must rest on character and that character must rest on a common understanding of the meaning and purpose of human life—something given by the oral traditions and narrative history of society if not by nature itself. Aristotle had so much to teach us because he perceived that virtue is related to the skills involved in living a good human life; living in this manner depends in turn upon grasping what a good human life looks like by reference to natural and historical ends, the kind of aims disclosed when a life is seen as a story rather than as a series of isolated acts and events, as a narrative rather than an abstract and timeless cross section.

Moving from the Aristotelian to his own neo-Aristotelian conception of morals, MacIntyre can thus argue that the exercise of virtue always exhibits a "practice," namely, a "socially established cooperative human activity" with its own goods internal to the activity itself. A virtue in this sense is "an acquired human quality, the possession and exercise of which tends to enable us to achieve those goods which are internal to practices" (*AV*, 178). Despite the utilitarians, virtue therefore cannot be defined by external goods. Here MacIntyre is very close to Oakeshott. Yet, despite Kant, virtue cannot be defined by the subjugation of the passions to rational will either, and thus cannot be equated with altruism. Virtues conjure up skills appropriate to practices, which is Oakeshott's point; but they also conjure up a way of living harmonious with the purposes of a life, which incorporates ends into practices in a fashion alien to Oakeshott. Virtues as such cannot be defined in isolation from human relationships or from the narrative histories in which relationships are necessarily embedded. A particular virtue thus always requires "acceptance of some prior account of certain features of social and moral life in terms of which it has to be defined and explained'' (*AV*, 174), and it may differ in content (although not in form) from one culture or one era to the next. ''Virtue'' has more the sense of the modern term ''excellence,'' which suggests a relativity with respect to different subjects quite alien to the more universalistic modern idea of (deontological or utilitarian) virtue.

In Homeric civilization, the relations of men in a warrior society created heroic virtues like courage and honor (replicated in the medieval Age of Chivalry) that are strongly reinforced by the common (Latin) etymology of virtue and virility. In early Athens, human relations were defined as political relations (relations within the polis), and political virtues, such as justice, that were deemed indispensable to the practice of politics came to define morality. In the Christian Middle Ages, the excellences of Christian relations in communities of faith were associated with virtues like faith, hope, and charity. Each of these conceptions is distinctive and may seem incompatible with the others. But they share virtue's form in that all describe a particular historical setting for human relations and all assume the authority of certain social purposes and human aims.

III

MacIntyre's conception of virtue, extrapolated from his intellectual history of morals, enables him to diagnose the calamity of modernity. We live after virtue in a cantankerous society that can agree upon nothing, and we associate morals with feuding academic schools not because we have forgotten the meaning of virtue but because we have lost the underlying sense of a community defined by common purposes on which virtue depends. Without a context of community within which our purposes are intelligible, the discussion of justice can proceed (as it does, for example, in John Rawls or Robert Nozick) only on the basis of individual interests and arbitrary ends. When identity becomes a matter of trying on roles (which, like masks, invent rather than disclose a persona), there cease to be characters in whom virtues can be in-

184

vested. Role players, whether they are Sartre's spontaneous crea tors of meaning or Erving Goffmann's playful manipulators of self-consciousness, are immune to virtue.

It follows from this that no one of the three chief players in MacIntyre's drama of modernity can be conversant with virtue or its practices. There is the aesthete ''who lounges so insolently at the entrance to the modern world.'' He is a cynical scoundrel who ''sees through the illusory and fictitious claims'' of moderns only in order to rub meaninglessness into their cowardly faces (AV, 70). And there is the therapist, who specializes not in disingenuous truth but in ingenuous deception (self-deception too), helping us to live with the lies that enable us to live without truth and mean- ing (which the aesthete has already demonstrated can no longer exist). And then there is that great modern facilitator, the man- ager, who offers the solace of a morally neutral expertise and—to fill the gap left by vanished virtue—proffers efficient means to any and all ends we might arbitrarily opt for. Here MacIntyre is not too far from the more dialectical Horkheimer and Adorno, who remind us that ''with full confirmation of the scientific system as the form of truth, thought seals its own nullity, for science is tech- nical practice, as far removed from reflective consideration of its own goal as are other forms of labor under the pressure of sys- tem.''[5] With the guidance of these soulless dissemblers, the aes- thete, the therapist, and the manager, we learn to live with, if hardly to love, life after virtue.

A powerful and revealing indictment of modernity. Yet, for all its argumentative ingenuity and its rhetorical conviction, Mac- Intyre's confrontation with the new age lacks the vital dialectical quality that has been so essential to modern assaults on modernity, such as Horkheimer and Adorno's. MacIntyre's undialectical, al- most Manichaean polarization of Western civilization into the era of virtue and the era after virtue compromises his search for a way out of the modern crisis and raises questions about the ultimate ideological tenor of his argument, which finally appears to be

[5] Max Horkheimer and Theodor W. Adorno, *Dialectic of Enlightenment* (New York: Herder and Herder, 1972), p. 85.

much more conservative than we (or perhaps MacIntyre himself, in his earlier incarnation) might expect. There is no modern thinker from Diderot and Voltaire to Foucault and Oakeshott who has not, with Hegel, been impressed by the "cunning of reason" and has not, with T. S. Eliot, been troubled by a history in whose "contrived corridors . . . unnatural vices are fathered by our heroism [and] virtues are forced upon us by our impudent crimes."

Rousseau, Hegel, Marx, and their successors all greeted the modern era with an apt ambivalence. It was not that modernity brought with it ills to match its achievements and new forms of emptiness to compensate its liberties: it was that emptiness and liberty, corruption and achievement, were recognized as dialectical moments in a single ethos—the evolution of consciousness toward a reflexivity that was at once liberating and alienating. Thus Rousseau hopes for perfection even as he fears corruption and sees in the perdition of man's lost innocence the promise of his salvation. Thus Hegel gleans from the slaughter-bench of history signs of reason's progress and sees in every cross a budding rose that may explain and justify what is suffered in the cross's name. Thus Marx construes the extremes of wage slavery as the price of capitalism's progress toward centralization and efficiency, and perceives in exploitation and class war unhappy instruments of necessary historical change. Thus Horkheimer and Adorno, whose critique of positivistic science and the coerciveness of reason MacIntyre sometimes seems to echo, nonetheless sketch the progress of Enlightenment with a far greater sensitivity to dialectical ambiguity: "Heaven and hell," they remind us, "hang together . . . ," and "the curse of irresistible progress is irresistible repression."[6]

---

[6] Ibid., pp. 14, 36. The full flavor of their dialectics is evident in this passage: "The identity of everything with everything else is paid for in that nothing may at the same time be identical with itself. Enlightenment dissolves the injustice of the old inequality—unmediated lordship and mastery—but at the same time perpetuates it in universal mediation. . . . The blessing that the market does not enquire after one's birth is paid for by the barterer, in that he models the potentialities that are his by birth on the production of the commodities that can be bought in the

Yet for MacIntyre, bleak Manichaean that he often seems to become in the pages of *After Virtue*, there is no secret germ of redemption in modern despair, no rose thrusting from the cross, no hidden purpose served by the long fall from virtue that describes man's journey through Enlightenment into new darkness. Indeed, if the modern era is without promise, the era of virtue often seems in MacIntyre's vision to be without blemish. His Aristotle is faultless and thus beyond dialectic. Yet surely Thrasymachus plied Sophist wares in ancient times no less cynical and corrosive than those of the modern emotivists and interest mongers. "Justice is but the interest of the strongest," he proclaimed, leering at a dumbfounded Socrates, who never gave him a satisfactory answer. Nor was one to be expected, since the sparring philosophers spoke to one another across an impassable abyss that separated two worlds of moral discourse that have been incommensurable ever since. But the name of Thrasymachus is not to be found in the index of *After Virtue*, and MacIntyre treats emotivism and its variations as an invention of the moderns. MacIntyre is similarly shortsighted on questions of ancient citizenship: Athenian and Spartan men made virtuous citizens to be sure, but among them lived helots, slaves, and "barbarians" (and, of course, women!), for whom virtue meant the willing surrender of their humanity. Aristotle's treatment of slavery is not prominent in MacIntyre's treatment of Aristotle. "How can that which we adopt for no reason [modern morals] have any authority over us?" asks MacIntyre, identifying a central conundrum of the world after virtue. But he does not ask the dialectical counter-question— "How can that which in effect adopts us [ascriptive morals or natural teleology in the ancient world] be truly ours or permit us to be free?"—which is the central conundrum of the world in its earlier era "during virtue."

---

market. Men are given their individuality as unique in each case, different to all others, so that it might all the more surely be made the same as any other" (pp. 12–13). For a French perspective on the dialectic of Enlightenment, see Michel Foucault, "What Is Enlightenment" in P. Rabinow, ed., *The Foucault Reader* (New York: Pantheon, 1984).

IV

Modernity's modern score card finally tells a more complex story than the one narrated by MacIntyre. Modernity does, to be sure, have a difficult time with meaning, with community, and with natural authority, but it offers freedom and equality a great deal more hospitality than they enjoyed in earlier times. After virtue is after Eden, but it is also after hierarchy, after slavery, after absolutism, and after ignorance. When Voltaire inscribed the fateful words "Ecrasez l'infâme!" it was not ancient virtue he wished to extirpate but all the myriad vices that virtue (and the social conditions that sustained virtue) brought in its train. In the premodern world, with the craft of practices had come the diseases of class; with order had come oppression; with chivalry, prejudice; with belief, error; with community, inequality; with faith, superstition. For an assessment of what Voltaire and the French philosophes wrought—the vices Enlightenment destroyed and the vices it facilitated—we require a far more dialectical method than MacIntyre permits himself in *After Virtue*. The hidden costs of modernity—the costs of liberty in terms of rationalized and covert repression, the costs of equality in terms of spreading subterranean conformity, the costs of science in terms of new forms of epistemological dogmatism and the shrinking of the realm of Being to the smallish scale of science's own solipsism—must be measured against the genuine achievements they have entailed. That is Hegel's powerful secret: the rose growing from within the cross, reason rising from history's slaughter-bench.

Because he fails to assume a posture that is dialectical, MacIntyre's brilliant attack on the modern age risks assimilation to points of view that are dogmatically conservative or even reactionary. By refusing to recognize modernity's victories, he renders its vices demonic and irremediable. By remaining oblivious to the succor modern liberty and justice have brought to the weak and powerless and dispossessed, he gives inadvertent succor to those modernity has discomifited. How many tyrants, how many manorial barons, how many colonizers, how many irascible slavers, bullying patriarchs, and arrogant imperialists—remembering the

useful privileges and prejudices enjoyed by their forbearers in by-
gone times—would find an all too wieldy instrument of reaction
in MacIntyre's assault on modernity? How many would discover
an all too complacent and comfortable redoubt in his paen to the
ancient world of virtue? Would MacIntyre really wish to trade our
stumbling anxieties for the certainties of a new Inquisition? For it
is thus that heaven and hell hang together. Rousseau regretted the
costs of modernity no less profoundly than MacIntyre, but Rousseau knew enough of inequity to grasp that as the forces and faculties that improve humankind are the same forces and faculties
that deprave it, so too the forces and faculties that enslave humankind are those that can emancipate it. The faculties of reason,
imagination, and socialization, whose depredations are warned
against in the *Two Discourses*, are the selfsame faculties that are
put to constructive political use in the name of man's ennoblement
in *The Social Contract*.

MacIntyre never gets so far. When he comes to that inevitable
question facing every reflective modern wishing to change the
world—What is to be done?—his vision dims in two disquieting
and crucial ways. First, he seems to become uncertain about what
he is actually arguing. Have we experienced a history that places
us beyond both virtue and redemption, a state "so disastrous" that
nothing can be done? Or is it that we have committed too many
philosophical errors? "Was it right in the first place to reject Aristotle?" he queries (*AV*, 111), as if to rectify that mistake might
remake our world. "Can Aristotle's ethics . . . be vindicated?"
he wonders (ibid.), as if to set history straight we need only put
our arguments in order and reorient our philosophical curricula to
the advantage of Aristotle and Augustine and Aquinas and at the
expense of Hume and Nietzsche and Weber. This antihistorical
intellectualism is much closer to the bookish abstractions of a
Nozick than to real political argument: it depends on logic rather
than engaged political judgment to settle political arguments. On
the evidence of MacIntyre's own analysis, it is preposterous; the
crux of his argument is precisely that it is not so much virtue as
the social structures and cultural ethos from which virtue grew that
have been "irrevocably lost." Ancient virtue is gone because the

world of the ancients has passed. If this is so, vindicating Aristotle is an exercise in despair.

Second, if the explicit philosophical lessons to be learned from reading the history of morals are muddy, then we are left only with ideological lessons that, while MacIntyre leaves them implicit for the most part, are nevertheless fairly obvious: rue the past, detest the present, fear the future. Political movements organized around these injunctions, a far cry from MacIntyre's careful analysis, have done less to re-establish past virtues than to destroy what vestiges of them remain to prop up our civilization.

What in fact *is* to be done? MacIntyre's only piece of explicit political counsel is this: "What matters at this stage is the construction of local forms of community within which civility and the intellectual and moral life can be sustained through the new dark ages which are already upon us" (*AV*, 245). What he can possibly mean in an era of multinational corporations, economic interdependence, irredentist nationalism, religious fundamentalism, and the constant threat of nuclear oblivion is not spelled out. Communes? (Run by dropouts?) Universities? (God forbid!) Churches? (Run by Reverend Falwell and company?) Does MacIntyre perhaps want those governmental bureaucrats whom he elsewhere decries to take matters in their own hands and, as Lord Devlin has urged, see to the "enforcement of morals"?[7] Or are the therapeutic communes that not so long ago dotted the Pacific palisades to be reinvigorated so that EST can save the West? There are no answers in *After Virtue*, only a sermon of despair.

The lesson with which MacIntyre leaves us is in fact deeply conservative, a lugubrious rejection of all that is modern but with

[7] See Patrick (Lord) Devlin, *The Enforcement of Morals* (Oxford: Oxford University Press, 1965). This is of course the solution preferred by a variety of social conservatives who have in recent years interrupted their campaign to constrain government as an instrument of social justice to inaugurate a campaign to empower it as an instrument of coercive morals. For the now rather aged debate around these issues (one that parallels the debate between John Stuart Mill in *On Liberty* and James Fitzjames Stephen in *Liberty, Equality, Fraternity* (1874), see H.L.A. Hart, *Law, Liberty and Morality* (Oxford: Oxford University Press, 1963) as well as the Devlin book.

no possibility of retrieving the virtues of a past irrevocably lost. He still does obeisance to Trotsky and St. Benedict, but he offers a counsel of bitterness. Liberalism as the legitimating philosophy of an age of emancipation may well have run its course; earlier chapters in this book certainly point to significant deficiencies in the arguments of its current champions. But a revolt against liberalism that appeals only to a dead and irrecoverable past has little hope of filling the hollowness that characterizes the postmodern era. Living, as we do, not only after virtue but also after liberty, we require a philosophy of the political that realizes and reconciles both rather than a philosophy of nostalgia that aspires to restore the first at the expense of the second. From MacIntyre comes only a sense of paralytic sorrow. In place of Marshall Berman's ambiguous joy in wandering among the spinning artifacts of a modern world in whirl, there is regret for old worlds forever lost. In place of an indulgent American delight in empty space, free movement, and the great open road (leading nowhere), there is a European longing for the orderliness of confined space and well-defined motion. There is in the accent with which MacIntyre inflects his arguments something fearful, something cramped, something profoundly anxious. A voice suited perhaps to our age, but unsuited to a successful revolt against liberalism and the spirit of political renovation it would demand.

It may simply be that MacIntyre has spent too much time in cities like Boston, where he has taught in recent years. Boston is too arch and reserved to be a truly corrupt capital city in Rousseau's sense, but it is urbane, cosmopolitan, immoral, uprooted, and otherwise resplendent with the corruptions of the age. Perhaps in assuming his chair at Vanderbilt (to which he has now relocated), in that seat of all that is "country," he will discover the consolations of a simpler age and find reason for hope. After all, Rousseau conceived his attack on modernity while living in Paris and composed his more sanguine works, like *Emile* and the *Social Contract*, in bucolic exile.

Of course, Nashville is also closer to the Bible Belt and that American heartland where racism is still an honest man's option, and MacIntyre may also discover, along with a simpler life more in tune with virtue, all of virtue's ancient vices that make some of us glad, for all the perils of modernity, that we live in its lengthening shadow rather than under the parching sun of ancient Athens.

EIGHT

Political Judgment: Philosophy as Practice

> Governments are instituted for practical benefit not
> for subjects of speculative reasoning.
> Daniel Webster

IN THE trail of its vices, modernity may bring virtues that compensate the loss of ancient solidarity; nevertheless, modernity's vices weigh on us. To live in modern times is to live at the end of a long corridor flanked by hundreds of closed and closing doors. The liberty we have won at the cost of ancient virtue must now be survived without virtue's succor.

Yet none of the philosophers reviewed here adequately prepare us for such a task. In conquering the muddled uncertainties of politics and suborning reasonableness to rationality, they have served the ideal of enlightenment better than they have informed our political judgment. In substituting reason for common sense, they have declared the sense of commoners to be nonsense. Rights are philosophically vindicated, but only as abstractions that undermine the democratic communities that breathe life into rights; justice is given an unimpeachable credential in epistemology, but no firm hold on action or on the deliberative processes from which political action stems; talk is revivified as the heart of a political process and then recommended to citizens, but in a form that answers to the constraints not of citizenship but of philosophy; civility is celebrated, but construed as incompatible with the sorts of collective human choice and communal purposes that give civility its political meaning; the past is resurrected, but only in order to disdain the present and mock the future.

The question these sorry conclusions leave behind is whether there is or can be some genuinely *political* philosophy that orders

193

our understanding of politics and informs the political judgment necessary to survival in democratic times without eviscerating politics of its essential character. What seems called for is a political philosophy of judgment, a theory of political judgment that renders judgment in political terms rather than reducing politics to the terms of formal reason. In this final chapter, I would like to examine political judgment, first by looking at certain recent discussions of its meanings—particularly Ronald Beiner's—and then by offering a view of judgment more in keeping with my own understanding of it.

What in fact (or in theory) is political judgment? Are we to think of it as a form of cognition and thus a species of the underlying genus judgment—an approach quite suitable to philosophy? Or should we regard it as an activity of politics rather than as a faculty of the mind—a perspective that leaves politics intact and bends judgment to its peculiarities? Take these examples: a scientist pores over her spectrascopic data trying to determine whether the interference lines suggest traces of a new element; a Catholic ponders whether he can reconcile the divorce papers he is about to file with his religion; a critic muses over whether the performar. 'e aesthetic of a new production of *Mother Courage* conceals or reveals Brecht's ideological intentions; a citizen asks herself whether the pornography ban she is campaigning for is compatible with the First Amendment. In each of these instances, an individual is apparently called upon to exercise the faculty of judgment, which looks upon first examination like little more than a particular kind of mental faculty. In each, the particulars of a specific situation are to be measured by, brought into conformity with, or rendered intelligible by means of a more general standard (say, a Marxist aesthetic) or principal (say, the sanctity of marriage vows) or law (say, the Bill of Rights).

Judgment evidently entails more than mere observation, but it falls short of full nomothetic explanation (adducing deterministic laws). Less subjective than the expression of rank personal prejudice, it is nonetheless less objective than the claim to scientific or metaphysical truth. It occupies precisely the ambiguous realm that lies between opinion and certainty.

If judging of every kind was a matter of fitting particulars together with universals in this fashion, then political judgment would be nothing more than the application of judgment *tout court* to politics in particular. Citizens and statesmen would do what scientists, philosophers, critics, moralists, and ministers do, namely, pursue a mediate form of human reasoning that avoids error and cant without achieving or even claiming the status of absolute truth (whatever that is).

In reality, however, the attempt to separate one form of judgment from another has usually led to versions of the faculty radically at variance with one another. Most modern commentators have aspired to segregate science from judgment, reserving the latter to the domain of what the ancients called right opinion. With the ancients, they suggest that judgment ought to pertain to praxis, a realm defined neither by man (subject) nor world (object) but by man-in-the-world or man-applying-himself-to-the-world. Science may incorporate judgment in the phase identified with the "logic of discovery," where hypotheses are first formulated and posited, but it relies on exacting forms of reasoning, such as induction and deduction, and eschews mere judgment in its crucial "logic of confirmation," where hypotheses are given the status of lawlike generalizations.

Kant went further and excluded morals from judgment as well. He offered a tripartition of the cognitive faculties that segregated both pure reason (the faculty by which we know and order the "real" world of necessity as mediated by our senses) and practical reason (the faculty by which we know and order the free world of ends in themselves) from judgment—a residual faculty with which we are left to explore such residual realms as the aesthetic. If judgment for Kant is radically distinct not only from pure reason but also from practical reason, it seems possible that political judgment may be radically distinct from moral reasoning and aesthetic judgment. That at least is the question that faces anyone who wishes to know the character not of judgment in general but of political judgment in particular.

To pose the question "What is political judgment?" is to be thrust into a philosophical debate as old as philosophy, a debate

195

that is given its modern form by Kant. The Kantian and neo-Kantian argument has been the focus of a good deal of discussion, most recently in the form of a provocative essay by the young Canadian theorist Ronald Beiner called *Political Judgment*.[1] Although the attention given to the problem of political judgment is welcome, the preoccupation with the German school and its antecedents in Kant and Aristotle is not, as I will try to show. Of course, the school is German only in the broadest sense, since it encompasses Hannah Arendt and Aristotle as well as such *echt* Germans as Habermas, Gadamer, and Kant himself. Aristotle can perhaps be viewed as an honorary German by virtue of the continuing tyranny of Greece over the modern German mind, but by the same token Hannah Arendt is more an American than a German (despite her birth and education) as a consequence of the continuing tyranny of Germany over the American mind. We might also include Ernst Vollrath in our survey (although Beiner overlooks him), since Vollrath's neo-Kantian essay on political judgment published in 1977 was in the requisite mode and was also dedicated to Hannah Arendt.[2] Indeed, Vollrath comes a great deal closer than any other theorist in the German school to recognizing the essentially political nature of political judgment.

Political judgment is not exclusively a subject of the German school, although anyone who reads only Beiner on the subject might be led to think so. The American pragmatists, in particular Charles Peirce, are clearly pertinent, as recent students of political epistemology like Richard Bernstein, Richard Rorty, and Charles Taylor make clear.[3] Indeed, anyone who has thought about politics, prudence, or practicality in their English or American mani-

[1] Ronald Beiner, *Political Judgment* (Chicago: University of Chicago Press, 1983).

[2] Ernst Vollrath, *Die Rekonstruktion der politischen Urteilskraft* (Stuttgart: Ernst Klett Verlag, 1977).

[3] See, for example, Richard J. Bernstein, *The Restructuring of Social and Political Theory* (Philadelphia: University of Pennsylvania Press, 1978); Richard Rorty, *Philosophy and the Mirror of Nature* (Princeton: Princeton University Press, 1979); and Charles Taylor, *Philosophical Papers*, vol. 1 (Cambridge: Cambridge University Press, 1986).

196

festations—which is to say, anyone who has read Jefferson oɪ
Madison or Tocqueville—will immediately realize that to treat
judgment exclusively as a form of reason, as both Beiner and his
German subjects appear to do, destroys its political character by
reducing it to a problem of individual cognition. As such, it can
(in Kant's definition) be limited to "thinking about the particular
as contained under the universal." Judgment here is made a function of a private mental faculty and thus becomes a problem in
epistemology: how conscious individuals come to know the world
and how they *know* they know what they know. Once judgment is
assimilated to epistemology, it becomes all too easy to overlook
the impact that the modifier *political* might have upon it. Political
judgment becomes simply one kind of judgment, namely, the
judgment of things political.

Kant's modern protégés are not merely Kant clones; they lean
hard on Kant's rationalistic walls. For example, Ronald Beiner is
anxious to invigorate Kantian rationalism with a healthy dose of
Aristotelian praxis. He knows that political judgment implicates a
world of activity distinct from other forms of judgment, and he
consults Aristotle precisely in order to account for the relationship
between judgment and rhetoric, judgment and friendship, and
judgment and sympathy. With Aristotle, he hopes to get around
the Kantian shortcomings of Arendt, Gadamer, and Habermas
(who themselves wish to get around their own self-acknowledged
Kantian shortcomings). From still another German, Max Weber,
Beiner borrows his ideal definition of political judgment as a
happy marriage of detachment and commitment. Here distance
(impartiality) is represented by Kant, and engagement (passion) is
represented by Aristotle. To judge is to disengage our private perspective and engage a public sympathy. We judge apart, yet we
also judge "with," judge as a friend might judge. Friendship ties
judgment to rhetoric (Aristotle's insight) and is like rhetoric in that
it wants to be "convincing and persuading without being able to
prove" (Gadamer's phrase).

Like Gadamer and Habermas, Beiner aspires to dialectic. But
their defects are his, and his conceptualization of political judgment, though ambitious, seems unrealized. By exposing Kant to

Aristotle, Beiner thinks the former can be infected with the latter's sense of sympathy and praxis. But Aristotle too had ultimately classified judgment (*phronesis*) as a form of wisdom or knowledge—as a "mode of true cognition."

In Beiner's account, Arendt also thrashes against the confines of rationalism. After all, in her view activity (the *vita activa*) is the key to man's political life. But she cannot escape the embrace of Kant, into whose arms she seemed about to recommit herself at the end of her life. At her death, Arendt was beginning work on a study of judgment that was to be the third volume in her trilogy *The Life of the Mind* (the volumes *Thinking* and *Willing* had already appeared).[4] But *vita activa* or no, judgment remained for Arendt a product of detachment, more the function of spectators than of actors. In her *Lectures on Kant's Political Philosophy* she continued to insist that "the public realm is constituted by the critics and the spectators, not by the actors or the makers";[5] and in her provocative study of Adolf Eichmann she explicitly barred love from the realm of judgment. Despite the outrage this seeming sangfroid inspired among many of her otherwise admiring Jewish readers, she reaffirmed the need to insulate her verdict on Eichmann from her own Jewishness. "Love belongs outside of politics because it impairs judgment," she stubbornly reiterated; "love, by reason of its passion, destroys the in-between which relates us to and separates us from others."[6] Political judgment might apply to a common world of praxis but for Arendt it originates in a solitary mental faculty exercised by individuals operating under constraints such as impartiality.

All of this theoretical byplay—Beiner on Arendt, Arendt as Kant, Kant plus Aristotle, Aristotle via Gadamer, Beiner on Gad-

---

[4] The Kantian mood of this entire enterprise is evident in the titles. In her last work, Arendt seemed to be reverting to the themes of her early Heideggerian education; see *The Life of the Mind*, 2 vols. (New York: Harcourt Brace Jovanovich, 1978).

[5] Hannah Arendt, *Lectures on Kant's Political Philosophy*, ed. R. Beiner (Chicago: University of Chicago Press, 1982), p. 65.

[6] Compare these words with the Epilogue of *Eichmann in Jerusalem* (New York: Viking, 1963), pp. 213–214ff.

amer—leaves us a long way from really understanding what the citizen does when she deliberates the pros and cons of pornography and how what she does differs from what critics or moralists do when they render judgments on the aesthetic or ethical domains. The critic can sit in the dark and compare what he sees before him with certain tenets of socialist realism. The Catholic can set his projected course of divorce litigation next to the tenets of the Holy Roman Church. Both can render judgment in solitude simply by following certain rules, for which Kant's categorical imperative is perhaps the archetype. Reason provides the measuring rod; philosophy offers the litmus test.

What the citizen does is altogether different. She cannot simply hold up her antipornography writ to the Bill of Rights and see whether it conforms to the First Amendment. Even were she a high court judge, she might do more than this; and she is in any case not a judge at all in that sense. She may come to the issue holding certain private opinions, but those opinions do not become political judgments without further activity involving others. Indeed, common civic activity constitutes what we mean by political judgment. The journey from private opinion to political judgment does not follow a road from prejudice to true knowledge; it proceeds from solitude to sociability. To travel this road, the citizen must put her private views to a test that is anything but epistemological: she must debate them with her fellow citizens, run them through the courts, offer them as a program for a political party, try them out in the press, reformulate them as a legislative initiative, experiment with them in local, state, and federal forums, and, in every other way possible, subject them to the civic scrutiny and public activity of the community to which she belongs.

Now, to suggest that political judgment entails a whirl of public activity is to argue that it is in essence political and not cognitive—that political judgment is defined by activity in common rather than by thinking alone. It is what politics produces and not what produces politics. What is missing from the German school is quite precisely politics. The philosophical preoccupation with reason and its conditions overwhelms the practical character of politics and its conditions. The civic community engaged in

199

public thinking is displaced by the rational individual engaged in private thinking as the source of judgment, so that cognition rather than common activity necessarily becomes the target of inquiry. But if, as I will argue, political judgment is public thinking, then it is not the meaning of *thinking* and its constraints but the meaning of *public* and its constraints that demand our attention.

My argument draws on the Anglo-American experience with praxis and looks to theorists of political action such as Burke, Tocqueville, and Dewey for justification. It construes political judgment as a function of commonality that can be exercised only by citizens interacting with one another in the context of mutual deliberation and decision. Solitary individuals may make moral or aesthetic judgments, solitary judges sitting on the bench may render legal judgments, but citizens can produce political judgments only as a body acting corporately.[7] And if one objects that a king, at least, can render political judgment in solitude, I can only respond that he does so because he *is* the citizenry acting in common. Since he must judge in the absence of civic interaction, however, he will often be a poor judge. By the same token, democracy turns out to be uniquely supportive of political judgment, because it maximizes interaction and thus guarantees the diversity and generality that is crucial to prudent judgment. To the degree that an adequate politics depends on political judgment, it might even be argued that democracy alone provides for an adequate politics.

The most important fact about citizens is that they are defined by membership in a political community and enact their civic identities only to the extent that they interact with other citizens in a mutualistic and common manner. Political judgment is thus ''we-judgment'' or public judgment or common-willing (in Rousseau's phrase, general-willing). *I* cannot judge politically, only *we* can judge politically; in assuming the mantle of citizenship, the I

---

[7] Whether court judges exercise a form of judgment that is more like civic or political judgment, or more like individual judgment is itself controversial; but whether they are conditioned by their social environment or are merely applied logicians of a prior body of constitutional precedent, they do not resemble citizens, who are judges *only* as members of a community in interaction with one another and who expressly *create* a world of common ends.

becomes a We. This transformation naturally requires an under-standing of citizenship more vigorous and mutualistic than the one favored by modern social scientists, which identifies citizens as private agents pursuing private interests in a political marketplace. It also explains why experts can never displace citizens as decision makers in a democracy. Critics of democracy often make the mis-take of conflating expertise and political judgment, perhaps be-cause the result conveniently allows them to question the capacity of sovereign people to govern in times when issues are complex and policy questions highly technical. But expertise is not political judgment. The wise citizen, like the wise politician or the wise president, need not master the full technical details of every issue up for decision. It is his duty to offer general principles for the application of policy—broad normative guidelines that set param-eters for the execution and interpretation of policy. No American president takes office with the aggregate expertise of an econo-mist, an international lawyer, an environmental scientist, and a strategic weapons expert. Yet he will be called upon to initiate policies and make decisions about fiscal matters, diplomatic trea-ties, environmental issues, and strategic policy. And, it is gener-ally agreed, his capacity to do so will depend upon his political experience, his prudence, the quality of discussions afforded by his staff, and his willingness to listen and learn—all of which con-stitute his capacity for sound political judgment. The expert pres-ident can be distracted by his specialized knowledge (President Carter?) from the broad normative questions that are the true busi-ness of political judgment. Nor does there seem to be the slightest correlation between expertise and moral or political judgment. Ex-pert doctors at Buchenwald were anything but prudent judges of the value or ends of medical research in a just society, any more than expert rocket engineers at Peenemunde were prudent judges of a wise foreign policy for Germany. Expertise may facilitate judgment, but it does not constitute judgment.

Take, for example, the current debate over safety standards for genetic engineering. The point for presidents and citizens alike is not to arbitrate between the technical claims of competing molec-ular biologists about the risks of gene-altering laboratory experiments. The point is only to reach a judgment, given the uncertainty of the experts, about *how much risk* they are willing to tolerate. Their decision will take the form: "Given the lack of consensus among the experts and the fact that all foresee some risk of grave consequences, and given that the benefits are not altogether certain and lie well into the future, we believe that no genetically altered agents ought to be licenced by the government for the next three years." As with so many other political judgments, this one is about the acceptability of risks, the allocation of resources (how much risk for how much potential gain at what potential costs?), and the desirability of broad principles. Such decisions are the mainstay of politics and are debated by legislators, statesmen, and other politicians regularly. And there is no reason why citizens cannot debate and reach decisions of this kind as effectively as their leaders. In doing so, they come to acquire the kind of civic competence we associate with wise political judgment, as well as the specialized knowledge we associate with expertise. We require not that citizens become as expert as specialists, only that they become as insightful and prudent as congressmen or presidents. A recent study of the effects of citizen participation on technocratic decision making in the field of DNA research suggests this expectation is not unrealistic. "The rDNA case provides one of the most interesting and promising examples of productive citizen participation in recent years . . . after the initial period of sensationalism and political posturing had passed, the deliberations of the citizen's advisory group demonstrated that when a participatory body is given sufficient time, information, and opportunity to make decisions that will have a real impact on issues that truly matter to the participants, it can achieve a high level of sophistication and understanding. And it can produce decisions and recommendations on complex technological problems that are as well informed and reasonable as those made by expert, professional elites."[8] Here, citizens apparently became not only wise but expert as well—more than mere judgment demands.

[8] Bruce Jennings, "Representation and Participation in the Democratic Govern-

I have been focusing here on the mutuality of political judgment. This emphasis is not without antecedents in the German school. For Kant as well as for Beiner, to render moral or aesthetic judgments is to respond to a community of standards. Philosophers who are impatient with the radical dichotomy between private subjectivity and objective truth and who remain sensitive to caveats about the communal character of all standards and paradigms (including those that are "scientific") acknowledge mutualism when they resort to the term *intersubjectivity*. Intersubjectivity is meant to convey the idea of minds in congruence, minds that produce identical judgments, which, though less than objective, may nonetheless be regarded as more than merely subjective.

Political judgment takes us well beyond intersubjectivity, however. It entails not simply the congruence of opinions arrived at by independent individuals, but the integrity of a single whole judgment produced by the interaction of independent opinions. Political judgment in this sense is common judgment in its highest form, what by the measure of our discussion in Chapter One we may call sovereign judgment. Thus, political judgment is something produced by politics rather than by cognition; its concomitant is citizenship rather than individual consciousness. Where intersubjectivity suggests individuals in agreement, citizenship suggest individuals transformed by membership in a political association into common seers who produce a common judgment.

This line of argument would seem to ally political judgment closely with the Rousseauian concept of the general will. Indeed, the German school would benefit enormously by shifting its gaze from Kant to Kant's practical and all-too-human hero, Rousseau. The general will depends on particular citizens practicing the craft of citizenship in a particular time and place; its content can thus never be posited in the abstract or defined universally. It pertains to particular communities and is sensitive to history, mores, common actions, and the world of ends created by common membership. It arises out of the intersection of interests but is disclosed

ance of Science and Technology," in M. L. Goggin, *Governing Science and Technology in a Democracy* (Knoxville: University of Tennessee Press, 1986), p. 240.

by their collision. For in Rousseau's conception it is only when individual interests collide and sectarian biases cancel one another out that citizens can eventually discover in the residue of their combative interaction what they share in common—that which unites them as citizens and permits them to call themselves a community. Rousseau thus writes: "There is often a great deal of difference between the will of all and the general will; the latter considers only the common interest, while the former takes private interest into account, and is no more than a sum of particular wills: but take away from these same wills the pluses and minuses that cancel one another, and the general will remains as the sum of the differences."[9] What citizens share is this residue precipitated by the clash of their private interests publicly confronted. Political judgment is possible only when they meet and act in common. Private men, even when they are prudent private judges, will not be able to figure out what the public good is, for it depends on—indeed, it only exists through—the interaction of that public assembled and voting.

Kant was Rousseau's most ardent fan, bestowing upon him the august title "Newton of the moral world." But by trying to forge from practical reason and private will a tool that would accomplish for individuals what Rousseau's general will achieved for the community, Kant perverted the character of political judgment and undid what was the greatest virtue of Rousseau's method: that it depended neither on reason nor on good will, but ("taking men as they are and laws as they ought to be") asked only that men interact in a civic community in accordance with their interests as they saw them. Wise political judgment demanded no special cognitive faculty, no virtuous altruist, no universal imperative; it required only that all members of a community participate in a political process of deliberation and decision making aimed at disclosing what they shared in common and thus what constituted their being as a community. Kant makes Rousseau the patron of universal reason and so of private conscience as a discoverer of the good. In his *Emile*, Rousseau might have given Kant cause.

[9] Jean-Jacques Rousseau, *The Social Contract*, bk. II, ch. 3.

But in his politics, above all in the *Social Contract*, he offered us a portrait of political judgment in which politics was much and reason little.

In scrutinizing political judgment, we have as much to learn from Rousseau as from Kant. We may even prefer Machiavelli to Aristotle for our perspective on the morality of common action, Oakeshott to Gadamer for insight into the meaning of civility and civic judgment, Pierce to Habermas for a model of social reasoning rooted in activity, and William James to Hannah Arendt on the importance of outcomes rather than origins in assessing judgment. Rationalist idealism and German cognitivism have produced many things, but a healthy political practice does not loom large among them. Neither in its bureaucratic/legalistic phase nor in its demagogic/fascist phase has German politics offered us a very prudent model of political judgment. It would be perverse to blame German political pathology entirely on the German philosophical conviction that political judgment is a function of knowledge, but it certainly seems fair to identify radical philosophical idealism— whether in Plato, Kant, or Hegel—as an impediment to a flexible and lively political practice. Where reason claims to speak, politics is silent; where men profess to agree upon what is true, there is no need to devise methods to live and act together in the face of uncertainty and conflict; where right is purportedly given, common justice need not be invented.

The German tradition looks to solve philosophically the very problems that in the Anglo-American tradition are the occasion of politics. Where philosophy stops, experience, history, common sense, and common action begin: enter politics and political judgment. For suitable texts, we need only look to the *Federalist Papers*, Madison's Notes on the Constitutional Convention, or de Tocqueville's account of his American journey. For a suitable method we do better to consult our political skills than to cultivate our mental faculties. What we need, then, if we are to understand political judgment, is to understand the conditions of politics.

I commented in Chapter One on such integral features of politics as action, autonomy, and sovereignty. These suggest a particular conception of the domain of politics (one that I have spelled out in some detail in *Strong Democracy*) that bears brief recapitulation here. This conception understands politics as being circumscribed by conditions that impose a necessity for public action, and thus for reasonable public choice, in the presence of conflict and in the absence of private or independent grounds for judgment. While a philosophical question may take the form "What is true and how do we know it to be so?" and a moral question the form "What is right and how do I act in accord with the good?" a political question takes the form: "What shall we do when something has to be done that will affect us all and we wish to be reasonable, yet we disagree on means and ends and are without independent grounds by which we might arbitrate our differences?" This formulation makes clear that the real political problem is one of action under conditions of uncertainty, not one of truth or even justice in the abstract. The advantage of this viewpoint, recognized by Machiavelli and celebrated by Burke, is that it eschews metaphysics and circumvents issues of final truth or absolute morals that trouble students of judgment in the abstract. It requires a proximate solution for real problems that will persist whether or not an ultimate measure of judgment is available. *Some reasonable judgment must be reached even where none can be epistemologically warranted.*

On this view the political judge, as an actor, can afford neither the luxury of agnosticism nor the Olympian nonchalance of skepticism that are available to philosophical judges.[10] To be political is to have to judge, to choose, to act when the grounds of choice are not given a priori or by fiat or by unimpeachable cognition. To be political is thus to be free with a vengeance—to have to make judgments without guiding standards or determining norms, yet under an ineluctable pressure to act.

At play here is that form of necessity we associate with the do-

---

[10] Without trying to judge the case for or against Robert Bork as a prospective justice of the Supreme Court, we may acknowledge that the position of a law professor speaking hypothetically on consitutional law and that of a working judge compelled to take concrete decisions with effect in the real world are radically incommensurable and that arguments developed as a function of professional reflection may not be predictive of decisions taken while sitting on the bench.

main of action, to which I first alluded in Chapter One. But I must again stress that the domain of action entails the tyranny of action, for politics encompasses the realm not simply of action but of necessary action. It is enmeshed in events that are part of a train of cause and effect already at work in the world. This engagement guarantees that even the choice not to make some decision—the failure to reach a common judgment—will have public consequences of political significance. As I noted earlier, nondecisions and nonjudgments are thus part of the logic produced by what we may call the first law of inertial politics: that events set in motion in the public realm will continue to their logical conclusion (their inertial terminus) if there are no contrary inputs from conscious political actors. "Nonactors" and citizens who refrain from passing judgment thereby bear responsibility for whatever results their nonactions have allowed the momentum of events to produce.

There is little to startle us in the first law of inertial politics. It is the political analog of consequentialism, which, as the moral posture that evaluates conduct on the basis of its effects rather than its intentions, bears a not surprising pertinence to the political domain. As Kant specified the logic of intentions (deontology), so Machiavelli had earlier specified the logic of consequences (although he certainly did not call it that). In his most vivid example, Machiavelli chides the overly scrupulous Prince, who in his short-sighted mercy abstains from executing the children of enemies who have betrayed him and his principality; once the children mature into men, they will transform the wrongs of childhood into a sword of vengeance and wreak civil war and fratricide on their principality.[11] Cruel as it may seem when measured by the deontological standards of private moral conduct, the public conduct of public actors—princes and citizens alike—must always necessarily answer to the standard of consequences for the community. Do you use a morally repugnant weapon to end a morally horrific war? Are capital crimes to be met with capital penalties? As Hegel reminds us, what makes public decision making so morally intimidating is that the choice is usually between evil and lesser evil.

[11] Machiavelli, in *The Prince*, ch. 17.

"It is a fearsome thing to kill," confesses Brecht in *Man Is Man*, "but it is not granted to us not to kill." It is not granted to political judges not to judge, and that knowledge alters the character of judgment itself.

If politics requires judgment in the face of uncertainty, it also demands judgment in the face of conflict. One of the perils of the German school is that, in assimilating judgment to cognition, it ascribes conflict to error rather than interest. Power and interest scarcely appear at all in the pages of Beiner's *Political Judgment*, and the idealist framework leaves little room for them. Yet, as Rousseau writes in remonstrating with enthusiasts of the general will who imagine it acts as a mirror to natural consensus, "If there were no different interests, the common interest would be barely felt, as it would encounter no obstacle; all would go on of its own accord, and politics would cease to be an art."[12] Conflict is the very essence of politics: it is what political judgment is called upon to treat with. Those political judges whom we call citizens cannot impose cognitive consensus as a solution to the collision of opposing interests. The problem is not one of knowledge but one of interests in opposition, and interests in opposition can be adjudicated only by such political means as bargaining and exchange or—better from the perspective of strong democracy—the artificial creation of civic communities that transform how individuals perceive themselves and their particular interests.

The appeal of abstract principle to the German school in the face of uncertainty is perfectly understandable given the muddy ambiguities typical of actual politics. Politics is a good deal less tidy than the intellectual faculties with which philosophers hope to apprehend it. It is an arena of the practical and the concrete, the everyday and the ambiguous, the malleable and the evanescent. There is no firm stairway to a higher realm from which one can borrow shaping norms and fixed standards to guide political judgment. The only kind of cognitive truth to be found in politics is the kind made, in William James's phrase, in the course of experience. The pragmatists yield better clues to the nature of political

---

[12] Jean-Jacques Rousseau, *The Social Contract*.

judgment than the idealists. What is required of political judgment is captured perfectly by James's definition of pragmatism as "the attitude of looking away from first things, principles, 'categories,' supposed necessities; and of looking toward last things, fruits, consequences, facts."[13]

Similarly, it is not so much Burke's conservatism as his sense of the concreteness of politics that leads him to reject the possibility of approaching the science of commonwealth a priori. The political condition is engendered by history, circumstance, and context. Real political actors, confronted with controversies and dilemmas issuing out of fundamental conflicts of interest and value in a changing society, are required to exercise judgment in common on matters they cannot agree upon as individuals. Citizens take over where individuals are thwarted. The philosopher, like Minerva's owl, arrives only at dusk, too late to aid the political actor. Or, if he has somehow arrived promptly, the dilemmas are superseded by virtue of his arrival, and the need for political judgment vanishes.

The citizen wishes in any case only to act rightly, not to know for certain; only to choose reasonably, not to reason scientifically; only to overcome conflict and secure transient peace, not to discover eternity; only to cooperate with others, not to acheive moral oneness; only to formulate common causes, not to obliterate all differences. Politics is what men do when metaphysics fails; it is not metaphysics reified as a constitution. By the same token, political judgment is not the application of abstract, independent standards to political actuality; it is the forging of common actuality in the absence of abstract, independent standards. It entails dynamic, ongoing, common deliberation and action, and it is feasible only when individuals are transformed by social interaction into citizens. It is sovereign with respect to other forms of judgment exactly in the sense that politics is sovereign with respect to other forms of association: it governs judgment among men in

[13] William James, *Pragmatism and the Meaning of Truth* (Cambridge, Mass.: Harvard University Press, 1978), p. 32.

209

general, coming into operation precisely at the point where other kinds of judgment fail.

Political judgment is thus the sovereign faculty of the body politic, operating through its citizenry as a single whole. It integrates us, making individuals into citizens and creating from disparate parts a single people. Machiavelli, Rousseau, and Jefferson (among many others) have reminded us that the individual is foolish, the multitude wise. Political judgment is the multitude deliberating, the multitude in action. It is the secret of democracy's success—and the most powerful argument that can be offered against the benevolent tyrannies foisted on us over the ages by Plato and his modern German heirs.

Yet the multitude in action presents its own clear and present dangers, for the multitude is a creature of many aspects. To loosen political judgment from its moorings in epistemological certainty (however contested) and set it afloat in the name of democracy will seem to many to leave the forging of political wisdom not to a ship of state but to a ship of fools. If democracy is mistaken for its parodistic cousin, mob rule, then political judgment becomes indistinguishable from public opinion, that is to say, mass prejudice. If democratic political practice is understood as little more than the bartering of private interests in a quasi-public market setting, then political judgment will come to resemble nothing so much as a crude economic calculus. The mob also reasons, it will be said, but do we really wish to install its rantings as the ultimate arbiter of political judgment?

Naturally not. As I have tried to suggest elsewhere, strong forms of democracy are premised on the activity of citizens, and citizens are as far from being masses as Kant's rational seekers of autonomous ends are from being compulsive calculators of selfish interests. The citizen is an adept participant in the polity, schooled in the arts of social interaction and marked by the capacity to distinguish the requirements of ''we'' styles of thinking from those of ''me'' styles of thinking. To speak of democratic political judgment is to speak of civic education and also of styles of political participation that go well beyond occasional voting. The adept political judge is what we mean when we refer to the competent cit-

210

izen; and, as we have noticed, both citizenship and competence depend on continuous political engagement and experience.

If political judgment is understood as an artful political practice conducted by adept citizens, then to improve our judgment we must strengthen our democratic practices. To think aright about politics, we must act aright, and to act aright calls for better citizens rather than better philosophers. If we find our political judgment defective, it may be the fault of too little rather than too much democracy. Thomas Jefferson, a rather more aristocratic advocate of democracy than generally perceived, nevertheless believed that when a people saddled with democratic responsibilities showed too little discretion in their judgment, the remedy was to burden them with still more democracy and thereby to inform their discretion.

The secret of political judgment is neither to discover absolute standards by which the wise might take the measure of political justice nor to refine the mental faculties of the citizenry by teaching them philosophy so that they might emulate the wise. It is rather to inform their discretion and enlarge their political experience. A citizenry in action, capable of thinking as a "we" in the name of public goods, is about as much political judgment—for better or for worse—as humankind is likely to be permitted. In democratic times, philosophers will always be a luxury—the morticians but never the movers of a free state—while citizens with a well-developed capacity for political judgment will be an indispensable necessity. It is a sad and telling commentary on the condition of our democracy that philosophers may today be a good deal more plentiful than citizens.

211

Index

Library of Congress Cataloging-in-Publication Data

Barber, Benjamin R., 1939–
The conquest of politics: liberal philosophy in democratic times /
Benjamin Barber.
p. cm.
Includes index.
1. Political science. 2. Liberalism. 3. Democracy. I. Title.
ISBN 0–691–07764–9 (alk. paper)
JA83.B2483 1988
320—dc19   87–37687
CIP